Honey, We're Going to Africa!

Harvey T. Hoekstra

Winepress Publishing
MUKILTEO, WA 98275

DEDICATED

To my wife, Lavina, so beautifully genuine, unpretentious, never seeking acclaim -- a missionary-mother with a servant heart, able to convert mud-walls or sticks and grass with dirt floors into an attractive home in which there was contentment and love and where our people in Africa knew they were always welcome and could find help in times of need.

To our six children, Denny, Jim, Dave, Carol, Mark, and Paul who shared our adventures in Africa and the pain we experienced as a family during those long months of seperation while away from home in a distant mission boarding school.

To my missionary colleagues with whom we were privileged to live and work and without whose encouragement and help our task could not have been accomplished.

To God be all the honor and praise for the incredible privilege He gave to us that we should be Christ's missionaries for nearly thirty years among people who might otherwise never have heard of Him!

TABLE OF CONTENTS

CHAPTER ONE

HOW
IT ALL BEGAN

The year was 1946. My 1932 Ford V-8 was making a fast trip from Holland to Grand Haven in Michigan. I had twenty one miles to go. I could hardly wait to get home to my wife, Lavina. I wondered what she'd say when I came bounding through the door with the words, "Honey, guess what — we are going to Africa!"

I was on my way home from the seminary where I was preparing for the ministry. We'd just been listening to a "red headed, rash, religious" Presbyterian missionary from Africa, named Don McClure. He had a gift to excite the imagination and challenge one to action. He told how he had come from the South Sudan beyond the Nile River, where people had never heard of Jesus Christ. God had given this man a great vision and a bold, innovative plan. They called it the "Anuak Plan" - fifteen missionaries for fifteen years to evangelize an entire tribe and then move on.

He wanted to return to Africa with competent missionary recruits. People needed included a doctor, a nurse, an educationalist, an agriculturalist, an evangelist and he was searching for someone to translate the Bible into the Anuak language. This captured my attention. I liked working with foreign languages. While a student at Hope College I'd taken German, Latin and Greek during the same semester.

As he spoke my heart was strangely warmed and I sensed that God wanted me to be that man. After chapel was over, we gathered around and peppered our speaker with questions, wanting to learn all we could about this tremendous challenge. With these small glimpses of what was involved, I was hurrying home to tell Lavina all about it.

As I raced homeward about as fast as I thought was prudent, I fantasized that Lavina would collapse, falling to the floor in shock and that I'd have to revive her. And then, again, I'd think, "No, it's not going to be that great a surprise. We've talked sometimes, albeit superficially, about being missionaries, possibly to Japan." But Africa was something else. She'd picture lions chasing her up trees and snakes slithering in the grass waiting to strike.

Bouncing along in my Ford with its worn out shock absorbers, I also pondered the commitment Lavina had given me before we were married. I sometimes had kidded her that she wanted me real bad, because she promised she'd go with me wherever the Lord called me. She'd said, "Honey, I know that ministers move from place to place and have to go wherever God calls them. I can do that with you. I'll go with you wherever the Lord calls you."

But to go out to Africa? It was still considered a dark continent and a risky place with wild animals, strange people and threatening diseases? Our image of Africa had been shaped by Livingston and Stanley. Neither of us had thought that far ahead when we were madly in love making far reaching commitments to each other. One side of my brain was racing in high gear with all these and a myriad other conflicting thoughts. The opposite side was praying earnestly that God would prepare Lavina's heart with a positive response. — Anyway, there'd be a long while before we'd have to make a final decision. I still had another year at the seminary. That'd make for a total of three years driving back and forth those twenty one miles to attend classes while serving as student pastor at Bignell Chapel.

I'll never forget the flow of adrenaline and the boundless enthusiasm with which I shared what I thought God had been showing me that morning about our going to Africa. She never collapsed and I didn't have to pick her off the floor, but it was a turn of events she'd never anticipated. We prayed about it often, talked about it regularly until finally one night, when sleep eluded us, we got out of our bed around two o'clock in the morning and told the Lord we were ready to go to Africa if that was what He wanted us to do. That night, on our knees, our hearts were at peace and we heard His word of promise, "I will be with you always, even to the end of the world." The old translation came to mind because to us, that's exactly where we'd be going. A scant two years later, a lion was in our front yard while we slept peacefully in our mud-walled house with only a mosquito net between us and him. We were at Akobo in the Sudan.

*****

Our story really begins much earlier than that fateful day when God used Don McClure to spark our interest in Africa.

It begins in a tiny eight room hospital upstairs over the pharmacy where I promised Jesus that if He'd make we well again, I'd try to be a preacher of the Gospel.

It was November, 1935. I had just celebrated my fifteenth birthday.

GROWING UP ON THE FARM

My boyhood home was in Minnesota. I grew up in a Christian family with five brothers. We never had a sister. I'm sure my mother must have been at least a little disappointed when the doctor said, "We have another boy here." I was number four!

We all went to catechism, Sunday School and attended church as a family. When itinerant evangelists held services nearby, our family sat near the front. We lived on a dirt road five miles from Maple Lake. The closest school was two miles away and we walked both ways except when it rained or the weather was too forbidding during the winter. Sometimes we were lucky to catch a ride if my dad or a neighbor happened to be going into town.

Ours was a small farm of eighty acres. Six or seven acres of that grew a wide assortment of vegetables which my dad and we boys peddled out on retail routes to homes in the various towns and among resort people spending their summer on one of the several nearby lakes. We also sold to stores and vegetable markets in the neighboring towns, reaching out as far as St. Cloud some 27 miles distant. All of this was excellent preparation for learning how to communicate and make a sale. My dad was good at this and he taught his boys these same skills. I can still hear him saying, "Harvey, take a head of cabbage and run up to that house. Tell the lady it's ten cents for one and if she'll take three she can have all three of them for a quarter." That boyhood experience, trying to sell vegetables and meeting people in public was excellent preparation for a future preacher.

I graduated from grade school when I was twelve years of age, went to high school a few weeks and quit. I never went back to high school until four and a half years later. It was during those years that I promised Jesus I'd try to become a preacher of the Gospel.

ILLNESS STRIKES

On October 10th, in the evening, I was out beside the barn feeding the calves their evening milk. I began to feel ill with chills. It was the evening for our young people's meeting at church, and I didn't want to miss it. I went, but was miserable with chills and fever. I could hardly wait for the meeting to end so that I could go home and crawl into bed. Three days later when the fever had left and I came downstairs, my mother remarked that she didn't like the way I was walking all bent over. Concerned about that, later in the week they took me to old Dr. Rousseau in Maple Lake. He said that I had had an attack of appendicitis but he didn't recommend surgery.

Ten days after that first attack, the fever and chills returned. Around six o'clock, my folks took me to Buffalo, sixteen miles from home where I was admitted for surgery later that evening. On the way, they stopped at uncle Ralph's farm to pick up my Aunt Marie who was a registered nurse. The hospital was small and up a flight of stairs above the drug store. In preparation for the surgery, I was given a spinal injection. My mother cautioned me to lie real still when they pricked me. She said, "Alfred Naagkteborn, a neighbor boy who lived across the field from us, nearly died when they broke off the needle while attempting to give him a spinal before his operation." I never moved!

During the surgery I was fully conscious and able to hear part of the conversation as Dr. Catlin and his son, Dr. Bob, performed the surgery. I recall how Dr. Catlin said, "I had hoped we could have gotten that thing out of there in time."

I knew then that I had a ruptured appendix and was a very sick boy. They saved the dirty black pieces of it and I later saw them in the little bottle floating in liquid. Eventually we threw them out!

Two weeks and two days after the first surgery, these same doctors again performed a second operation to deal with an abscess that had formed behind the bladder. I was desperately ill following the surgery and it wasn't at all sure that I'd make it. This was before the miracle drugs of penicillin and sulfa had been discovered. My Aunt Marie, a registered nurse, was in the same room with me taking care of me night and day.

A LIFE CHANGING EXPERIENCE

On November 20, we celebrated my fifteenth birthday in the hospital. Two days later, at noon the doctor came in, pulled back the covers, tapped me on the abdomen and said, "We're going to have to go in there once more." Another abscess had formed into which they would insert a tube through which it could drain.

My favorite aunt, Ella Mae, mother's younger sister, was "babysitting" me, keeping me company that same day. She knew that I was afraid to die. When the doctors left the room, she got out of her chair, took hold of my trembling hand, knelt down beside my bed and prayed. I don't know what she said. I only know that as she prayed I had an indescribable experience of God's grace and peace. My fear was totally gone. I felt I was bathed in God's love and goodness. My heart was inexpressibly glad. It seemed that a thousand lights were brightening up the room. I am unable, adequately, to describe the wonder of that experience. I felt, joy — waves of joy and God's peace washing over me. It made no difference whether I lived or died. It would be alright. I knew that God loved me!

Two hours later my folks drove in from the country. They'd been phoned and told of the impending surgery. My mother was crying. She fully expected me to die. I remember sharing my experience with her then and telling her not to be sad or afraid.

Well, as you can tell, the operation was a success and God mercifully healed me. I went home on December 5th. I had been in the hospital 45 days and had lost 27 pounds of weight. But before I left for home, another wonderful thing happened.

A LIFE CHANGING PROMISE

On one of those days after the third operation, a retired farmer, Peter Schermer by name, stopped by to visit me. He had been there once or twice before. To a boy just fifteen years of age, he looked pretty ancient. Even so, I really appreciated his coming and making my time go just a little faster.

This last visit of his, however, was surely ordained of God. Sitting just beyond the foot end of my bed, this elderly man shared with me about the experience they'd had with their son when he was a boy like me and was ill. He said, "I had a son like you and when he was a boy he, too, was desperately ill. One day when I came into the hospital there was a black sheet over his bed and he wasn't there. When I saw that black sheet, I put my hands in the air and said, 'Oh,

God, if only you'd have spared my son, I'd have given him to you.'" He continued,"As it turned out, my son was still alive. They had put him in a room across the hall expecting him to die." And then he said, "But God spared his life and when he became a young man, he went to the seminary and became a preacher of the Gospel."

When I heard those words, I said in my heart, "Dear God, if you'll spare my life and make me well again, I'll try to be a preacher of the Gospel." It was a commitment which by God's grace I kept and from which I was never seriously tempted to turn aside. I knew that God had spoken to me through that retired farmer.

On December 5, 1935 I was released from the hospital. At home I was gradually regaining strength. Two years went by and I was still not in school. I often prayed about it, wondering how it would ever be possible for me to become a preacher. I had been called and had made a promise to God, but I was no nearer getting into school two and a half years after leaving the hospital than I was when I'd said I'd be a preacher.

But God has his own timing in things like that and brings it all together at His appointed time. We don't always understand these matters, but we know it to be so.

PLANS FOR GETTING INTO SCHOOL

In the summer of 1937 our little country church was having a week of special evangelist meetings. A man named Isaac Van Westenberg came from Chicago to be the week's speaker. On one of those nights, he called for testimonies. Among others, I also shared from my experiences. This man had never heard of me, but that evening when I sat down, he pointed his finger straight at me and said, "Now, there's a young man for the ministry." It was the finger of God!

After the service a few gathered around my folks and urged that a way be found for me to go to school. The next day, I was out hoeing cabbage in the field across the road just opposite our house. A car came over the hill from the direction of the church and turned into our yard. It was Rev. Van Westenberg. He'd come to follow up on the events of the preceding night at the church.

I was called out of the cabbage patch and my folks, the visiting preacher and I sat around the kitchen table. It was agreed that I should get into school and prepare. We all decided that it might be good for me to enroll in Northwestern Bible School in Minneapolis at the beginning of the second semester in January. That would allow me to help with the farm work through the busy fall months too.

When January came, my folks, my brother, Gerrit, and his wife, Glorene, who were living in the little house next door, took me and my trunk to the Bible School in Minneapolis. We went two weeks early so that I could seek out a job and support myself. I actually found a meal job in the restaurant next to the Orpheum theatre on Hennipin Avenue. It looked like I was all set to become a student at Northwestern Bible College.   But this was to change dramatically.

When the folks and Gerrit and Glorene returned home the day they had dropped me off in the city, Gerrit shared with my folks that I'd sometimes talked with him about wanting some day to attend our own theological seminary in Holland, Michigan. That conversation triggered in my Dad's mind that he should visit with the superintendent of schools in Annandale and explore the possibility of my starting highschool. I really don't know what I was thinking when I spoke of going to our own seminary when I didn't even have a high school education. But my dad realized what would first have to happen. He wasn't a strong advocate of education for his boys, but he knew that I needed one if I was to become a preacher of the Gospel.

Ten days after they'd dropped me and my trunk off at Northwestern Bible College, at two o'clock in the afternoon I received a letter from my father. In it he told how he'd been to see the superintendent of Annandale High. Mr. Tripp, the superintendent then, had said that if I began high school immediately I could probably catch up with the others and graduate in three and a half years. There was precedent for that kind of accelerated attempt. Henry (Hank) Schut, who later married my cousin, Hazel, had gone back to school when he was older. He'd graduated in three years and I'd heard a lot of people talk about what he'd done. By four o'clock that afternoon I was out on the road hitchhiking the fifty miles home. Once in Maple Lake, I called my dad and he collected me. It was already past eight o'clock in the evening before we arrived home. We sat together around the kitchen table discussing this new possibility. By ten o'clock that night the decision had been made. I would go back to the city the next afternoon, Sunday, collect my trunk and begin high school in Annandale. Wilbert Schut drove me to the school in Minneapolis that afternoon.

ATTENDING HIGH SCHOOL IN ANNANDALE

The next day, Monday morning, January 24, 1938, the school bus stopped at our mailbox to pick me up. Annandale was seven miles from home. I began my high school education that day.

Two and one half years later I graduated with honor. It had been hard work, but God had marvelously helped me. I never took an examination without asking the Lord to help me. Some sacrifices were necessary to achieve. To catch up with the other students, I spent the first few Saturdays studying the entire day in the little, vacant house on our farm. It was a great challenge and I loved it. I often studied late into the evenings. Sometimes I'd go to bed real early, set the alarm and begin studying at 2:30 in the morning. We always had cows to milk and chores to do as well. During my second year, I even took seven weeks off from school on Thursdays to go out alone with the truck to sell vegetables on a route I had in Monticello.

During the school year I didn't participate in most of the young people's social activities and "good times". I did continue teaching Sunday School and always attended the weekly teacher's meeting. Rev. Adolphus Dykstra, our young pastor, was such an excellent teacher none of us who taught on Sunday wanted to miss out.

ATTENDING HOPE COLLEGE IN MICHIGAN

In May 1940, I graduated from high school. That same fall my folks and I travelled from Minnesota to Michigan in their nice 1937 Chevy. My dad always kept his car in tiptop shape, so it was a first class ride all the way! I was excited. The first hurdle of finishing high school was behind me. I was eager to start at Hope College and complete my formal education. I was highly motivated because of the promise I'd made when I'd been so ill. It never occurred to me that I wouldn't make it.

The college had a job lined up for me taking care of a woman's furnace and yard on Thirteenth Street right near the school. We met this lady in the afternoon and I expected to move into my room in the morning. My dad handed me a dollar bill just before they left for Chicago where they'd visit relatives on their way home. His last word, as I recall it, was, "You'd better get yourself a haircut."

I had no idea what lay ahead. In the morning, I learned that the lady had changed her mind. I don't know whether she didn't like my looks or what went wrong! I ended up staying with an older lady named Miss Doesburg, living on Tenth Street between College and Central Ave. It was close to the college, and I liked that. My duties were easy enough. Carry in the coal for the space heater and empty out the ashes, help with odd jobs around the place, and be available in case of need.

I also found a job in the Dutch Mill Restaurant where I could earn my meals. That first semester, I skipped classes three days each month so that I could read light and water meters for the city. When my friend, Howard Van Egmond, quit his job as night clerk in the Hotel Netherlands, I applied and was accepted. John Schut, a boyhood friend from Maple Lake who was also attending Hope College, was rooming with me at Miss Doesburg's. At this juncture he took over my responsibilities in the house. Employment at the Netherlands Hotel involved long hours, seven nights a week, but it was a good job for a college student having to work. It gave me the opportunity to study on the job. My classes were in the morning and I slept afternoons. When I received my first grades, I was surprised to find I'd done better than I'd hoped for. I suspect I'd set my academic sights a little too low and never thought that I might be able to maintain the good record I'd finished up with in high school. But sensing that I could probably finish near the top of my class if I really tried, I began to study more seriously like I had in high school.

Taking nine hours of credit work summers, I could come close to graduating in three years. I did this and finished the remaining several hours required to graduate during my first year at Western Seminary. One of my summer school courses was in Japanese history. Dr. Albertus Pieters, who'd spent years in Japan as an RCA missionary and later taught at Western Seminary, was the teacher. He'd retired by then but former students still talked about how they'd never go into his classroom unprepared. Dr. Pieters, for some strange reason, wasn't much in favor of students working and studying at the same time. I was holding down a full time job nights while going to school during the summer. I've always considered that Dr. Pieters paid me one of my highest compliments during my college years when he gave me a grade of 99 1/4 on one of his comprehensive examinations. As he returned my paper he snorted in his mustache in his inimicable manner saying, "Mr. Hoekstra, I don't know how you do it, but I can't deny the facts." I still chuckle whenever I recall how he said it. When I received my diploma it was "Cum Laude" (with honor). I knew it was because God had helped me and gave Him thanks and praise!

MARRIED WHILE STILL AT HOPE

I was a very busy young man during those student years. Even so, I managed to court an attractive young lady, Lavina

Hoffman, and we were married while I was still at Hope. She was God's gift to me, beautiful, sensible, supportive and never prepared to give up. Looking back, we concede that getting married when we did may not have been the smartest thing to do. But God sometimes graciously overrules for good even when we may not know what's best for ourselves.

It wasn't easy! Lavina and I were normally poor and lacking some of the amenities of life. But we had each other. When our first son, Denny, made his debut, eleven months after we were married, we knew we had our work cut out for us. Sometimes, we wondered where our next meal would come from. Many a can of soup made its way to our table. Occasionally, we'd look at each other and say, "The Lord must be getting us ready for Arabia or something!" At that time, we had no idea that it was Africa.

Though the going was tough, we both worked to put food on the table and pay our way. Quitting school was never an option. It never occurred to either of us that we wouldn't make it or that I should drop out. It simply wasn't an option. We would look to God to see us through and we were willing to do whatever was required.

I think our lowest point came one day when, during the college year, out of work, I had taken a day out from classes to look for a job. All prospects for job openings had come to a dead end. Nothing was available. I finally stopped at one of the factories where a man, whom I didn't know but who said his name was Ed Boevie, gave me hope. He said I should go to the Boone Aluminum company and ask to speak to the man in charge. He said "I'll call him and tell him you'll be showing up."

This was encouraging because most of those places were simply taking names down and one never got in to see anyone at all. Eventually, I was at the little opening in the outer lobby where you filled out the forms. After waiting longer than I had hoped would be the case, in as much as Mr. Boevie was supposed to have called them, the manager invited me into his office. He confirmed that he'd been contacted.

At one point I said, "I don't care what job I have to do. I'm willing to clean spittoons or do anything. I need work." This kind man, raised his hand and stopped me saying, "Take it easy, fellow. Take it easy. We'll find something for you."

They gave me a job working nights in the tool crib where I'd sharpen tools and give them out to the workers whenever they needed to turn in their dull cutting tools for replacements I would have sharpened. I'd never seen the inside of a factory before. To learn the job, I had to skip classes at Hope for one week. The following week I began at mid-night, came home in the morning after eight o['clock, changed into clean clothes quickly to make classes at Hope. In the afternoon and early evening I tried to sleep.

It was a good job. The pay was three times what I'd earned at the hotel, and I could still study on the job. Some of the factory workers knew I was studying and tried to avoid disturbing me as much as possible. Some even sharpened their own tools. I suspect they could do it better than this college student with his limited experience at that. The Lord was so kind and merciful to me! Later when I started seminary, Lavina began working nights and switched back and forth between the second and third shifts. Denny was just a little tyke then. Jenny Schut, a dear friend from Minnesota who was living next door, took care of him. Jenny and her daughter, Elsie, were like a grandmother and auntie to Denny. During one period, every morning before going to class, I would transport Denny in a basket on the front of my bike to get him over to our friends, Bill and Kay Vandenberg. If it rained, we covered him with plastic. This was when Lavina was working the day shift and I was in seminary.

OUR FIRST SUMMER ASSIGNMENT TO PREACH

Seminary students were normlly sent out on summer assignments. Some went to help in local church ministries and two or three students always went to the Indian mission fields in New Mexico or Nebraska. We were the only married couple in seminary at that time, so Lavina and I, with our two year old son, Denny, would be going out together. We'd been assigned to Winnebego, Nebraska, but before this was finalized, we were reassigned to Bignell Chapel near Grand Haven. The change was made because during that time Lavina's mother, living in Holland, Michigan was gravely ill.

Again, we saw the marvelous providence of God at work in these events. First of all, we met Franklin and Gladys Kieft who in later years would play such an important role in our lives and ministry. When our summer assignment ended, this little preaching post called Bignell Chapel, where I'd been preaching two sermons every Sunday, invited us to continue on as their student pastor. They wanted us to keep on living there and serve them like a pastor until I completed my seminary training.

Every day during the school year, I drove our '32 Ford V8 the 21 miles back and forth to seminary. Every Sunday two more sermons were waiting to be preached. It was my great joy, but also my ever present burden. More than one message received it's final touches well past Saturday at midnight!

It was great that Lavina didn't have to work those long hours outside the home any longer. She loved watching Denny develop and teaching him all those things a good mother does. I suspect her stories included the boys and girls from Africa. Sometimes Lavina and I talked about the peoples of the world who had never heard of Jesus. We'd talk about America where the churches were so plentiful and where radio programs put the Gospel within reach of almost everyone. We sometimes spoke about our becoming missionaries to Japan, but not really seriously. We never talked about becoming missionaries to Africa, that is, until that day when Don McClure visited our seminary.

AFRICA IN OUR BLOOD

In the summer of '46, Lavina and I attended the New Wilmington Missionary Conference in Ohio. We met a number of missionaries there on furlough and some who were new recruits. We felt right at home with them and Africa was in our blood. It was a summer that confirmed our call to Africa.

Lavina and I talked incessantly about Africa. We must have talked about the rivers, rain and mud as we speculated and tried to visualize what living in Africa might be like. That we were doing a lot of this became apparent one rainy day when we drove out to the country over muddy roads to pick up a side of pork from a local farmer. Denny was in the back seat and when the car came to a halt, he excitedly started hitting his mother on the shoulder to get her attention. What do you think he wanted to know? His question, "Is this Africut? Mommy, is this Africut?" To him Africa was a place of rain and mud and he thought we were there!

APPOINTED BY THE RCA

During this time when God was calling us to serve in Africa, the Reformed Church in America (RCA) was making its decision to expand its missionary program to include Africa. The RCA and the United Presbyterians were to become partners in the work of the American Mission (the name of the Presbyterian Mission) in the Sudan. The RCA had caught this vision from this same Don McClure. Bob and Morrie Swart and Wilma Kats would be the first to go out. We'd be following them in a few short months. But before all that happened, there were still some hurdles to overcome and training we needed to be ready for the tasks lying ahead.

During our last year at Western Seminary, we formally applied to be accepted by the RCA to serve with the Presbyterians in Africa. The forms to be filled out seemed long and complicated. There were hurdles to overcome, but eventually one night the phone rang. We were just about to step out of the house to leave for our weekly young peoples' meeting in the church. Bev Vandermeiden, a young teen aged neighbor girl, was standing there waiting to ride with us when the phone rang. On the line was Miss Ruth Ransom from the RCA's Board of World Mission meeting in Kalamazoo. She was calling to tell us that Lavina and I had just been appointed by them to serve in Africa. They wanted us to come to Kalamazoo the next day to be introduced to the entire Board and to meet with her committee to make future plans. It was a night we can never forget.

That same year in May, 1947, I graduated from Western Theological Seminary in Holland. We'd had three marvelous years serving as student pastor while attending seminary. Suddenly this was all past tense. The RCA mapped out the additional preparation we should have before leaving for overseas.

After a year at Scarrit and Peabody Colleges in Nashville Tennessee and a summer at the University of Oklahoma in the Summer Institute of Linguistics (SIL) of the Wycliffe Bible Translators, we were ready to push off. But there were innumerable details needing attention. Passport forms to fill out; inoculations that gave us fevers and sore arms; furniture, food supplies and tools to accompany us. Visits to family members and visits to a number of supporting congregations eager to meet their new missionaries and bid them Godspeed. Everywhere we went, people encouraged us and tried to help in any way possible. Several men helped build wooden cases that could also serve as cabinets for furniture. Going to Africa, we needed guns and ammunition for hunting. Our meat supply was out there somewhere in the tall grass, or perhaps flying overhead. We'd become expert shots as we kept meat on the table. We'd be in lion and leopard country so we'd also need guns for our own protection

SAILING FOR AFRICA

It was July 2, 1948 when we sailed for Africa. Our dear friends, Arnie and Marge Vanlummel, had come from where they were serving a church in New Jersey to see us off. Rev. Bert Bosenbroek, representing the Board, gave us their official send off and he led us in prayer.

We were on a newly refurbished freighter, named "The SS Steel Apprentice". They allowed eleven passengers. To carry more meant they'd have to include a doctor.

Late in the afternoon our friends had already left and we started moving out to sea. We were all out on the deck watching the shoreline gradually recede in the distance. It was beginning to darken. As the Statue of Liberty was fading in the distance, we, suddenly, felt an indescribable sense of aloneness. Nobody was with us and we were desolate. I thought to myself, "What have I done? I'm taking my family to a place I've never seen and where there are dangers I can't even imagine?" Lavina wasn't feeling that chipper either. It was the moment of truth. There was no turning back. We were committed. The bands had stopped playing! All the nice words said about our courage and how great it was that we were willing to go out as missionaries were past history. We were alone and nobody spoke to us.

About that time, we took Denny, who was five and a half years, and Jimmy who was just three months old, and went into our cabin. We opened the Bible and it fell to Psalm 105 where we read these beautiful, unforgetable words:

"When they were few in number,
of little account, and sojourners in it,
wandering from nation to nation,
from one kingdom to another people,
he allowed no one to oppress them;
he rebuked kings on their account,
saying, 'Touch not my anointed ones,
do my prophets no harm!'"

We closed the book, got on our knees together and prayed. When we opened our eyes it was like we were in another world. The loneliness and desolation had been lifted. Our hearts were at peace and we experienced His presence and peace. This terrible feeling never returned, but it was a moment we will never forget. How precious, indeed, are the promises of God to strengthen the hearts of those who lean on Him.

Sixteen days later we docked at Port Said in Egypt. We would soon set our feet on African soil.

CHAPTER TWO

OUR FIRST DAYS IN THE SUDAN

We'd flown all night, hitching a ride on that small aircraft flying from Cairo to South Africa. When we landed in Khartoum about eleven in the morning, we felt as if we had stepped into a blast furnace. It was 110 degrees and rising! For a moment I wondered if we'd missed our calling. It was hot! It was worse than Norman, Oklahoma! We'd never felt anything quite that hot before. People seemed to be lying around in whatever shade from buildings could be found. We thought everyone must be suffocating from the heat. Later we learned that this was the time when Muslims fasted for thirty days. They'd been up feasting all night and were now sleeping and resting during the day. Not being permitted to drink or even swallow their own saliva during the day, was reason enough for them to be less than energetic.

It was a different world from which we had come. Wearing those wide-bottomed, white shorts I'd bought in Cairo, and wearing that white pith-helmet hat didn't make me feel very comfortable. I worried a little on the plane about arriving in Khartoum on Sunday wearing those shorts. I didn't feel any more secure when sedate, impeccably dressed Dr. Shields with his wife, Mildred, met us at the airport and he was wearing neatly pressed, tan trousers. I felt a little better about it when Dr. Shields came to the table the next (first morning for us) wearing shorts. But when I made an innocent comment like, " I see you wear shorts also" and Dr. Shields responded with "Yes, when it's not the Sabbath", I felt badly!

Dr. Shields seemed rather forbidding at first, but we soon came to realize that both he and Mildred were tremendous people who cared for others and were always extremely helpful. The lesson we learned was not to be so quick to pass judgment and to learn to appreciate others however different they may be from one's own way of seeing and doing things. Coming from a somewhat parochial background, I needed to learn tolerance. I was challenged to cherish my basically conservative views and theology, while learning to be flexible in my attitudes and more readily adaptable. In a cross-cultural environment, we'd constantly be challenged to distinguish between form and substance.

We survived the first shock and were told that as we travelled further south to Malakal and eventually to Akobo, some 750 miles south of Khartoum, the weather would be much more pleasant because the rainy season had already begun in that region.

There was much to learn in this difficult and forbidding country. The Shields, who had met us at the airport, ran the mission guest house where we stayed until a way could be arranged to get us further south to our destination. They took care of everything and shared from their experiences. We soon learned that one of the primary virtues we needed to learn to survive and be content was "patience". Everything would take longer and we'd be dependent upon others making decisions over which we would have little control. And then, there was always the uncertainty of it all. There might be a plane in two weeks, or then again, there might not be one indefinitely. We'd just have to wait and see how things developed. Don't be in a hurry! Patience!

We were shown to our room in the back where guests stayed. It was spartan and clean except for evidences of a liberal layer of dust which had been already dealt with. We were told that this was "haboob" season and these strong winds off the desert could develop unpredictably and make a real mess of things.

Each afternoon, everyone disappeared into these rooms, shut the door, turned on that huge overhead fan and rested from about two until four p.m. At four thirty, the Shields and any other missionary guests gathered on the veranda for a refreshing "tea time." We later learned that this was a British custom which missionaries had also adopted. These were delightful times of rich fellowship when in this relaxed atmosphere experiences and plans were shared.

After this "tea break," everyone went into "high gear" and rushed off to the office or the market. Dr. Shields and I returned to government offices to finish what had been started and hadn't been completed during the cooler morning hours.

We learned that the evening dinner hour was also according to British custom. The Sudan was still peacefully ruled by the British during those years, and their good influence was exhibited in innumerable ways. Influenced by their customs, missionaries also fed their children first around six or six thirty in the evening. After the children had bathed, had their evening meal and were safely tucked away for the night, the adults had a quiet evening dinner. It began around eight p.m. and lasted for nearly an hour. During the meal, conversations stopped while everyone listened to the 8 o'clock news on BBC (British Broadcasting Corporation). Rarely was an evening dinner or a morning breakfast completed without the BBC being turned on. It was every missionary's indispensable contact with the outside world. This was supplemented by a subscription to TIME or NEWSWEEK. We soon learned that most missionaries were real news hounds!

OUR FIRST HABOOB

We were in Khartoum less than a week. During that time, however, we experienced that inevitable haboob with its powerful wind and blinding dust.

The night it happened, we were all sleeping on the veranda. Every night those single width beds were rolled out of our rooms onto the veranda to catch the cooler night air. The rooms stayed hot until nearly daybreak. If you wanted to sleep, you slept outside. It was a beautiful experience to feel the fresh air coming in and to see the thousands of stars overhead. Dogs were barking everywhere and when daylight broke, the donkeys were braying in some neighboring Arab's yard, sounding like a dry farm pump that needed a good greasing. The bustle of people on the street getting to their places of activity were part of our new experience. It was often less than quiet when we were there because of the feasting during the night and the fasting during the day. We were there

Ramadan, the month Muslims fasted and feasted. We wondered then, how this could be!

The morning after the haboob, Lavina picked Jimmy out of his basket, and found him covered with dust. His little eyes were okay and his one thumb had been sucked clean, but he was covered with dust. Where he had lain, was clean and you could see his shape in the basket marked out with boundaries set by the dust. Dust had gotten into our suitcases and everything else as well. Nothing escaped receiving its uninvited layer of dust. We actually thought it was pretty bad. Our hosts, Dr. and Mrs. Shields, however, insisted that this one wasn't that bad and that we really ought to see a real haboob sometime. We realized then, that the old timers knew a lot and that we young missionaries had a lot to learn yet!

Dr. Shields knew his way around government offices in Khartoum. He knew exactly what had to be done before we could move on. Permits to travel to the south, considered a closed district by the British, required special permission to enter that area. We were told later that this was, in part, a way to control the spread of Islam in the South by restricting the movement of Muslim merchants who introduced Islam wherever they went.

STOCKING UP IN KHARTOUM

Dr. Shields took us to Morhigs, a large, general store belonging to a Greek merchant. In this store, one could find almost everything needed from lumber and nails to pots and pans and foodstuffs. This store had what we needed to purchase before moving south to Akobo. Morhigs would pack whatever we bought and ship them to Akobo. We were surprised how extremely helpful these Greek merchants in the Sudan were to the missionaries. Most of them were genuine friends.

We bought huge amounts of staples, including big 30 gallon baked earthen pots called zeers and smaller two to three quart earthen jars called gulas. At Akobo, we'd be having our water carried up from the river to the house. Every day, the person who carried up the water would fill those zeers. The zeers, in turn, would drip the water drop by drop into a bucket underneath. We learned that these were essential pieces of equipment for our safety and survival. Without a senior missionary like Dr. Shields helping us, we wouldn't have had a clue. Later at Akobo, we learned how to clean the zeers periodically by having them emptied and rubbed down with a soft brick. Then we let them dry out good before refilling. Between cleanings they'd be useable for another two or three weeks, depending on how dirty the river was before cleaning was again required. The clean water in the bucket was put on a fire and boiled, cooled and poured into the smaller, clay jars called gulas, which aerated the water and cooled it. This was a daily chore that Lavina learned never to neglect. If one did, by afternoon when it was hot, that cool, refreshing drink might become an occasion for drinking lukewarm water! We learned fast!

Supplies from Khartoum, would be put on a train by the Greek merchant. His agent would transfer them from the train to the Nile steamer at Kosti, about 19 hours by rail from where they had started out. Three days later, a resident missionary in Malakal would meet the steamer and off-load these supplies destined for Akobo, another 300 river miles up country. Akobo was approximately 700 miles south of Khartoum. It'd take from two weeks to a month before they'd arrive. At Akobo, we'd be off loading them from a provincial, paddle wheel steamer. They couldn't get there too quickly!

MALAKAL — JULY 17, 1948

So there we were flying to Malakal with all the business of getting supplies and permits accomplished. We were so excited to be heading south this quickly. Older missionaries commented that we'd broken all records. Normally, missionaries had been travelling a couple of months to reach the Sudan. God was indeed blessing us and we daily thanked and praised Him.

What a thrill to land in Malakal. There was a different feel to the air. The atmosphere seemed fresh and clean. This was rainy season in the South. We sensed immediately how much more pleasant the weather was.

Mat and Ruby Gilliland, missionaries based in Malakal, along with Robb McLaughlin, a young, short-term volunteer working as a builder met us at the plane. An earliest memory is of the beautiful cooing of the morning dove perched somewhere in one of the tall trees in front of the house on the riverbank where the Gillilands were living.

Malakal was the capital of the Upper Nile Province. In 1948, when we first arrived in Malakal, the British were in control. The provincial governor, deputy governor, a chief police officer, an education officer and a public works officer were people we came to know well. They were generally very helpful to the mission. In the field of education the government and the mission cooperated closely. The British administered a vast area covering thousands of square miles and numerous tribes, each with its own customs and language. Some of these officials were deeply committed Christians and had the welfare of the people under their jurisdiction at heart. We learned to respect them and greatly benefitted from their wisdom and assistance.

Before moving south from Malakal to Akobo, some 300 river miles away, a lot had to happen first. Was there a steamer going soon? If one was going up river, could we find space on it? How long would we have to wait, if we missed the first one going? If it went too soon, would we be able to get the additional supplies we needed and would there be room for them on that steamer?

STOCKING UP IN MALAKAL

Mat Gilliland and I did a lot of walking back and forth the quarter mile from the mission into the town. We went to and fro between government offices and between the two Greek merchants. These Greek merchants had been in Malakal a long time and were the only source of groceries and supplies for missionaries and government people.

Having just come from America, the shelves in these small, Greek merchant shops didn't look like much to us. There wasn't a great variety on those shelves. One item I remember as being in abundance was a mixed, canned fruit from South Africa called "Compote." We later got so tired of it at Akobo that we began to refer to it as "Compost." Not too complimentary!

We'd gotten the big items in Khartoum, but not knowing when they'd show up at Akobo, we had to purchase basic supplies again and with less variety available in Malakal. Now we purchased a five gallon tin of cooking oil, a two hundred pound sack of sugar, salt, kerosene, beans, rice, powdered milk — all in quantity.

Later, at Akobo, we learned that once a year, Lavina would be returning to Malakal to order the next year's supply of most things. These would be supplemented with orders placed by letter or telegram we'd send to these same Greek merchants who would pack things up and send them to us at Akobo. We were amazed how thoughtful and helpful these merchants were. We were utterly dependent upon them and for the frequent good offices of the resident missionary if something out of the ordinary was needed. We would learn to help each other and depend upon each other. The mission family is unique and precious. Ties between us would become strong and bind us together like one large family working together, laughing and sometimes crying together.

The "TAMAI"

We were in Malakal only a few days before we boarded a wood burning, paddle wheel steamer, called the "TAMAI." It was painted white and was really picturesque. The first class barge on which we travelled had two small bedrooms, a dining room and a lovely screened in veranda across the front with comfortable, cushioned reed chairs. The kitchen was down below immediately beneath the dining room. It was dark and dirty and smelled like smoke. This was where a person hired for that task normally cooked the food on a wood fire. When all was ready, he would send the food up on a "dumb waiter," operated in something like a chute in which dirty clothes are sent to the basement to be laundered. It was brought up to the kitchen and lowered again by pulling on a rope attached to the shelf on which the food was coming up and on which the dirty dishes would be lowered. We'd never seen one of these and it was intriguing to this young missionary family!

We brought with us all our food needed for the remaining estimated 300 mile, seven day journey up the Sobat and Pibor rivers. We also had on board our supplies for Akobo. Paul Musser and his wife, along with Mildred Heasty, who'd grown up on a mission station and whose parents were still there, were traveling with us. They chaperoned us as far as Nasir, located on the Sobat about 90 miles from Akobo. They got off there, visited missionary friends, and we proceeded on the last 90 miles alone to Akobo, just off the Western tip of Ethiopia.

Travelling by paddle-wheel steamer was a marvelous, calming experience for us. With the gentle breezes created by the slow, forward movement of the TAMAI, we relaxed and reflected on God's goodness and mercies. So much had already happened. It was good to have time to reflect. The leisurely journey on the TAMAI provided that delightful opportunity. Ours was a rare privilege.

STOPPING AT NASIR MISSION STATION

We were on the TAMAI seven days and nights. Ninety miles from Akobo, on the Sobat river, was Nasir where Presbyterian missionaries had been at work for many years. The work among the Nuer had been started there by Dr. Lambie befored he moved on to Ethiopia. Dr. and Mrs. Smith were still there and about to retire, but their daughter, Mary, was now back at Nasir. She had recently completed her medical training and was serving as a medical missionary doctor. We were met at the steamer by Charles

(Chuck) and Mary Alice Jordan. Chuck was a trained Agriculturalist. We didn't know then that within a few years the Jordans would be moving to Akobo and become dear colleagues of ours living in the same mission station. Several things stick in my memory from those 24 hours we stopped at Nasir. First impressions have a way of writing themselves indelibly on the mind! The flies were so numerous as we walked from the steamer to the mission house, that the next time out, I put on my army surplus, bee bonnet. During that time, most young missionaries going to remote areas stocked up on things like that at the army surplus stores. We'd done it too. We were ready for anything!

I must have looked like an idiot and I wonder what those missionaries must have thought about this naive, foolish young missionary. The Arab merchants sitting in front of their small, thatch roofed shops must have had a good laugh too. We weren't in the Sudan many days when we realized that coping with flies was normal and one didn't wear a bee bonnet! The missionaries at Nasir must have shaken their heads and had some hilarious laughs after we returned to the TAMAI.

Another recollection is of the food these missionaries served us. At Mr. and Mrs. Smith's for breakfast, they came out with a very dark colored porridge which hardly looked like something one would eat. It looked like mud! In fact, however, it tasted great, much like our ralston cereal. We learned that missionaries ate this porridge almost every morning. It was their home made cereal, prepared by roasting the ripened dura (kaffir corn). This particular variety had a purple color, and consequently the dirty looking appearance when cooked. We learned later that the dura had a number of varieties and colors and we often had beautiful tasting, as well as nice colored, porridge with which to start our days.

At Akobo, our problem wasn't the color of the porridge, but quality of the milk we put on it. Before the mission had its own herd of cattle, we'd buy milk from village people.

One could never be sure that the gourd in which they brought the milk hadn't been washed in cow urine and that a little may have remained in the bottom of the gourd. It didn't take more than a swallow to know thing's weren't right!! A few such experiences, and we missionaries were strongly motivated to have a mission herd. Each cow produced only a little, but we had good quality control and that's what was important for a good dish of home grown, home roasted, dura porridge at the beginning of every day.

On that stop at Nasir, back in July of 1948, the single, lady missionaries served up a delicious noon meal. I still remember how much better it tasted than it looked. We were served a fruit we hadn't tasted in the states. They called it papaw (papaya), deep orange in color and, as we learned in the months ahead, normally eaten when the flesh is firm. Theirs must have fallen off the tree because it was soft and gushy, not nice and firm as we imagined this unknown fruit, which sort of reminded us of a cantaloupe,should be. Once we gingerly tasted it, we found it quite good, especially when we squeezed a little lime on it as per their instructions on how it should be eaten. Then at the close of the meal, they came out with a very "runny" lemon (lime) pie. It was much too thin to pass the test, but it tasted so good that no one complained. We soon learned that lime pie just was that way in this hot country and that regardless of how it appeared, it was "special." We loved it, and a good lime pie like that often graced our table in the years ahead.

Once settled in, we raised papaya all the time. We grew to love them and I suspect that we ate papaya at least 300 days out of the year. Our morning breakfast rarely lacked a generous half of a papaya with a slice of lemon beside it to spruce it up just a bit! Papaya mixed with bananas, oranges and some home grown pineapple was "missionary-desert" that can't be matched anywhere in the world! We loved it then and miss it now!

Stopping and staying overnight with the missionaries at Nasir was a great experience. These were folks from whom we could learn so much. They would become our dearest friends and colleagues in the Lord's work in the years ahead. We were glad to stop, but itching to move on to complete the last 90 miles up river to Akobo. We'd been on the way for 25 days. Seemed long, but everyone told us we were breaking all records. It'd taken the Swarts more than two months to make it, including their delay enroute in Egypt. So far as this young missionary couple was concerned, we just wanted to get there as soon as possible. Excitement was mounting! So, when the steamer, having unloaded its cargo for Nasir and having loaded the grain and other supplies for Akobo, blew its first warning whistle indicating a sailing time was approaching, we collected our things, put Jimmy back in the basket, and with the resident missionaries leading the way, we threaded our way through the busy local market, stepping it off in the direction of the TAMAI.

HEADING FOR AKOBO

Finally, it happened! The narrow gang planks connecting the steamer with the shore were pulled on board. The ropes tying the steamer to secure posts were loosened and dragged onto the barge. A last whistle blew and the boat began to move. This was it! We were slowly churning our way upstream, heading for Akobo. We were alone now, just the four of us, Lavina, Dennis our five year old, Jimmy, then four months, and myself. This was adventure of the highest sort. We were on our own!

As we picked up just a little speed, the gentle breeze began blowing through the screen on the sitting veranda. It was pleasant and refreshing. We drew close to one another, put our arms around each other and praised God for His watch-care, protection and leading. We knew His good hand had been on us all the way. Our hearts sang to be His missionaries in this far away land of Africa. We were glad because we knew that He was taking us to a place where without our being there a task He was entrusting to us would remain undone. My hope and dream was to be the translator for the New Testament in the Anuak language. Time would tell!

29

"...offer your bodies as living sacrifices, holy and pleasing to God--this is your spiritual act of worship."

Romans 12:1

CHAPTER THREE

OUR NEW HOME
AKOBO

WELCOMED BY THE LIGHT OF AN ALADDIN LAMP

According to folks at Akobo, we were 24 hours ahead of schedule. It was already dark, nearly 7:30 p.m. when the TAMAI finally stopped and tied up. We discovered that we were directly in front of Don and Lyda McClure's house. It was less than 75 yards up the bank and down the short path from the steamer into their house. What a night to remember!

As the steamer was docking, we could see a bright light coming down the steep bank toward us. It turned out to be Lyda McClure carrying a kerosene burning lamp to light her way. She was surrounded on all sides by about fifty school boys wearing their white shoulder cloths. Their white teeth and white cloths were about all we could make out, but the chatter of excited voices filled the air. What an unforgettable night! The journey was over! Twenty seven days — via ocean freighter, train, airplanes and the last seven days by a slow, wood burning, paddle wheel steamer. School boys meant willing hands. They helped with the luggage and the supplies we'd brought from Malakal.

Lyda quickly apologized that Don was not there to welcome us. They had thought the steamer was coming the next day. Don and Wilma Kats, a single missionary who was still living with the McClures until the single ladies'

31

house was built, had gone by boat up river to shoot some ducks for meat. They weren't home yet. She explained that Bob and Morrie Swart were living in a vacant government house at the government post about a mile away. She said, "They'll know you're here when they hear the steamer's whistle. They'll be joining us for dinner once Don get's back."

By this time we had made our way up the bank — pitch dark, except for the light of the Aladdin lamp. We shall never forget the awesome, unforgettable experience of entering by the front door into the McClure house with Lyda and that Aladdin lamp. The room we entered was a huge round tukl (mud-walled and round with a grass roof). Overhead was a grass roof, held in space by 2 inch coils of woven grass rings that went round and around to make a conical covering. It was so beautiful and rustic. We had never seen anything like it. The roof was made of poles, those rings of grass and thick thatch which we would see better the next day. It was poetic, picturesque and made an indelible impression on these young missionaries. We knew then that we had truly arrived. This was Africa and these missionaries, like the Anuaks, lived in houses made from mud and grass. We were home in Africa. Praise be to God.

We soon heard the drone of the outboard approaching in the darkness. Don and Wilma came in with guns and a handful of ducks. Don apologized all over the place for not being there to welcome us, but explained that we'd come so fast they just weren't expecting us for another day. Don had a great sense of humor. Having been on the TAMAI seven long days and nights, it didn't seem that we could sneak up on anyone unexpectedly. But that's the way things were in the Sudan. We were often in the dark. No mail! No news! And sometimes no lights!

Bob and Morrie Swart and their two little girls, Valarie and Gayle, soon arrived in their jeep. We were all so excited. Questions flew thick and fast from both directions. We learned that we'd be going home with them in the jeep and that we'd be living with them until our house was ready.

Lyda had a fantastic meal ready in no time, including a delicious cherry pie for desert. We learned that they, too, had been to Leggett's wholesale store in New York before coming out to purchase basic supplies of tinned fruit and vegetables. Without Leggetts, missionaries would have been hurting. We hoped our freight would catch up with us soon with our order of tinned food. Lyda had a real gift at homemaking and was known for her good cooking and creative table displays. We ate by candlelight with candlewick dishes in a mud house with a grass roof. We were pleased and surprised!

LEARNING TO LIVE IN A DIFFERENT WORLD

During the meal we learned more about what to expect. Additional missionaries were scheduled to come in the months ahead. Once the rains ended in a few more weeks, Don and Bob would be busy with a big building program to provide houses, school buildings and a clinic. As soon as Bob and Morrie's house was built, they planned to move from the government house a mile away to the mission compound. The single ladies were scheduled to have the next new house. When completed, Wilma Kats would move out of the spare bedroom in the McClure house to be joined by a United Presbyterian missionary expected at Akobo early in the new year.

We learned that we'd be living temporarily with the Swarts. Our more permanent house was a little over a mile away in the opposite direction, downstream from the mission. That would put it a little over two miles from the Swarts. This house had been started by another mission while Don was on furlough. It was abandoned when the two missions deemed it best not to work that closely together when large unreached areas remained with no missionaries at all. Good sense prevailed and any possible tension between the two missions had been averted. God overruled it all for good and it proved to be a great blessing for us personally.

The building needed a lot of additional work on it before one could move in. It had walls and a roof only. It needed a floor, doors and window openings needed frames with mosquito netting on all the openings until screen was available to replace the cloth. Everyone agreed that netting was good for mosquitoes and flies but not too formidable against lions! To work on the house I'd be walking the more than two miles back and forth each day until it was finished. The jeep couldn't make it because the river had backed up and the swamp enroute was impassable. I later learned that I'd have to wade in water nearly up to my waist to get there. Once through the swamp things dried up quite rapidly.

So Bob and Morrie took us along with them that night and we had our first night on army cots under a mosquito net. Some new missionaries experience several weeks with the stomach and digestive tracts making their adjustment to the new environment. I was one of them! I still recall how sick the smell of fresh guavas made me feel. I could never believe then that one day I'd learn to love them and eat them in all sorts of combinations.

Lavina seemed real strong and took everything in stride. This surprised us because back home, I was the strong one and she had frequently had minor health problems. In fact, I was to give her liver shots the first few months to help her build up her iron! During those first few weeks when food just didn't sit well, I often felt I was the one who needed the shot more than she!

The physical adjustment for the body was more difficult than our emotional adjustment. We were so grateful to be missionaries at Akobo. We counted it an unspeakable privilege. Any difficulties and inconveniences were part of a missionary's experience. We remembered Paul's testimony,"I have learned in whatsoever state I am, therewith to be content." Phil 4:11. The excitement, the new things we were constantly learning, and the challenge to be available to the Lord shaped our mind-set. When we were tempted to be anxious, we found ourselves often remembering the exhortation of the Psalmist, "Commit thy way unto the Lord; trust also in Him and He will bring it to pass." Psalm 37:5.

WE LIVE OFF THE MISSION COMPOUND

Akobo mission station anticipated rapid growth. The Anuak plan called for a total of fifteen missionaries to work among the Anuak for fifteen years. Additional stations were on the drawing board. But in the beginning, most of the new missionaries would likely get their start at Akobo. Houses were needed. To get started the mission would put people where there was a roof that didn't leak. And if the roof did leak, they'd put them there anyway!! That's why Bob and Morrie Swart were a mile up stream from the mission where the McClure's lived and we were to be a good mile down stream on the other side. We were scattered out along the Akobo river. We were connected either by walking or using a canoe or outboard during the rains and by jeep during the dry season. Later I also had a Whizzer bike with a motor on it.

Lavina and I had ambivalent feelings about living in isolation down-stream from the mission. At first we were tempted to feel isolated and somewhat deprived. But once we got our roots down, we began to realize that living off the compound at this place called Pakang, located near a large Anuak village, gave us a unique advantage. We were forced to use the Anuak language to be understood. We would learn the Anuak language more quickly and more idiomatically. Once we were able to speak a little, we had a marvelous evangelistic opportunity to share the Gospel in those nearby villages. Living there, we found our fulfillment in relationships with our new friends and neighbors, the Anuaks. Were we to live on the mission station, we'd likely find our social relationships with fellow missionaries tending to take center stage. These and many other thoughts made us ponder it all. There were advantages and disadvantages to living some distance from our colleagues. On balance, we concluded that we had received a blessing and opportunity in disguise and we gave God daily thanks. Our hearts were overflowing with joy. Lavina and I were both supremely happy and content.

LETTERS HOME INDICATE THE ADJUSTMENTS

Letters to our families during those early days, indicate how things were going and what we were thinking.

September 8, 1948:

"All of us are just fine. Our bodies have made the adjustment now. Our appetites have returned and we are all feeling fine. I was pretty soft when we first came, but now my body is strong, my feet are tough and I am a real farmer. There is much physical work that must be done out here to get things organized. The village workmen help a great deal, but still there is always the special work to do one's self...

"Almost three weeks ago we moved from the Swarts into our new house. It is not complete yet, but a unit of it is finished so we moved into it with odds and ends of furniture provided by the other two families. Luckily, McClures still had their old refrigerator so we are using that too. Our own things have not arrived, nor do we know yet if they are on the way. I have had word that my guns have left Egypt and are on the way. I have borrowed a couple of Don's guns for now. I use a shotgun constantly for ducks for food. I shot four in one shot the other day.

"Our home is located about 1 1/4 miles down stream from the mission. It faces the river along the South side and is set back about 100 to 150 yards from the water. It is a rectangular building at present with three rooms and a washroom. The three rooms are about 12' by 16' with a hallway and bathroom between two of the rooms. The walls are about a foot thick, made of mud bricks covered with solid mud. The roof comes down low and extends out over the side about 5 feet. It is a grass roof. We have no glass. The windows and doors are full size and are covered with mosquito netting. We use one room for sleeping, one for a sitting and dining room, and the other for a kitchen. Lavina cooks on three single burner kerosene stoves. Not too handy for her.

"There is a small house, formerly intended for a kitchen in back of our house. So in it, I fixed up a stove — building it out of a type of sand brick. I made the stove pipe out of five gallon kerosene tins. I made the cover over the stove out of one tin I had opened up flat. Then for an oven I took the end out of the can and fixed a wooden and tin door in it. Well — believe it or not, we baked bread in it yesterday and it worked slick. The bread was very good! Out here a person makes a little bit go a long way. We would not think of throwing a rag, a piece of paper or a piece of string away. I made a table for Lavina to use temporarily out of a little grocery box about 20" square. For legs I used some long sticks of firewood. For nails I used the old crooked nails out of the box. Everything is useful out here. We enjoy making things a lot. Sometimes it puzzles us just how we are going to do it, but after awhile we figure something out. For funnels we are just using a tin can bent shut on one side for a spout. And so it goes with making something out of nothing almost every day.

"We like our place here very much. We are away from the mission which has some disadvantages. We have, however, the advantage of being near a big village and this will give us a big opportunity to learn the language and to carry on evangelistic work. Every day we have about 20 or 25 women, men and children hanging around the yard. Often they come and sit right under the eaves of our house where it is nice and cool. When we know the language we will be able to have Bible story hours for them and what an opportunity it will be to bring them the message of salvation. Then, too, in some ways, I think it is an advantage to be more or less alone. I think one would tend to tire of living too close together. As it is we can get together whenever we want to. Don has a motor boat and we can get back and forth easily. Else there is always an Anuak canoe around and we can get an Anuak to take us. It is a common sight to see us on the river in a driving rain. We are used to that here.

"We have tall grass out away from the house a ways and it is a good place for the wild animals. Every night we hear *the hyenas howling. Last week one morning we had a lion track across our front yard. The following night we were both awakened about mid-night by the roaring of a lion. It is a blood curdling roar they have and he was very close by. We got up and I loaded my heavy rifle. Lavina and I each sat by the mosquito netting covered window openings looking for him. My light was not strong enough so we did not get him, but now I have a search light and car battery from the mission. We are hoping he returns. Sunday morning we had a hyena track less than 6 feet from our front door. In the evening, right after we were in bed we heard him howl in the back yard. You should have seen Lavina and me out there in the terrible mosquitoes with the searchlight and gun. He got away in the tall grass, but during the dry season it will not be so easy for him.*

"While building our house, one morning we discovered a leopard track right under our window. So, you see we have lots of animals around here. How would you like to sleep with just a thin mosquito net between you and an angry lion? We are so used to it that we think nothing of it anymore. Can you imagine? Even Lavina isn't afraid of them! It is just part of our life here — as trucks and cars and airplanes are back home. I think I have seen about two or three planes since we left Malakal!"

June 27, 1950:

"Last night we were rudely awakened at 2. a. m. by an invasion of army ants. They were all over my study and bedroom. They awakened me first and then Dennis, Lavina and Jimmy. Do they ever bite! Scorpions were fleeing for their lives before their carnivorous march. I killed 8 scorpions which had fled out of the grass roof down the walls unto the floor. I walked in the dark the first time, not realizing their presence and missed a couple of them by a matter of inches. I think the Lord was caring for his own again. We had to spend the rest of the night on the davenport, in chairs and on the floor in another part of the house."

September 18, 1950:

"Just before coming in for the night we took the children down to the river to wash the mud off from them. Right now I am at my desk sitting under what I call a 'mosquito house.' It is a huge net about 7 feet high and 8 feet square, tied to the roof sticks and surrounding my desk, typewriter stand and chairs for Lavina and myself. This is our first evening with it. We are borrowing it from Lee and Kitty Crandall as their house is alright. Our house is literally so full of mosquitoes that they tend to get in our eyes and ears.

"We have a very fine mosquito repellant made in Khartoum, and with long trousers or house coats we have managed for awhile in the earlier part of the evening, but it was pretty rugged. We think this little cage will be pretty nice." (We soon discovered that it became very hot under there because inside we also had to have an aladdin lamp burning and it used up the limited supply of oxygen.)

"I wish you could see just how we live out here. We so often take these things for granted, but I suppose you would be quite surprised."

March 10, 1949:

"We are all sick here except Jimmy. We've been in bed for a week with a burning fever and a terrifying headache in the back of the head and down the back. We have to take aspirins every couple of hours to keep going. Sulfa or penicillin don't touch it. Our doctor doesn't know what it is yet. He thinks we may have typhoid fever, but wont know until he sends our blood samples tomorrow via car and flies them to Khartoum. ... We're having a pretty rugged time of it, but don't worry about us. The Lord will most surely see us through. ...

"Dr. Harry Hagar is here for two days and leaves tomorrow. Blood samples were refrigerated in thermoses and taken by Dr. Hangar and his travelling companion Dr. Weber, the 185 miles by road to Malakal. These were then

put on a plane and flown another 500 miles to Khartoum. A telegram from Khartoum confirmed that we had Typhoid fever. Fortunately for us, our inoculations help reduce the pain and duration of the disease. ...."

HOW LAVINA COPED
THOSE FIRST MONTHS AT PAKANG

Those first six months at Pakang were an extended camp-out. We survived and thrived on borrowed pots and pans, mismatched dishes and cutlery, army cots and improvised cooking utensils.

Lavina, like all the missionaries, baked her own bread and prepared everything that went into our mouths. The bread deal was quite something. She had a 200 pound bag of flour when she started out. Gradually, it went down, but as it went down the weevils and worms in it went up! She taught an Anuak to sift it, sometimes running it through an old silk stocking to separate the weevils and worms from the flour we wanted to save and use. The sifted flour was set in the sun in large, round, eight inch high, copper wash tubs called a "tish" which we'd brought down from Khartoum. Chickens and goats had to be kept away and whenever a sudden shower appeared these heavy tubs had to be brought in quickly.

At first Lavina mixed her bread and let it rise at home. But after she'd carried it that 1 1/4 miles to the mission to bake it in Lyda McClure's oven, she found herself baking unleavened bread. The "rise" in it was gone! To solve the problem, she took to carrying the flour and yeast and mixing it at Lyda's and waiting for it to rise there before baking it. This way she came home with some mighty fine looking bread.

But baking it in the back yard worked out much better. That kerosene tin with a partial, mahogany wooden door swinging on a nail driven through the tin on each side worked just fine. The only problem was that about every three weeks, the door would dry out so badly that it started to burn and would have to be replaced.

Lavina not only baked on that outside arrangement of bricks, but also did a good bit of cooking out there when things needed to simmer longer. This economized on kerosene and, anyway, those kerosene pressure burners were often a headache. They operated under pressure and the little pump often needed a new leather which we didn't have.

We were counting the days until our freight would arrive. Week after week went by and still no certain word on where it was or whether it would arrive before the last steamer for the season would come. In the end, our things from America made it to Malakal from Port Sudan in time to be loaded on the very last steamer before the river would be too shallow to navigate. It finally arrived at Akobo on January 6th.

The arrival of our stove, kerosene refrigerator, beds, pots and pans and dishes and cases of canned fruit and vegetable from Leggetts wholesale house in New York really lifted our spirits. We were as happy as kids with new toys. And what a difference it made in the comfort with which we lived. Never did that good food taste so delicious. Now Lavina could really cook again and bake her bread right in her own oven. She'd made do with very little and had made our little house into an attractive, homey place, but now she could really enjoy some of the essentials which would make everything easier for her. She's a great cook and homemaker under any conditions, but having the essentials again, would make it so very much easier.

Lavina was a truly happy, fulfilled missionary wife and mother. She was more than busy. Each of the children was taught during their first years at home. It took a lot of skill and perseverance to keep busy children at their schooling. Still, in addition to these inescapable responsibilities, Lavina found time to help me with primer construction, teaching some of the women and just making time for anyone who came. Our home was always open and many hours were spent sharing with women and girls who dropped by. Lavina set a terrific example for Anuak women as to what it means to be a wife and mother who modeled the love of Jesus Christ. I don't recall an Anuak, or for that matter, a

Mesengo who ever criticized Lavina for some failure in character or demeanor. She set a great example for all of us in our home and in relationships with others. Her's was honoring to Christ! In all our years on the field, I never once heard her pine to return to America. To God be the glory!

Lavina was a brave woman. She showed no signs of the fear she had once expressed about living in Africa among the lions and crocodiles. She had come a long way since that day when I came home from seminary and suggested the Lord might be calling us to "the dark continent." A vision of being up a tree in Africa with a hungry lion at the base had long since evaporated. She learned to cope with ants, rats and snakes in the house, plus scorpions that hid in the grass roof and would drop down on our beds when the army ants invaded us. Once when she was resting on the bed on an afternoon and looking up into the grass roof, she saw a snake in the grass weaving its way forward just overhead. And still another time, she was cleaning out a small cabinet we'd made out of a packing box. Immediately behind this little three foot cabinet she discovered a poisonous puff adder sleeping. Once she had a six-foot red cobra in the dining room. She, and the rest of us too, were all so very aware of our daily need for the Lord's protection and care.

DANGERS AND INCONVENIENCES

There were plenty of dangers and inconveniences to cope with in Africa. I sometimes said, "Everything is done the hard way out here." The modern conveniences that make life easier for women in our homes in America weren't possible out there. Clothes were washed by hand. Washed clothes were hung on an outside line to dry. No problem during the dry season, but a real headache during the rains. The responsible person always had one eye on the clouds! Ironing was with a heavy, cast metal, charcoal burning iron. Floors were mopped daily to keep ahead of the dust and dirt. There was no wall to wall carpeting and only a few throw rugs. Inside plumbing was a faucet attached to a pipe through the wall coming out of an elevated barrel positioned on a platform. Water was carried up from the river morning and night to keep the barrels full. Another barrel stood outside the bathroom and was connected to a faucet and a shower. This too was filled by hiking it up from the river. Much more could be said, but the question is, "How does a woman cope and still have time for ministry?"

The answer was found in training people for those tasks. Taking people right out of the village who wore little or no clothes and had no experience in how foreigners lived and teaching them was a challenge and sometimes a frustrating experience. People trained to help in these tasks were known as "servants" or "house-boys". Sometimes new missionaries didn't like the idea of having "servants" and would try to do all these tasks themselves. It was interesting to see how many of these "idealists" gradually came around and decided that coping with all these mundane tasks was taking too much valuable time and robbing one of time for an effective ministry. Servants were a necessary evil. In fact, they were a mixed blessing. On balance, we couldn't have coped without them. Many of those who worked as servants stayed for years. They enjoyed the security of their position and the benefits that flowed from it. We missionaries learned to live with servants and tried to lead them to Christ and set a good example before them. Our servants, particularly those who worked in our houses became trusted friends — more like family members than employees. We thanked God for them. But had there been a choice between modern washers and driers, carpets and vacuum cleaners, we'd have opted for the latter.

With this background, you can now appreciate the pathos and humor of several of our experiences during those early years at Akobo.

THAT FASCINATING PIT

Servants were great baby-sitters, but sometimes they let us down. I recall twice when our children played with things and in places that were out of bounds.

We had an 18-foot pit for our toilet or latrine. It was dug under the backside eave of the roof and enclosed with a mud wall. Its advantage was that we had access to it without having to go outside during the rains.

For some inexplicable reason, that little room seemed to have a special attraction, on occasion, for our little children. Once when we came home from the mission, we learned that David had been playing over the hole with my set of keys to all the trunks and doors dangling from a chain in his hand. I guess it was great fun to see the pendulum of the keys in motion until they slipped out of his hand and sank to the bottom. The keys were never recovered!

On another occasion, however, the situation was quite a bit more serious. The clothes hamper also stood, out of the way, in that same little room having the box with the hole in it. This time, the servant was preoccupied with something, and, sure enough, the children were in there again. This time they took to dropping pieces of laundry down the hole. It must have been great sport because, the hamper was nearly empty when we discovered it. With the help of a flashlight I discovered what had happened. Fortunately, the things were still retrievable. With the help of a garden rake, I think I recovered every last piece. The final solution was a hook on the door out of reach! The barn was locked after the horse had escaped! How human we missionaries proved to be.

A GREEN THUMB PUTS FOOD ON THE TABLE

Lavina can put a terrific meal on the table, but if you don't have any food in the house its impossible. Perhaps that's where a little team work makes the difference. I was challenged to provide vegetables, fruit and meat so it could happen. I had grown up on a farm in Minnesota and we'd also been truck gardeners along with having cows, horses, chickens and pigs, so gardening was easy and fun for me. I have to qualify that word "easy" somewhat because nothing is really easy in the Sudan. The cotton soil was so hard where we started our garden that I added sand to the soil. The sand, itself, had come from a pit dug by Bob and Don along the river bank in connection with the building program. That cotton soil was so tightly packed that their sand pit went right down beside the water, going 15 or more feet below the water level only a few feet from the river, without water ever leaking into the pit.

In addition to adding a little sand, we encouraged things with a liberal dose of sheep manure from the village. Then to protect the young seeds and seedlings, I put a thin layer of grass on a lattice work over each of the seed beds. These were gradually thinned out as the plants grew and needed more exposure to the sun. Water was carried up from the river by one or two Anuaks. They'd carry two five- gallon tins of water, on each end of a four-foot pole that they put across their shoulders. Many months later the First Reformed Church in Orange City, Iowa sent us a gasoline- powered engine and pump which we positioned on a small barge floating on empty barrels. Vegetables and fruit began to thrive in abundance!

It was a lot of work to survive. But growing a garden was good for me, as it gave me a useful hobby which fit in with my translation work so very handily. Eventually, I had a couple of Anuaks who could do most of the work, and I would just keep an eye on it, so to speak. Late in the afternoons, when the sun was smaller and the work in the office had been set aside, I enjoyed "playing" in the garden. It was a real relaxation and renewing experience for me. The other missionaries liked it too as we grew more than we needed and could often share with those whose thumbs were less green or who were so busy with other things they found little time or inclination to garden.

Lavina, the little children and I frequently moved around in the garden in the late afternoon as the temperature was beginning to go down and the sun was getting ready to retire for the night. It was family time and we enjoyed our time together so very much. Sometimes, we'd get in the boat and take a little ride up the river just to cool off as the breeze we created evaporated the perspiration.

A FISH FROM HEAVEN

One late afternoon episode in the garden is unforgettable. The river, of course, flowed peacefully, with only a long, inclined bank separating the garden and it. On that river scores, sometimes hundreds, of pelicans were floating, swimming and catching their fish.

This particular afternoon, one of them took off, circled in the direction of the garden and was nearly overhead. From its mouth was dangling his catch—a live fish. It looked large enough to make us a meal. Lavina, looking up longingly said,"How I'd like that fish for supper tonight." The thought had hardly formed and the words had scarcely taken shape, when that pelican dropped his fish almost at our feet in the garden. It couldn't have been more freshly delivered. And, it couldn't have been delivered at a more appropriate time — just in time for supper and providing our first meat in several days! Our thanks to the Lord for our food took on special significance that evening. Our children had a first class object lesson in our Lord's ability to meet the needs of his missionaries, even in extraordinary ways! The lesson wasn't lost on their parents either! Thirty years later, the memory of that experience still triggers the joy bells ringing in our hearts. Is anything too hard for the Lord? God is so good!

HUNTING TO PUT MEAT ON THE TABLE

At Akobo, we missionaries had different gifts, training and responsibilities. The practical jobs were divided among us taking these factors into account. Don and Bob did a great job with the cattle. The mission herd grew steadily and after a few years we had all the fresh milk and home-made butter we needed. As the herd increased, the men would sometimes butcher an animal and we'd have beef instead of wild animal meat in our refrigerators.

During our early years, we depended on our ability to locate and shoot one of the numerous kinds of wild animals for meat. We would usually work all day and then around four or five in the afternoon we'd go out looking for animals. Bob and I frequently went out together. We had a lot of fun kidding each other on who was the best shot. He used a .306 calibre bolt action, and I had a .348 lever action because I shoot left-handed.

Hunting was great fun at first, but gradually it lost some of its appeal. A lot of hard work was involved in going out for meat. Once the animal was shot, we either skinned it or supervised the skinning of it. Some of the meat and all the intestines were given to the local people to divide as they saw fit. We learned early on not to try to divide the meat for them ourselves. This had great potential for misunderstanding! Sometimes the Anuaks and Nuers would quarrel as to who should get what. That really took the fun out of it.

Once the animal was skinned and each missionary home had its chunk of meat, we still had to cut it into appropriate size pieces so our wives could handle it. By the time we finished all of this, it was often between nine and ten at night. Since we also arose early in the Sudan, any night activities tended to be limited. At the mission, the generator was set to go off around nine-thirty at night.

During the rainy season, which usually lasted from late April until early October, we depended more on our hunting ducks, geese and guinea fowl. We really became excellent shots with all that practice. I had a smaller calibre shotgun, a .410 pump action. Many a spur-winged goose tumbled out of the sky and into our kettle. Ducks often congregated along the river in thick concentrations. More than once I shot five to eight ducks with one shot. Without our guns our table would have looked quite different. They were our lifeline for meat just as our garden was for vegetables. There was no meat market, vegetable stand or bakery at Akobo. Our missionary wives cooked everything from scratch. And they were all experts at it.

TRAVELLING ON THE RIVERS BY OUTBOARD

Looking back on our years in the Sudan, I have often marvelled that we had no serious, life threatening accidents on the river. The river was our road to get places. We visited villages up and down the river for preaching purposes. During the rains, we'd go out to shoot ourselves some ducks or geese to keep meat on the table. Sometimes we'd go on picnics and stop under some thorn tree on the river bank where ubiquitous Anuaks or Nuers always showed up from nowhere. We spent hours and hours in outboards on short trips and long ones.

Several times each year we'd do the trip of 90 miles each way to our neighboring missionaries working in Nasir.

Once when Lavina was ill, I left her behind at Akobo and took Jimmy along with me so that she could have the needed rest. Jimmy was about five years then. Eager to get back home to Lavina, we turned around at Nasir that afternoon, intending, at least, to get a start. We'd go a couple of hours and then sleep in the boat. By the time we started going up the Pibor river, it was already getting pretty dark. We pulled into the tall grass beside the flooded river and put up our net in the boat to sleep. Jimmy fell asleep in the bottom of our 16 foot boat, but I never did succeed in overcoming the mosquito problem. There were just too many to cope with. Finally, after a couple of hours of this, I decided we'd do better just travelling slowly up the river, creating enough breeze to lick the mosquitoes. I left Jimmy sleeping on the bottom under the net which was now serving as his blanket.

We travelled all night like that making our way toward Akobo. On a narrow, crooked river with floating logs and grass, it was quite a strain. At first we went quite slowly, but gradually, as I became more brave and accustomed to the darkness our speed increased to where we were travelling at full speed. I have never been on the river when it was darker or more difficult to see. Only our defeat by the mosquitoes and my eagerness to get back to Lavina made us foolish enough to keep going. Once in awhile, we'd hit a floating stick. It was really difficult to see where the banks of the river were.

Finally, about 4 a.m. I thought we were passing a bayou where the river would turn in the direction of Akobo. In the darkness, I turned sharply and soon found myself stopped in the tall swamp-grass beside the river. It wasn't the place I thought it was. In veering off into the grass, I had killed the engine and had broken off the sheer pin in the propeller. Fortunately, I had a flashlight with me and was able to take the motor off in the pitch darkness, lay it down beside Jimmy who slept through it all, replace it, put it back on the boat and get back into the river again.

By this time, it was beginning to get just a wee bit lighter. An hour later we were safely home tied up on the river bank in front of the house. I carried Jimmy up, unloaded our things and crawled into bed. Lavina was so pleased and surprised that we were back already and could hardly believe it.

Less than a half hour later, a colossal rain storm crashed down around us. That's why it had been so unusually dark on the river. There hadn't been a star in the sky. But the Lord mercifully held off the rain until Jimmy and I were safely home. When I awakened and went out after the storm had passed, I discovered our boat out front was nearly sinking. It had rained some 4 1/2 inches of water. We sang the doxology in our hearts, marvelled at the Lord's mercy and said, "I must never be so foolish again!"

KEEPING SPIRITUALLY FIT

In a letter written a year earlier, dated April 27, 1949, after telling of some of the rats, scorpions, mosquitoes and flies, I shared my thoughts about our challenge to keep spiritually alive.

49

April 27, 1949:

"I suppose when you read things like this back home you think this is an awful land, but once living out here these things become part and parcel of life and one takes them as a matter of course. There is real danger in this for us too, in that we fail to realize sometimes how completely dependent we are upon the Lord for our well being. How we must pray constantly, and how we need your prayers, that we will always be aware of how dependent we are upon our Heavenly Father's care and that we stay in the very center of His will. The old Devil is just as real here and attempts to deceive us just as much, even as he does in more or less Christianized America. The final test, wherever a Christian is living, remains the inner relationship he nurtures with the abiding presence of Christ. It is as easy for us to drift away from Him here as it is for you at home — and perhaps even a little easier, because we have so little in the way of things to aid us and inspire us. So much, so much we need the constant prayers of the Church at home that we may be absolutely and fully committed to the sacred trust as Ambassadors of Christ."

BUILDING AND MAINTENANCE

Bob and Don and, later the other men as well, often spent weeks and months overseeing the work on new buildings and maintenance of the old ones. During the dry season a lot of hard work was involved in the blazing hot sun getting the roofs in shape before the rains returned. The men saw to it that before another rainy season rolled around, everything was in order and the roofs had been patched or re-thatched so as to withstand the downpour of rains coming. Once our house at Pakang was finished, I didn't get involved in building activities to any great extent. I was assigned to work on the language and to work on the translation of the New Testament into Anuak. I must confess that I sometimes felt guilty about being so privileged and not doing my share with the other men in those hard tasks. But both Don and Bob helped me by strongly encouraging me to stick to the translation and leave these things to them. I can still hear Don saying, "Harvey, you stick to that translation. It's the most important thing you can do. Our time is short and we want you to complete it before we all have to leave."

I am forever grateful to God for the encouragement these men and the other missionaries gave to me to stick with it. Without their words, I may never have completed it in twelve years and have it printed before we all were forced to leave the Sudan. It was truly a team effort.

Harvey and James Buya,
his first Anuak Bible translator assistant.

An Anuak learning to read.

CHAPTER FOUR

LEARNING A NEW LANGUAGE

As soon as we were moved into our partially completed house, I began a disciplined language study. We'd been trained at the Summer Institute of Linguistics (SIL) in Norman, Oklahoma in how to analyze a language and reduce it to writing. Without that background, we wouldn't have known where to begin. There were no grammatical aids of any kind. What little writing existed had been improvised from the Shullik and we soon realized that It was inconsistent, inadequate and incomplete.

DISCIPLINE OF DAILY LANGUAGE STUDY

I'd spend 5 hours a day with one or two informants. These were Anuak teachers or students with not more than four to six years of formal education. Their use of English was limited and I was often unsure that the information given me was accurate. One could never be certain that what you asked for and what your informant told you were the same. Once I asked for the word "house" and later learned I had been given the word for "horse." A little further along, when I tried to get a translation for the verse, "Surely He has borne our griefs and carried our sorrows," I discovered he was using the word "to give birth to." When we really got into serious translation, a possible mis-communication became much more significant and dangerous. The challenge to figure out what was being said and how to write it down was totally consuming. I wanted to work at it night and day!

We'd been taught at SIL how to identify the different kinds of sounds found in different languages. We had learned the international alphabet so that we could write down accurately what we heard and then reproduce it by looking at the paper. We knew reasonably well how to handle the phonetics involved, but when it came to phonemics, we were pioneering in unknown territory. Our challenge was to determine what phonetic sounds were psychologically significant and should be represented in the final alphabet used for spelling and printing. They'd told us that phonemics was the science of cooking the phonetics until what was pure remained. As you know, all languages have many conditioned sounds which slide and glide together.

Then, too, we had to figure out what actually constituted a "word." It was difficult at first to know what was a "word" or a "phrase." We needed to determine how words were formed, that is, what were the different parts of a "word" (i. e. the morphemes). We needed not only to determine where the "word" boundaries were, but we needed also to figure out the grammar. It was like working on a gigantic jigsaw puzzle — totally captivating and in the back of one's mind night and day. Sometimes long periods of "pumping sand" with little apparent progress in language study was suddenly illuminated with a brilliant flash of insight which made several things fall into place and now seem simple. It was a task that never really ended before we had to leave the Sudan.

The essentials we were dealing with are technically described as matters of phonetics, phonemics, morphology and syntax. Anuak proved to be a tonal language with words that were basically a consonant, vowel and a consonant, making it one of the more difficult languages in the world to speak and write accurately. The words were short. Thus the vowels were extremely important. Each vowel could be high or low in tone, short or long in length, and it could be tense or lax in quality. To pronounce or write the vowel inaccurately resulted in a difference in meaning. To complicate matters further, the quality of the vowel with respect to tone, tenseness or laxness changed according to its grammatical position in the sentence. In contrast to some tonal languages where the tone remains constant, in Anuak the tones were changing depending on where the word was found in the grammatical structure of a sentence.

To be understood, we had to learn these basic tonal patterns of the various kinds of sentences we use in speech. Many times we had the words all correct, but when using them in the villages, people couldn't understand us. We would observe Anuaks asking each other, "What is he saying?" This caused a lot of heartache and frustration. When we conversed with mission employees and folks close to the mission, they seemed to understand us because they'd learned how to second guess what we were saying in context. In the villages, it was a different matter. Visiting village folks taught us how much we still had to learn! I made visiting villages and spending nights in villages sitting around the fire with Anuaks an essential part of my language study effort. I learned a lot under my mosquito net, just listening, when folks thought I was asleep. What they said about missionaries was also instructive!

My method in studying the language was to write every word or expression on a separate 3 by 5 card. I'd shuffle these cards daily, gradually separating those I could safely put "on the back burner" and review less frquently. After five hours with informants, I'd normally go to a nearby village or find people outside the office with whom I could practice as I tried to speak and listen. There were plateaus of learning and sometimes it seemed no progress was made. Language study called for the most serious kind of discipline. I kept telling myself to study the language just as faithfully as you studied for an exam in college. Without that kind of discipline, the goal of speaking, being understood and understanding the Anuak would never be realized.

DANGER OF BEING DIVERTED

Lack of discipline wasn't the only thing that could sabotage one's language study. There was always the pressure of other useful activities. In every mission station the school and the clinic require people to work in them. Someone has to do it. Some are trained specifically for that purpose. They are medical and educational missionaries. But in a new station like Akobo, the first missionaries, untrained for these tasks had to do them. I was no exception.

I was assigned to teach 4th grade arithmetic. I had never taught arithmetic in my life. It never occurred to me during all my preparation to serve as a missionary that I'd become an arithmetic teacher. I walked back and forth to the school from our home a mile and a quarter each way every day. In the afternoons, I'd sometimes walk back again to give a hand with the new buildings. Not much language study was going on during that period. I determined in my own heart that God hadn't called me to Africa to teach arithmetic. It wasn't that I didn't enjoy it to a certain extent, but I knew this wasn't my calling.

I praise God that my colleagues soon recognized this too and in one of our regular station meetings, it was voted unanimously that I should be set free from that arithmetic class, devote full time to language study and prepare myself to translate the New Testament for the Anuak people. That was why we had come and now the mission, too, recognized it and confirmed that call with their blessing by assigning me to the task. The joy bells were ringing!

This is what I wrote home to my folks in a letter dated December 19, 1948:

"I have been asked by the station to analyze the language and to reduce it to a proper writing system. ... Also, I have the task of translating the Bible into the Anuak tongue. My soul thrills at this glorious task. I started with three informants on Monday of this past week. ... Pray for us and may the church pray for us in

this tremendous task. One feels so weak and incapable. It is really baffling. Only the same Holy Spirit who inspired the original writers can qualify us for this task. In the passage where we read that John baptized with water, but you shall be baptized with the Holy Spirit, we translated it, 'John led people to the river to wash their livers with water, but you shall have your livers washed by the spirit of light.' The Anuak have a saying, that if one is angry with his friend that he should wash his liver with his friend — this leads us to make that translation." (This translation later proved to be inadequate as it suggested a kind of "baptismal regeneration". It was later changed)

LANGUAGE STUDY
PRACTICING IN THE VILLAGES

I made rapid progress in my language study. Living near the village, along with careful discipline and persistence, all helped.

The letter to my folks dated October 2, 1948 tells how I was going about it then:

"I am getting along nicely with the language. I can see progress every day and that is encouraging. These past ten days I have been doing some real missionary work and it has been a thrill and blessing to me as well as to the Anuaks. I have been writing a simple story of the Gospel in English and then I write it in Anuak with the help of an informant. With this in hand, I go out to the various villages and get the people of the village together under a tree and tell them that I want to tell them a story. We sing a couple of songs in Anuak and then I read them the story in Anuak. This does two things. It helps me learn the language and at the same time I bear testimony to the significance of Jesus Christ. It seems to me that this is almost an ideal way to start out.

"I wish you might see me some afternoon as I start out in just my shorts — no shoes or shirt! I go down the trail and when I get to the village there are usually a large number of men sitting around and some kids. The kids run out to meet me and then we either call the women or start to sing so that many of them come.

When the service is finished I walk around through the village and stop here and there to talk with the various men or women sitting around or working with the flour which the women pound out with a long pole in a hole in a hollowed out block of wood placed in the ground. Often they will ask for soap or a piece of cloth or for money. Other times they ask me to try to help them as they are sick. How I would love to be a doctor and be able to help them both of body and soul. It seems to me that almost the ideal way to work out here would be as a doctor going in and out the villages healing and telling the gospel message. This would be the closest approximation of Jesus ministry of healing and teaching.

"When the service in one village is finished, I go on to the next, which is usually about 1/2 to 1/4 mile away. After three or four, I turn around and come back home greatly blessed for having born withness to Jesus Christ. In all the villages visited so far I have found an eagerness for the message that is most encouraging. The door for Christ stands wide open here. If the church is not asleep she will work here now before the Muslims come and they become hardened to the Gospel. Our need here is for a consecration and for men and women."

WANTING TO SPEAK LIKE AN ANUAK

Language study with informants, spending week-ends in villages to practice, listen and learn became a way of life for me. I enjoyed preaching in the villages and doing the work of an evangelist. But my real task was to translate the New Testament to give the Anuak people God's word in their own language. Progress was sometimes slow, but gradually, I was able to understand most of what was said and could express myself effectively in the Anuak language. My goal was to speak it so well that in the dark Anuaks wouldn't know that I was a foreigner speaking.

To communicate the way Anuaks did, we also had to learn their body language and sign language. We soon learned that one never beckoned to another with the finger as we do in America. Among the Anuak as in many other parts of the non-western world, you beckon for someone to come with the hand turned downward and one uses the entire hand to motion for one to come. One points with the tongue — a bad habit when one is home on furlough and accidentally points with the tongue to indicate to the clerk the item one wants. We learned that the size of animals and fish required the hand to be either stretched out straight, palm down, or to have the palm stretched out with the hand on its side. Chickens were indicated by the crooked finger. But perhaps the most important use of the hand which one wanted to be sure to use correctly was when speaking about the size of a child. The Anuak never wanted anyone to indicate the height of a child by putting out one's hand with the palm down as we would in America to indicate how tall the child was. To do so, for the Anuak, was to stunt the growth of the child. On furloughs I enjoyed so much telling about these various ways of using our hands when speaking Anuak. It was a joy to challenge the children in our congregations to give their hearts to Christ and to grow up swiftly loving Him and being ready to serve Him -- perhaps even as a missionary. I would hold up my hands as in Africa and say,"Today, I'm holding up my hands (palms showing with fingers up at the level of a child's head) because I want you to grow up quickly and to be strong and ready to do what Jesus asks of you. He loves you and is helping you grow up quickly so that you may go somewhere for Him, His missionary to take our places as we quickly grow too old."

To speak like an Anuak we had to have the sounds pronounced correctly, the length of the vowels and the tones the right length, quality and level, and we had to use our hands with body movements that communicated accurately and effectively. A lifetime challenge and never fully realized!

ADULTS VERSUS SCHOOL CHILDREN

In that same letter I put down some of my concerns about what I then perceived to be a disproportionate emphasis on schools and too little effort to reach adults with the message of Jesus Christ.

"I am preaching this evening on II Corinthians 5:17-21. This morning I rode my bike, as I did last week, and went out about six miles on the trail. I held four services in different villages. There was a very good response and it thrilled my heart to tell them the wonderful message about how Christ was sent by God to save them. We just sat around under the trees, sang some songs in Anuak, and then I told them about Jesus. I prayed in Anuak and then moved on to another village. I think this is the only way to win Africa to Christ. It can never be done in the school alone. It will come through village evangelism and the teaching of adults to read so that they may read the Word of God for themselves."

The longer I was in the Sudan, the more convinced I became that missions were making a mistake in their putting so much emphasis on teaching the children in the schools to the neglect of evangelizing adults. I said we should go right to the top and meet with village chiefs and elders and tell them the great truths from the Bible. These were the decision makers. If they became believers, whole villages would follow them, other heads of households, their wives and their children. Concentrating on the schools sent the wrong message to village leaders. Concentrating on schools suggested that we missionaries may have lost confidence in the power of the Gospel to convert adult people and their ability to change. Perhaps, we were, unconsciously, giving up on adults because we thought only children could change enough to qualify as Christians. There was a lot to ponder as we considered where God would have us place our effort. Years later in graduate study at Fuller's School of World Mission, Dr. Tippet helped me understand a bit more clearly what I was wrestling with in my spirit during those first years in the Sudan.

The fundamental issue was a question of power. We were dealing with a "power encounter." The question for the adult villager, especially, was a question of who has the power for good or for evil over one's life in all its aspects. The Gospel made sense when, under the Holy Spirit, those who heard recognized that Jesus Christ was powerfully alive and present and had power to protect one from every threat, including sickness, demons and death. The Gospel was seen to be fantastically good news when Christ was proclaimed as Savior and powerful Lord, alive and present to save and to protect anyone who committed one's self to Him in faith. This was a message that made good sense to adults and could give whole households a new way to live in freedom and without fear. We didn't need to teach them how to play our kind of church, but, rather to introduce them to Jesus and create the opportunity for them to look into God's written word. The Holy Spirit could be their final guide. Exciting possibilities with dramatic change, contextually relevant would occur. I was feeling things deeply as I tried to think through for myself where my priorities and emphasis should be.

PAKANG

Pakang was a little over a mile from the mission where our colleagues lived. At Pakang we lived near Anuak villages. People were coming constantly to see what we were doing. They pointed to things and asked questions. At first, we understood very little, but it was a marvelous opportunity to practice our language skills with our many curious visitors.

Living near the people gave us a good feel for the African village. I was frequently in those villages, some close by and later when I had an outboard, I'd go further from home. I came to feel strongly about the importance of the African village and how it related to the evangelization of the Anuak, and possibly of Africa. Sometimes I wrote about it in my letters home. I tried to picture for my family what I observed and shared my reactions with them. Many of the convictions formed during those early months in Africa remain unchanged today.

ANUAK FIELDS AND VILLAGES

The Anuak were fastidious farmers. Seeds were planted using five or six foot sticks to make the hole in the wet, sticky cotton soil into which the seed was dropped and stepped on. Men used simple single bladed hoes which were about three inches in width with a small channel into which a two or three foot stick, about an inch in diameter, had been tightly jammed. They prepared their plots of land meticulously and worked hard to keep the growing crop clean of weeds. They planted both dura (kaffir corn) and maize.

When the crop was ripening, crude temporary six- foot platforms were erected on poles and situated as needed throughout their fields to protect the harvest from the sparrow-sized dura birds, so numerous that an unguarded field would be completely destroyed. The children and young people made these platforms their homes and ate and slept there during harvest season, abandoning them only during the severest rain storms. With three-foot willowy sticks to which they attached marble sized mud-balls, these "field watchers" successfully kept their losses to a minimum.

Women, with the sporadic help of men, gathered the ripened grain in baskets woven from grass and stored their bounty in small, circular storehouses positioned so that their bottoms were about three feet off the ground. These were covered with small thatched roofs which the women would tilt up and then lower again on days grain or corn was needed for pounding into flour. Such graineries were located close beside the houses in which people lived.

Every village had a few cows, sheep, goats and chickens. These belonged to individual families and the cattle were frequently kept in a common building which was similar to other Anuak houses in size and shape.

Chickens were usually in limited numbers because a brood of eight or ten tiny chicks was easy prey for the hawks. The mother hens did their best to warn and protect their babies, but only a few reached maturity. And, of course, every village had its quota of barking dogs.

When we went out to the villages, we passed through these Anuak fields, unable to see anything except the path underfoot until we emerged on the opposite side. During the rainy season these paths were often muddy and some had low spots with standing water and filthy areas one had to pass through. Canvas shoes were the shoes of choice to wade through these low areas as they could dry on one's feet. During the dry season these same paths were baked dry and in the previously sticky cotton soil there would now be deep and sometimes treacherous cracks going down a depth of several feet. One could now see great distances whereas only a few months earlier we were "walking blind".. It was fun to travel on these dry paths riding my small, whizzer trail bike propelled by its tiny gasoline engine.

Some of our impressions, being formed during those early months in the Sudan, are reflected in a letter home dated May 9, 1949:

"The key to the heart of Africa lies in her villages. It is in the African village with its mud houses and grass roofs with lounging men, playful children and hard working women that the real victory for Christ will be won.

"If I could take you with me to one of our villages, you would find, perhaps, ten to twenty of these small huts. The walls are made of mud and sticks and are about as tall as a short man. You cannot see these walls from the outside because long grass from the roof comes down to the ground protecting them from the rains. On one side we notice a small opening. We enter but see nothing until our eyes become accustomed to the darkness.

"Inside the hut we see a small baby lying on an animal skin on the floor. The mother sits nearby. Flies are crawling all over the little baby. If we look more closely, we will likely find the baby's eyes are sore and infected. How could it be different with hundreds of flies crawling over its little body every day. The marvel is that any of these babies grow up considering that they have no clothing and no protection except their mother's love.

"From the roof of the hut we notice a wing or two of a bird, possibly the shriveled up head of a chicken, several horns from cattle

and some tobacco hanging to dry. Each of these items has some special relation to the spirits of whom the Anuak lives in constant fear.

"Walking through the village, we notice that here and there are mounds of dirt with several tall sticks on the top of which are the horns of some former cow. Tied to the sticks are ears of corn. Buried beneath the mound of dirt are the fetish bones and charms and even, possibly, the body of some relative who has died and is buried there.

"To this shrine the Anuak turns at specific times to offer prayer to the spirits of the dead. They have greatest fear and respect for these shrines and in no case would they walk on them or be disrespectful to them.

"Often, as I preach in the villages, I see on either side of me these pagan shrines and know that only as Jesus comes into their hearts and transforms them will the fear and superstition that haunts our people's hearts be taken away. Often I will ask them if the Gospel is not a good word from God (Anuaks ask a question with a particle that anticipates a positive answer) and they will answer, 'It is a good word.'

"Then I ask them, 'Will you not trust in Jesus, God's only son, to care for you and save you?'

"They answer that they want to, but then I point to their shrines and tell them that if they trust in Jesus they must throw these things out in the field because Jesus wants them to trust in Him only. They smile and know that what Odola (that is my African name) said is true, but in their hearts they are still afraid to do so.

"We can bring them just that far and then we know that we must wait for the Holy Spirit to take all fear and superstition away and to plant within them the new life. Pray for the power of God to be released here in the heart of Africa."

Every village has its graves. Some are buried just beside the house where they are protected by an enclosure of thorn branches. It is normally several years later before the grave site is no longer revered and respected as a place where one communes with the spirit of the departed one. During the first few weeks after the burial, the women relatives mourn loudly and hauntingly every morning long before the sun rises. In our memory bank these haunting cries of hopelessness and despair are indelibly written.

Some burials take place in the house of the person who has died. A letter home describes what happens.

May 20, 1949:

"Last week one day while at Bob's house we heard a lady go by wailing loudly and knew that it meant a woman was mourning the loss of a relative. We decided to walk over to the village and see.

"There inside the grass wall we found about 25 women wailing loudly and a couple of men. We asked if we might come inside the village fence and sit down to observe. This we did and then presently saw the mound of dirt outside the hut and the man who had died lying under the cloth lying nearby. Inside the house several women were digging the grave.

"In a short while this man would be buried inside the house. A grass mat would be put up to cover the opening into the house and the house would be sealed shut until it caved in upon the grave.

"Another soul without Christ had slipped into eternity. Bob and I asked if we might have a prayer in the village, but they refused, saying we weren't relatives of the man. Things like this write themselves deeply on our hearts out here. You have never heard anything quite like it at home. It makes us want to work even harder in the little time that is ours to live for and serve our Savior."

PREACHING IN THE VILLAGES

MAY 8, 1949:

"On Sundays I usually take my motor bike" (a whizzer bike with a motor) *"and go out for five or six miles along the rough trail (worse than our cow paths in the pastures at home by far) and hold five or six services in the villages.*

"In these services we either meet under a tree or in the cattle barn. Sometimes we have the cows and sheep and goats tethered

right beside us giving us competition with the message. I don't stand in these village services. Instead, I sit down with them, teach them some songs and then tell them about Jesus Christ. Often, I stop and ask questions and we talk it over as we carry on the service. Often one of the Anuak men will repeat after me each word I say. Now and again a person from another village walks by and one from our service exchanges greetings with him and they have a short conversation. Or it may be some baby is crying or children are talking in a slow, low mumble.

"You would be shocked to drop in out of the sky to see our service but it is Anuak and the way the Anuaks gather together and we must learn to accommodate ourselves to their patterns of behavior. It isn't always easy, but there is something about these village services that reaches deep down in one's soul and moves one to preach the wonderful Gospel of our Savior who is their only hope as he has never preached it before.

"If you folks at home could see for yourselves our people and the terrible weight of their sin, superstition and fear, it would fall upon you as a dreadful weight, and there would be no one who would not believe it worthwhile to come out hear to live for Christ. Not one of you would withhold the very best you have for Christ.

"We are moved to shame when we think of the complacency and ease of the Church and the believers back home when thousands and millions are dying every day in the terrible fear and guilt with no knowledge of Christ, the only Savior. How can it be right that one would not sacrifice a little for these folks for whom Christ died. Our people here are waiting for the messengers of God who are coming so late. Perhaps some son or daughter back home will feel the call of God to come to a pagan land to bring the glorious message of Salvation. Do not dissuade that boy or girl. Bid them Godspeed. Encourage them on their way of preparation to be His ambassadors to realms beyond the sea. God gave the very best that He had, His only begotten Son to die the shameful bitter death on Calvary for our salvation. We dare not withhold all that we are and have from Him for those for whom He died."

The letter quoted above indicates where our hearts were as we began our many years of missionary service in Africa.

Looking back, some forty five years later, our core convictions remain much the same as when we started. "There is no other name given among men by which we must be saved." Acts 4:12. True then and still true now!

DEADLY SNAKES - A LITTLE GIRL DIES

From a letter dated June 9, 1950:

"Last Sunday I had five nice services. In one village I found a friend whom I have been teaching to read. His little girl, about nine, was bitten by a snake the night before. He brought her to us at three Sunday afternoon. I took them to Lillian, but she said the poison was spread through the body and the only thing now was rest.

"We carried her back to the boat and home, but the next morning we had word at seven o'clock that she had died. It was so pitiful to hear the awful wail going up by those who have no hope but much fear. I've spoken to him once since then and will see him again soon to talk to him earnestly of the Eternal hope there is in Christ Jesus.

"I have been dealing with another young lad who had T.B. and am trying to show him the love of Christ and his hope for a better life. Pray for us in our personal work along with the translation. This morning, he stopped by on the way home from the clinic and I stepped outside the study and sat down in front of the door on the ground and told him so simply the beautiful message of Jesus. His face was interested. Pray that God may be pleased to touch his heart. He lives in a village near our friend, Dilok.

"Just this very minute I saw a blind Anuak passing by. He had a Muslim, long gown on. He is one whom the Arabs have supposedly converted to Islam. I didn't know him, but called him over and we sat down and I told him of Jesus and how he had died and rose again. We prayed and he promised to return soon to hear this new word. O, that God will give us power. I wish you could feel and see with us the tremendous challenge. How pitiful for this man — blind in soul as well as body."

LOW RIVERS - FISH IN ABUNDANCE

Every dry season the Pibor river became so shallow that we'd have to cut the speed of our outboards to avoid snapping off sheer pins in the propeller caused by hitting fish. The fish were so numerous that they were unable to escape quickly enough when an outboard was cutting through them at full speed. There were times when fish would jump out of the water into the air as they tried to get out of the way. More than once, I was struck in the chest by a flying fish. Rather painful too!

One night Lee and Kitty Crandall gave Lavina and me a ride home to Pakang from the mission following the regular mid-week prayer meeting. It was a delightful ride with the four of us in the boat — stars overhead in a brilliant sky with a gentle breeze blowing in our faces and keeping the mosquitoes away. Under a full, bright shining moon a night-time ride in an outboard on the river was intoxicating!

But this particular evening, when Lee and Kitty returned to the mission after dropping us off, it was far from that. With only the two of them in the boat, the outboard was skimming the water at a good clip. Lee and Kitty were just new on the field at that time and hadn't encountered fish jumping out of the water and hitting them in the boat. Kitty soon called back over the roar of the motor that she'd prefer walking. They parked the boat at the first little village, walked the rest of the way and picked the boat up the next day. We all had some good natured fun and laughs over that for several weeks.

DRY SEASON FISHING

During the dry season, we were fascinated with the way Anuaks herded fish ahead of them in a flotilla of a dozen or more canoes being paddled side by side. Each canoe usually had a father and a son in it, with the father in front with his harpoon and the young lad paddling very slowly from the rear. The men worked the harpoons and kept coming up with speared fish. There were so many fish now concentrated in the narrow, shallow river that their chances of spearing one were extremely good. They'd go about a fourth of a mile and then all would turn back in unison to do the same thing coming back to where they'd started out. They actually caught so many fish that the river banks smelled from decaying fish. During this time of the year, the Anuak virtually lived on fish, cooking them along the river bank rather than back in their villages. I often wondered if Jesus and His disciples prepared fish along the water's edge the way the Anuak did.

When the rains returned and the rivers began to rise, the flotillas were discontinued, but father and son kept on fishing, using a slightly different approach. Now the man in the front used his fish spear with its sharp, curved barbs and patiently waited for an unsuspecting fish to break water in front of the canoe. In an instant the man would throw his spear. Rarely was there a day when such a team returned to the village without at least one good sized fish and possibly several. A favorite time of the day for this was late in the afternoon when the sun was beginning to go down in the west.

We missionaries frequently were able to purchase a nice, fresh fish for only a few cents. Many a supper hour in our home saw fresh tasty fried fish on our table. Two varieties were known to be better than others, the Olok and the Orwedho. Once we learned the hard way that a certain type of fish had pin worms in their flesh. Needless to say, we were careful not to make the same mistake twice! One learns quickly under those conditions!

GETTING AROUND DURING THE DRY SEASON

Before Mission Aviation began operating in the Sudan, it was really difficult to get around. We not only moved about in a dugout canoe or with an outboard on the rivers, but during the dry season, we travelled either with some kind of mission vehicle or we'd hitch a ride on one of the

Arab merchant's trucks. These trucks were always overloaded —stacked high with goods and people. Breakdowns were frequent between Malakal and Akobo. While the driver would try to figure out what to do, we'd try to find a bit of shade to shield us from the sun, or at night we'd try to find a way to sleep in what seemed really cold weather after the hot daytime sun. We always carried extra food and water along for such emergencies. Our letters home during those early years bring back vivid memories of rugged trips.

A MOST DIFFICULT TRIP FROM MALAKAL

From a letter dated June 9, 1950:

"We had a rugged trip back to Akobo from Malakal. I drove the station wagon, which is a complete wreck, really, with nothing but the spring holding the back frame together. We started from Malakal in a rain storm, the fourth in four days. It took us four hours to do the first 12 miles and we were stuck several times. We had a long pry-pole in the car and when stuck, Lyda would drive and I would heave on it. We had soft roads all the way except about 20 miles.

"First of all, we broke the bottom water hose to the radiator and I had to tape that all up. We always carry plenty of water. We had about forty gallons with us this time and 55 gallons of gasoline.

"A little further out from Malakal we noticed a bad leak in the gas tank. By keeping it less than half full we overcame that problem. Then we hit real mud and were nearly stuck when we stopped about mid-night and threw the bedrolls on the wet ground and slept until daylight. We then cooked a breakfast and by that time the sun had dried the surface out sufficiently to move.

"The car over-heated very badly and for a long way we were using water every two miles exactly. We were dangerously low on water — in fact, so low that we scooped up water from the old car tracks to get enough to get us to the nearest water hole. It is quite a dangerous trip with fifty or more miles with not a soul living there and with no water anywhere. But we always send a telegram

when leaving Malakal just in case. If we do not arrive in sufficient time, someone will come out to look for us.

"Last of all, about 9 o'clock the second night about sixty miles from home we ran into a terrific pool of water running right across the road and with ditches on both sides of the road. We tried to roar through it but stalled out about four feet from the other side. Fortunately, we were near a Nuer village. I called for them to help, but only seven or eight Nuer women came out to give us a hand. We put a long rope unto the front of the car. Lyda drove and they pulled, while I heaved on the pry-pole. Even Lavina was pulling with the Nuer women.

"Finally, after much effort, we got out and from then on we managed somehow to get home. The tracks had been dug so deep by a truck that one time while travelling along about fifteen miles per hour we suddenly came to a dead stop. We were stuck fast on the high center. Again, the old pole and some heaving saved the day and out we came! We arrived home that morning at one-thirty a.m. — ever so glad, but tired! This is just a little idea of our trip home from Malakal."

DEPENDING ON MAF

Once Mission Aviation Fellowship (MAF) initiated their program in the Sudan, these gruelling trips would be past history!

MAF was vital to our mission in the Sudan. They saved us hours and hours of time to say nothing of energy. MAF flew in our supplies. They flew our children out to catch other modes of transportation which would eventually get them to school in Alexandria, Egypt. MAF enabled missionary families to move about on business and with MAF we could leave for annual vacations and still be rested when we arrived back home to resume our work. If there was an emergency, we could count on MAF to come to the rescue. Before MAF was there it was quite a different story.

In the Sudan, road trips that took a day and sometimes more, were flown by MAF in less than an hour. More importantly, there were many months when roads weren't useable. Because MAF had two planes, one of which was a float plane, we could get in and out during both the dry and rainy seasons.

It was interesting that when MAF first began to serve missions in the Sudan there was some question in the mission as to whether or not travelling by MAF should be considered a normal and legitimate way for us to travel, or whether we should use MAF only in an emergency. Missionaries living in remote places like Akobo opted for looking on MAF as a normal way to travel. Some missionaries living in the Malakal area at first questioned whether we shouldn't perhaps look on MAF as being available primarily for emergencies. In a few short months, the debate was academic. Everyone recognized that MAF had increased our efficiency so dramatically that it would be folly to wrestle on the roads and river with MAF there.

We used MAF all the time. And, on at least one or two occasions they came to the rescue in times of emergencies. I still recall well our concern when Vern Sikkema, Bill Roy and our son, Dennis, failed to return from a trip by Jeep to Waat, about 70 miles away. After waiting a day, when they failed to return, we called MAF on the radio and Betty Greene flew in with the float plane. She picked me up and we flew low over the road from Akobo in the direction of Waat. About 35 miles out, we spotted Vern and Denny wearily trudging toward Akobo. They looked so pitiful from the air. They had already walked some thirty miles and had a long hike ahead of them. To encourage them we dropped some cans of food and fresh water. Bill Roy had come on ahead, more quickly, to tell us what had happened, so we didn't see him on the road. But we had the information we needed and knew that the men would be home before night. Knowing this, Betty and I continued on to Malakal for a scheduled mission committee meeting.

When I returned home, Lavina said that Dennis, then only fourteen years old, was so tired from the nearly seventy mile hike in rain and mud that he was delirious during the night as he tossed back and forth fitfully from exhaustion.

It was an experience this young lad didn't soon forget. We all had a good reminder of just how much MAF meant to us.

We had one final lesson in the Sudan on just how much we had come to depend on MAF. This occurred only a few months before missionaries were forced to leave the Sudan by government order.

All of our missionaries from the outstations had been flown into Malakal by MAF for our annual mission meeting. We always spent a week together each year hearing reports, enjoying fellowship together and making decisions about the following year's work. These were great times in our missionary experience. On the next to the last day of our meetings, we were in for a rude surprise. The MAF pilot came in and said he had some disturbing news to share with us. They had had a slight accident the day before in which the prop of the plane was bent. It'd take about six weeks to get a replacement propeller from England. They had no way to get us to our homes.

Dry season roads were still not useable. We'd all have to, somehow, get home by river. Pibor, the furtherest station from Malakal was just over an estimated 400 river miles. Missionaries from Abwong, Nasir, Akobo and Pibor all needed to get back to their stations along the Sobat and Pibor rivers. The only way to get home would be by outboards on the river. The only person not having to get home was Bob Swart who had remained at Pibor to guard things from the flood which was threatening to inundate the mission station.

Outboards from nearer mission stations and Malakal were pressed into service. My assignment was to go on ahead by one day with the needed gasoline for the others who would be following. I'd drop the gasoline off at agreed upon places along the river so that the boats following could carry the maximum number of people with the minimum weight of additional fuel.

I started out on the appointed morning at six a.m. in a sixteen foot aluminum boat with two outboard motors attached. I was carrying a load — 34 five gallon tins of gasoline. When darkness fell, I had travelled nearly 200 miles and was approaching the Nasir station, now empty of missionaries who were still stuck in Malakal.

It's a trip I'll never forget. Just outside of Nasir, in the darkness I lost my way. With some shouting and sign language wherever I stopped to ask people the way, and with the help of lightning I found my way back into the main stream of the river. It was nearly 8 o'clock when I pulled up to the bank in front of the Nasir mission station. Pastor Moses Kwaich came out and welcomed me, inquired what was happening and then showed me to one of the vacant mission houses. After a time of devotions and conversation, he left and I slept.

The next day I did the 90 miles to Akobo and the following day went the remaining 125 miles to Pibor. I spent the remaining hours of the day getting rested up. Bob Swart and I started out that same night to fetch our wives from Nasir more than 200 river miles distant. Meanwhile, other missionaries and their children were making their way upstream toward Nasir in a flotilla of small boats. For the mothers with small children it wasn't an easy trip to make.

In one week, I had travelled more than 800 miles by outboard. It was as if I had travelled from Minneapolis to Chicago and back in a small boat on the river. It goes without saying, that no one among the missionaries ever has anything bad to say about MAF. Never, ever!

OUR FIRST PRIMER THE HARD WAY

But a lot of history would be written before that last emergency without MAF's services. Way back in 1949 we had just completed making our very first primer. Lavina and I worked together in our efforts to provide primers and books and to teach Anuaks how to read. We started from scratch, even before we had a mimeograph to run off our stencils.

During August in 1949, Lavina and I had cut stencils for our first primer. Not having a mimeograph machine, we travelled with the children via paddle wheel steamer downstream for three days, going some 200 miles to a mission station that had a mimeograph machine. Tal Wilson was living alone at Abwong when we arrived unannounced. We told him we planned to stay for at least a week and that while there we wanted to use his mimeograph. We told him we'd brought our own stencils and paper. The steamer was continuing on to Malakal and when it came back on its way to Akobo we'd be leaving again. I can hardly imagine putting forth that much effort to produce our first primer. But it was that or nothing under conditions that then prevailed. It proved to be well worth the effort. One of those primers was used by God to teach a young man, living some 150 miles from Akobo inside Ethiopia to read. That young man later became the first Anuak evangelist out of the Pokwo station and the first ordained Anuak pastor. His name was Akway war Achudhi. We'll tell you his remarkable story when we tell you about Pokwo.

JOY IN OUR WORK

Our contentment and joy from the very beginning of our missionary experience is indicated in my letter to the folks, dated February 18, 1949:

"That leads me to speak of Lavina. She has done very excellently out here. She has been a constant companion and a real missionary wife and mother. She has made a wonderful home for the children and all of us. In all the inconveniences, she did not complain or murmur. Never has she complained of loneliness or of a desire to go back home. We have all been so very happy in our work.

"The Lord has indeed been gracious to us. He works in marvelous ways in the hearts of His children. He has given us perfect and indescribable peace in our souls. Each day is a day of rejoicing in our work. We are perfectly happy and would not exchange our work for the largest salaries and the largest pulpits in the world. I don't know how many times I remark to Lavina how happy I am in my work and what a joy we have because God called us so clearly to our work. As you look at it, everything seems hard and difficult for us, but when your soul is at peace

everything seems easy and fun. I do not mean that there are not many difficult and hard trials, but when the will is in harmony with the will of our Lord, the greatest burdens are lifted off and we walk free. We praise Him again for the marvel of His grace and mercy in calling us here to suffer but a little to make Him known, loved, honored and obeyed."

CHAPTER FIVE

BAPTIZING NEW BELIEVERS

On this particular morning, we were busy at it in the little office with the narrow door. This tiny room had been added unto our bedroom veranda to make roofing problems less complicated and less likely to leak. To reach it from inside the house, I passed through the living room and the sleeping veranda.

Every day I was home, I tried to be in the office by 7 a.m. Morning prayers began at 6 a.m. with our workers and any visitors from the village. We'd have our breakfast and family prayers before my translation helpers arrived.

That morning, in the office, we'd barely completed the prayers with which we always asked the Holy Spirit to guide us as we handled God's Word, when there was a clap outside. Stepping outside, I was shocked. In front of me was a man so emaciated and ill that he, literally, took hold of his shriveled up, empty stomach and pulled it out, a flabby, empty piece of flesh. Still holding the extra skin and flesh in his hands, he pleaded with me to do something or he would die.

We didn't have a doctor in the station yet, so we were helping as we were able in situations like this. I often remembered Don McClure's furlough story of how he'd sometimes go to the medicine chest in situations like this and say, "Ini mini maini mo" and pull out whatever bottle was so identified! I wasn't at all sure what to do, but finally settled on giving him medicine for dysentery. This would require his taking the medicine several times a day for seven days. What to do? I couldn't give him all the medicine then and there and tell him to take it to his village to use it as per instructions until the seven days were up. This would be far too risky. There was a good possibility that under those conditions, he would go home and take them all at once to be cured and made better immediately. Or again, he might just put the entire bottle up in the inside of the grass roof along with the other sacred things he had no doubt put up there at the word of the witchdoctor. I had seen those necks of chickens, backbones of fish and the sacred sticks in their houses, tucked in the grass where it came down and extended over the mud wall.

So this is what I did. I said, "Look, I'll give you medicine for now and the rest of the day. But in the morning you have to come back and get your medicine for tomorrow. I want you to do this for seven days. (I showed him on my fingers) This will help you and we will pray to Jesus every time you come to make you well again."

To my delight and surprise, this man, whose name was "Dilok" and who lived in a village called Wangdwar a little over a mile from our house, came back faithfully. Not only that, but he'd push open the narrow office door and sit on the floor listening to our discussions about the translation we were doing. His was an interruption we welcomed!

When the seven days had passed, Dilok still kept on coming back and sitting on the floor listening to the new translation as it developed. Finally, after several weeks, we finished the last two chapters of the Gospel of Mark. We took time out to read it all aloud so that Dilok could hear it also. When we were finished reading, he quietly said," I've been listening to everything you have been saying about Jesus. It has gone into my liver. I want to become a person of Yechu Kricho (Jesus Christ) and be baptized." I can scarcely express adequately my feelings that day. Besides the joy of hearing Dilok's words, I saw this experience as God's seal of approval upon my commitment to translate the entire New Testament for the Anuaks. God's word had proved to be powerful to open Dilok's eyes and cause him to believe. One day the entire Anuak tribe could have the opportunity to similarly hear and believe if my team of Anuak helpers and I stuck with it and were faithful.

Then some strange, unexpected things happened. I had been in Dilok's village and had seen the large shrine in the center of his village. I knew that he had sacrificed many sheep and goats at that shrine and that he and his wife kept beer in that small gourd attched to the bamboo pole standing in the center of their shrine, filling it regularly to appease the spirits. How could Dilok be baptized with that shrine there? He would have to remove it before he could be baptized. Did he realize this?

I spoke to him slowly and carefully. My Anuak usage was still limited but I knew I could explain it adequately for him to fully understand. This is a summary of what I tried to say, "Dilok, our livers are filled with happiness because of what you said. But there is one thing we need to talk with you about before you may be baptized. The shrine in your village! Are you prepared to pull up that shrine, turn away from the word of the witchdoctor and trust in the power of Jesus Christ alone to help you and protect you? If you truly trust in Jesus, you must trust him with 'one liver.' (your whole heart) No one can walk on two paths. As the paths get further and further apart, you have to choose to walk on one path or the other."

As I was speaking to him, I could see his face darken. It was as if a terrible heaviness had fallen upon his liver. He finally arose, walked slowly out the door, and without a word of explanation headed in the direction of his village.

DILOK IS BAPTIZED

It was three weeks before Dilok returned and pushed against, our narrow office door to enter. Now his face was radiant and he was eager to speak. He said, "I want to pull up my shrine and burn it. I want to follow Jesus with just one liver. I want to walk on his path alone." How we praised God as we prayed together for this tremendous victory of faith. Dilok was committing himself to Jesus in the confidence that Jesus was more powerful than any witchdoctor or any of the spirits he had tried so long to appease.

And then, I had a real shock and surprise. Dilok said, "But I don't want to be baptized yet. I want to wait for Odan (Don McClure) to return so that he can baptize me." Dilok wanted the top man, the chief of the mission, and no young, missionary newcomer for this momentous occasion. He was thinking like an Anuak. I learned a real lesson on how Anuaks think that morning.

When Don returned, he graciously arranged it so that I was, so to speak, his official representative and Dilok readily accepted Don's word. I had the joyous privilege of baptizing him. Dilok and I became very close friends and I learned from him, even as he learned from me and the Word.

In a letter written home following his baptism, I described it like this:

"Last week we had a thrilling service in which I baptized my first Anuak. He was the man who I had been teaching to read and had been trying to lead to Christ during these months. What a blessed day it was!

"We went to his village about a mile from our house for the service in this man's village. First we sang some songs and then Dilok spoke, standing beside his tall shrine . (a bamboo pole about 15 feet tall, several ears of corn tied on it, a gourd in which they would have been putting beer for the spirits, and then a mound of dirt about 14 inches high around it under which were buried the bones of the sheep which he had sacrificed)

"He told of how he had built this shrine a couple of years ago when a witchdoctor promised him that if he did so and sacrificed sheep for the spirit there, God would cause his barren wife to conceive and he, also, would have good health. He explained how

he had sacrificed ten sheep there and nothing had happened. He said he had been deceived, but that now he had learned to know of Jesus, the Son whom God had sent to save him, and he was leaving all of this and trusting only in Him.

"He then pulled up the shrine, chopped it up and burned it. They then dug up the bones and burned them. Then he still had some charms in his house and he asked his wife to bring them out to destroy them. The were brought out along with a special stick from the roof of the house, and these were all burned.

"Then I spoke a few words in Anuak and he knelt and I baptized him with these words in Anuak, 'Dilok, pi akithaa bat wii ni nyudhi. Yina dhanh Yechu Kricho, na ni war Jwok, ki nyeng jweiy Jwok ni en kur keere.'

"Following a few words spoken to him and prayer, all the Christians, that is, the baptized persons, gathered in a circle while the non-Christian village neighbors looked on. We were having our first communion service in an African village among Anuak people. Don took this part of the service. We used pancake like food for the element and tomato juice for the wine. We used a small gourd and Don went to each one of us and each took a sip. How our hearts were knit with one another as never before and how we felt that truly Christ was among us. It was an experience we shall never forget. Don said later, 'Harvey, it was the most beautiful and wonderful service I have ever been in.' The Lord was close to us that day as the sun began to set and we began making our way home on the trail.

"A couple of days later I came to Dilok's village and in place of the mound of dirt and the shrine, the mud floor in the village was smooth and clean. We are expecting great things from this man. He is truly a saved man. He is learning to read and says he wants to go out to teach his people. ... Dilok is the first Anuak to be baptized who is not an employee of the mission or a wife or relative of an employee. He lives about a mile from our home and about two miles from the mission. We just praise the Lord for giving us this joy and for calling Dilok for Himself. We feel this may be an opening wedge into the hearts of the people in the villages."

RITUAL EXPERTS, THE "WITCHDOCTORS"

Ritual experts, that is, "witchdoctors," had an enormous power over the lives of the Anuak people. They were greatly feared and were believed capable of causing death as well as giving blessings of health and prosperity. Illness, death, or unexplained, threatening situations brought people to the witchdoctor to have his interpretation of what went wrong and what was needed to appease the evil spirits and bring blessing rather than their curse. Both men and women had these special powers enabling them to be witchdoctors. Some were more powerful than others, but none were to be taken lightly. If a baby was ill, the witchdoctor identified the "jwok" (spirit) and prescribed what had to be given or sacrificed to entice the spirit causing the harm to leave.

These witchdoctors had a bag full of tricks and fetishes to ply their trade. There was little doubt that these persons had connections with the evil spirit world that gave them supernatural power. Some of it was pure deception, but there was much more to it than simply being more clever than others. Often a witchdoctor was a person who had had some unusual, unexplainable experience. If one had been rendered unconscious for some reason and his "jwok" (spirit) returned, this one might well be considered to have special powers associated with witchcraft. My observation was that many of those who functioned as witchdoctors were somewhat weird and eccentric. The Anuak had ambivalent feelings about these people. On the one hand, they were looked upon as benefactors, and on the other, they were seen as sinister and self-serving.

Before telling you about how one withdoctor, Odola Wenyari, turned to Christ and was baptized, I must say a word about amulets, charms, fetishes and shrines.

The Anuak were animists; that is, they believed that material objects had spiritual qualities. Spirits of many different kinds were identified with locations, objects, animals and things of all sorts. Certain trees were sacred locations and one never passed such places without showing reverence and usually offering a small gift of beads, a coin, or an offering of spilled beer or coffee.

Before crossing the river to set out on a journey to a distant village, older Anuaks would first make a small offering at the river's edge. If one were ill, the witchdoctor might require the villager to acquire a goat of a certain color or shape. This goat would be given special treatment in the village and given special gifts on a regular basis. These gifts might be a little beer or a little special grain — anything to keep it happy. In that goat the spirit that had attacked the sick person would live happily and no longer cause illness so long as it was given this special attention. Sometimes, the tip of the ear of such a goat would be cut off, put on a cord and worn around the neck of the person so honoring this animal.

The witchdoctors told the people what was wrong and what they had to do to correct the situation and to keep the spirit world happy. Their prescriptions ranged all the way from cutting one's own body until blood flowed to sacrificing a cow, a sheep or a goat. Nearly every Anuak had in his hut, his village or on his person some indication that a witchdoctor had been consulted. All were very aware of the reality of a spirit world which was hostile and needed to be appeased and kept happy.

The Creator God, giver of sunshine, rain and author of life was known and frequently invoked. Special people had power to influence the God who gave rain and produced the harvest. In general, however, it was apparent that the Anuak world-view perceived God to be far distant and, while ultimately with supreme power, He was not their primary concern. Romans 1:21 accurately describes what we observed then, "For even though they knew God, they did not honor Him as God, or give thanks; but they became futile in their speculations and their foolish heart was darkened." It was the fearful, essentially evil spirit world, that needed to be dealt with. For this, the witchdoctor was the person who knew what to do. These witchdoctors had the ultimate answer to matters of life and death. It was such a person as this that Christ loved, turned around and set free from the power of Satan and his evil accomplices.

ODOLA WENYARI IS BAPTIZED

It was a great moment when Odola Wenyari, the powerful, local witchdoctor professed his faith in Christ. He said he wanted to have the service in his village and to be baptized in the river in front of his house. He wanted all his neighbors to hear his testimony and see what he would do because of Jesus Christ. His village was on the river and less than 300 yards from the edge of the mission compound.

When the appointed afternoon came, Odola's village was crowded with more than a hundred men, women and children. Several local Arab merchants, who were Muslims and dressed in their long, white, traditional garments were there, too, to see what was going to happen.

Odola still looked like a witchdoctor because his one eye had long since ceased functioning and was focused at an awkward angle. His hair was always askew and standing up in a peculiar way. His actions were normally jerky and he seemed a bit eccentric. If you met him alone on a lonely path, your first reaction would be of some slight fear. That perception changed as we got to know him, but, so far as his outward appearance was concerned, it never did fade away completely.

He said, "You people all know that I am Odola Wenyari, the witchdoctor. What I am saying is being heard by God. This is no time to be lying. God will punish me if I fail to tell everything I know. ... I have deceived you by taking your cows and your sheep and your goats." .... Odola began speaking into the neck of the gourd as he had done so often in invoking the name and power of the spirits. Now, however, he was demonstrating how he had deceived the people with those strange sounds that came back from the neck of the gourd. He then, dramatically, lifted the gourd and smashed it on the ground in a hundred pieces. The people were awestruck. Unbelievers could scarcely believe their eyes. How could Odola do this and not be afraid that the spirits would strike him dead?

Odola went on to give his testimony. He wanted to be forgiven by God and to have peace with God. He said, "I want my liver to sit down." (to be at peace) "Because God has sent His son, Jesus, I have found that peace. Jesus, God's son, made the true sacrifice. We need not ever make another sacrifice of our sheep and our goats. We must all put our faith in the blood that Jesus shed. I am at peace because this Jesus was more powerful than death and those who killed him. This Jesus is alive because when his friends went to the place where they had buried him, it was empty. His friends saw him many times before he went back to God's place above. I never knew about this until these white missionaries came to tell us. At first I couldn't believe it. And, when I knew in my liver that they were telling the truth, I was afraid of what you all would do to me if I confessed how I had sinned before God and had deceived you by taking your sheep and goats. My liver was hard and I wanted to refuse to change. But when I realized that I must fear God more than you all, I said, 'I want to leave my evil things and be baptized so I can follow Jesus with one liver.'" (with my whole heart)

With these and many other words, Odola Wenyari confessed and professed his faith. It was a day none of us who were there would ever forget. We were reminded again that the Gospel is the power of God unto salvation for all who believe.

Eventually, the broken pieces of Odola's sacred gourd and other paraphernalia of a witchdoctor were all gathered up and carried by Odola and the other Christians down the steep riverbank and thrown in to be carried away or to sink out of sight forever. Odola, himself, then went into the river waist deep, turned around and faced the people crowding the bank. With a radiant face, and without fear, he was gently pushed under the water by the missionary and an ordained elder from the church. He was baptized in the precious, saving name of Jesus Christ, God's only appointed Savior.

Odola Wenyari became a true and faithful follower of Jesus Christ. He never wavered in his faith. He became a trusted elder in the Akobo Church. He was faithful in attendance and was always at the village prayer meetings. He continued to believe that God could speak to him directly. If he experienced a dream, he unfailingly shared it in the prayer meeting and closed his account with the words, "Now God, I have told the dream. Let it be so."

BAPTIZING IN A RIVER WITH CROCODILES

During our early years in the Sudan before the church building was done, we baptized most people in the river. Large crowds would be there on the river bank sharing in the happy event. Sometimes, people gave their testimonies of what Jesus meant to them. Not infrequently, someone had a sacred gourd or fetishes to part with and destroy. These ranged from small leather, homemade sandals to pieces of wire, a shriveled up chicken head or a tooth that had been sewed in a little leather pouch and worn as an amulet. This was clear evidence that Jesus was setting people free. In the power encounter, Jesus was winning! People knew deep down that Jesus was present and more powerful than everything they had always feared. True, they still needed to learn a lot about how to live out their faith in the context of their traditions, but on baptism Sundays they had already made the fundamental commitment to trust Jesus Christ to protect them from evil and to be their one and only Savior.

The baptisms themselves took considerable time when as many as thirty or forty were baptized in one service. Things weren't always routine either. I remember well the Sunday when people being baptized seemed a bit nervous. They had good reason to be as we soon discovered. Floating silently in the middle of the river was a huge crocodile. Just the knobs over his eyes were visible. We assumed he was hungry and unpredictable like all the crocodiles we'd ever known. I can tell you we baptized faster that Sunday than we had ever baptized before. We thought about the Lord shutting the mouths of lions to protect Daniel in the Old Testament and asked Him to please shut the mouths of crocodiles too!

That afternoon, as I sped off to the village with the outboard, this crocodile was still in that area. Chuck Jordan was on the river bank and I slowed to yell to him, "Chuck that croc is still there. Why don't you get your gun and see if you can get him?"

When I came back from the village about four miles out, where I had preached that afternoon, I stopped to ask Chuck how he'd made out. He said, "I got him. But by the time I shot him, he had one of our mission cow's calves in its throat."

I said, "Where is he? I've got to see that."

At that point, Chuck looked at me somewhat quizzically and said, "Don't you know that a croc doesn't come up for 24 hours after it's hit? We'll have to wait until tomorrow."

I knew that, but in my eagerness had failed to take it into account. The next noon, Chuck and I walked downstream along the river bank and, sure enough, there was our dead crocodile. It was at least 15 feet long and still stuck in its throat was the dead mission calf. God had closed the mouth of a hungry crocodile. Our silent prayers had been answered.

This experience encouraged us to baptize beside the river rather than in the river. We used locally grown gourds to pour water freely over those being baptized. Later when the church was built, we found ourselves using even less water and merely sprinkling. God seemed to honor and bless all three of these practices and, as in the book of Acts, "The Lord added to the church daily, those who believed." Well, in our case, it wasn't quite daily, but the Lord was calling his own and it was exciting to be part of it.

"For we do not preach ourselves, but Jesus Christ as Lord, and ourselves as your servants for Jesus' sake"

2 Cor 4:5

CHAPTER SIX

LETTERS HOME
ABOUT THE CHILDREN

The Lord gave us six healthy children, five boys and a girl. The youngest and the oldest were 20 years apart. Sometimes it seems that we raised two families because of the difference in ages. Dennis was born in October, 1942 and we sailed for Africa in July of '48. Jim was born in Nashville, Tennessee in March that same year. He was just four months old and still in his carrying basket when we headed for the Sudan. The following year, Dave was born at Akobo. Just fourteen months apart, they grew up having great times together. I recall how they played basketball at the Schutz American Mission school in Alexandria, Egypt. They had quite an advantage in yelling their strategies using the Anuak language. No one ever broke their code!

Carol Joy was born in the mission hospital in Dembidollo, Ethiopia in 1953. I'll never forget how overjoyed we were to have a little girl. But I'll save that story until later. Again, fourteen months later, running true to our pattern, Mark was born at Akobo. How he arrived is worthy of being told later in greater detail!

And then, to give us an even half dozen, six and a half years later our little caboose arrived when Paul was born at home when we were living at Pibor.

BY ROAD FROM AKOBO TO MALAKAL

Early letters give us an idea of what was involved to get by road between Akobo and Malakal from which all our supplies were bought or routed, when gotten from Khartoum in the North.

February 22, 1949: (written from Malakal)

"Dennis and I are leaving this afternoon about three o'clock for Akobo on a merchant's truck. We will have to ride on the back of it on top of a load of cement. Imagine doing that over that trail for 230 miles. We will stop about half way at an Arab merchants' center. Here we will be staying over for two days. We have one blanket with us and four water canteens and some soup and some cookies, so, I think we will get along alright. I have matches in my pocket for a fire and the camp cooking set I bought in Minneapolis.

"This will, indeed, be a rugged trip, traveling all night, but it will be a most interesting experience. It will be a little hard on Dennis, but we must get back to work and we will both be able to rest after getting home. I have my gun and field glasses with, so, it should be exciting."

DENNIS TO ATTEND SCHOOL IN ADDIS

April 27, 1949:

"Dennis and I came in on one of the merchant's trucks again (first leg of Dennis' trip to boarding school in Addis Ababa). *We had a faster and better trip, leaving Akobo about 3 p.m. on Monday and arriving here in Malakal the next day about the same hour.*

"We had an interesting trip and rather enjoyed it, although it was very hot during the day. The temperature was around 105 again. I shot a Tiang so the fellows had meat. ..."

May 8, 1949:

"Dennis is now in Addis. He left on the plane last Thursday (Mary Euwing was on that same flight and looked after him). I was so sorry I had to return home three days before the planes left so that I could not see him off. ... We had not thought it would be so hard to have him gone, but, truly, it has been lonely with him absent. I don't know how many times each day that we don't mention him. It is so early to have him go, but we know he is in a good school and that it is really better for him. We miss him so, though. He always had so much spark and pep and was so much fun. ... I don't know, but I think the sacrifice of one's children is perhaps the most deep cutting and trying experience for us missionaries. It is especially hard for Lavina as she misses him so much, but gradually now the intensity of it is diminishing and we are reconciled to it. I know that if we truly cast ourselves upon the Lord, His grace is sufficient even for this. If only he keeps well and strong now while away. It is when they are sick that they need a mother's loving care so much."

Commenting about Dennis at school Addis July 4, 1949:

"Dennis writes he is having a grand time in school. He is well and happy."

LETTERS FOR GRANDPA AND GRANDMA

June 24, 1949:

"Jimmy is still as strong and pretty as ever. ... he just loves to sing and to have us sing to him. He is really quite an affectionate and loving baby. When he finds a slip of paper on the floor, he sits down and starts rocking back and forth and sings. He sings, 'Jesus' over and over again. He's learned this because we sing 'Jesus loves me this I know' to him so often. Whenever I saw boards in the house, he either stands and keeps time with the saw, or he sits down and rocks back and forth keeping time with the music of the saw.

"This week Jimmy has had a case of sore eyes which are so common out here. They are caused by the flies which carry infections from the villages. He was awfully crabby and they are so painful. For several days they were stuck shut for more than half day at a time. It was so pitiful to see him sitting there trying to eat like a blind baby. But they are nearly better now and he is better natured too."

For his second year away from home, Dennis travelled with other mission children to Assuit in Egypt. They were chaperoned by one of the missionary wives or families. These trips were correlated with vacation times, which, incidentally, missionaries were required to take during those years. The weather and isolation dictated the wisdom of this mission regulation. One year, we took our holiday somewhere inside the Sudan and the next year, we had to leave the country and get away to where the climate was more favorable to good health.

GROWING UP IN AFRICA

In many ways, our children had a great time growing up in the Sudan. They loved to fish with the native children. They learned some of the ways the Anuak children had fun without toys. They learned to make things from sticks, grass and mud. It was great sport for them to make small mud balls, attach them to a willowy stick and sling them at birds to chase these dura birds out of the ripening dura. They'd sit up on the tall stands in the middle of the ripening corn and have a great time with the Anuak boys and girls who were up there from morning until night. Sometimes, they'd get a little rough, too, and have a mud-ball fight to see who could make the other person run first! We were always concerned that someone might get a mud ball in the eye.

The boys enjoyed their pellet guns and were fantastic shots. Many a rat suffered at their hands. They'd spend hours hunting for mourning-doves and came home with up to half a dozen which Lavina prepared and put on the table for that essential ingredient for another of her delicious, home cooked meals.

The boys learned to eat like the Anuak boys too. We weren't always so excited about that because we knew how easily dysentery and diarrhea could follow. Once, when I came in the back yard, Denny, who was then about six and a half years old, was sitting beside a little fire he had made. His legs were wide apart and he was holding a partially eaten fish. Just like the Anuaks, he was eating around the intestines and enjoying the meat. He looked up at me with a guilty grin and captivating smile that I shall never forget. We were still pretty strict about those things those first months, but seeing his endearing smile, even though tainted by disobedience, didn't make discipline any easier!

And then there was the time when I stepped out of the back door at Pibor. I was going down the back path and there, under the shade of a small bush, Dave was eating a tiny dura bird, about the size of a sparrow. He had plucked most of the feathers off and roasted it in a little fire he had going there. He looked up at me and, with the most satisfying smile, said with his childish lisp, "Thweet, dad. Thweet." Which by way of interpretation is, "Sweet, dad. Sweet." He was translating back from Murle into English!

When David was born, the Anuaks called him "Little Akobo." When he started growing up they began calling him "David Akobo." When Carol was born, they gave her the name, "Awile," which means, "the one who changed things around." She had broken the pattern from boys to our having a girl. Her older brothers still call her "Awile" sometimes as a playful expression of love and admiration, an indication of how glad they are to have such a lovely sister.

JIMMY AND THE ALADDIN LAMP

The children really loved the single missionary gal who lived at Pokwo with us after she came back from furlough. Having been there alone with their dad and mom for fifteen months, they were glad for a new face. Joan Yilek had a way with kids and when she'd come over for a meal with us, the conversation around the table was animated and frequently hilarious.

One evening Jimmy and Dave were so excited that they monopolized the conversation and we couldn't seem to get a word in edgewise. Finally, in good fun, I said,"Alright, now it's time for the adults to have a chance to talk. I want you children to keep silent unless you have something really special to say. But before you can talk, you have to raise your hand to get permission."

Everything seemed to have calmed down reasonably well, when Jimmy, who had had his hand up for some time and wasn't being recognized, began to sing softly, "I see something. I see something. I see something." He kept this up without our paying adequate attention. When, finally, we gave him the attention he should have had all along, under terms of the conditions playfully laid down, we saw that he was pointing to the Aladdin lamp. It was gradually going up in smoke as the wick became blacker and blacker. We had a good laugh and knew that Jimmy succeeded in having had the last word!

What fun we had as a family when the children were small and not some 2,000 plus miles away in school in Egypt. The pain of those empty beds that first night after the children left for school, has seared its way into our memories. The utter desolation and loneliness of those first nights were hard on Lavina, with a mother's heart. But we all felt it, even the little ones who weren't yet old enough to go away to school.

And then there were the letters we exchanged with our children. The school had a regulation that every child had to spend part of Sunday afternoon to produce a letter in an envelope for their parents. I suspect most kids would have written in any case. But those letters were very precious for both parents and the children. We shared many deep and meaningful conversations in those exchanges.

Some of the letters received produced joy and laughter. Dennis was always small for his age. He was just a little guy when he was in the third grade at Assuit in Egypt. One of his letters was unforgettable. It had only a couple of sentences but they got our attention.

He wrote, *"Please write Miss Duff a hot letter and tell her to stop opening my mail."*

After a good laugh over it, we thought an appropriate letter in response would be in order!

Other letters brought concern and pain, like when one of the boys would write about some perceived injustice in the classroom because of what a teacher had said. The painful incident would be described in detail to gain our sympathy and support. But we could sense that if we had been there, we could have helped the child appreciate some of the other factors that hadn't been taken into account. Had we been there we could have helped our child understand and the pain would have been less severe. But by the time this kind of letter came, it was far too late to be of much help. A month would have passed. By this time they would again be having fun with friends about which they normally wrote.

CHILDREN'S ESCAPADES AND ACCIDENTS

When Dave was about three years old, he gave us the fright of our lives. It was late afternoon and Lavina and I were enjoying the gradual cooling off of the day as we wandered through the garden, commenting on how the various vegetables were faring. During this time, David had climbed up on the steps that led up to the base where the water barrels were positioned. These steps allowed the water carrier to make his way up there with his five gallon tins to fill the barrels morning and evening. Water from the barrels ran through a lead pipe into the house to give us inside water. We had a faucet over the sink in the kitchen, one in the bathroom and a shower. All showers were cold, and they really felt that way, too, after the heat of the day.

This particular afternoon Dave had been playing quite contentedly on the steps and having a great time. However, during one of our frequent glances in his direction, we saw him sitting on the ground and he seemed to be in distress. He had fallen off the third or fourth step, landing on his small toy crane, striking it right across his windpipe. It seemed innocent enough, but almost immediately as the swelling began, it was apparent that the air passage was rapidly closing and he was having difficulty getting enough air.

We really didn't know what to do. We carried him into the house and put him on the bed and prayed that the Lord would cause the swelling to stop. We also contemplated driving him to Pibor, some 90 miles south where Dr. Roode was stationed. Of course, that would have been to no avail if the swelling had continued. Lillian Huiskens, our Akobo nurse, was soon there and she calmly kept a careful eye on him and together we committed Dave to the Lord's merciful, saving power. We look back on that experience with great thanks to God for His intervention and how He cared for Dave and taught us afresh how totally dependent we were upon Him.

Letters home are cute telling how Dave viewed the discipline of kindergarten every day.

November 9, 1954:

"David is in kindergarten with his mother teaching. There are rather frequent times when he shows up with 'I'm sick of school, mother. Let's not have school today.' He loves to play out with the Anuak children, roasting pigeons, fish, and corn in typical Anuak fireplaces. He speaks Anuak as if it were his native tongue!"

When Dave was a little older, he and the Jordan boys, Jack and Dave, had great times together. They had an interesting debate going among them as to whose Dad's dog was the strongest. One day these boys egged the two dogs on, each side hoping to prove the other to be wrong. I suspect they bit off more than they could handle. Before this inconclusive, furious contest was over the dogs had had the last bite. Dave came home by way of the clinic with stitches and a clean white bandage around his leg. He'd gotten a little too close to the action! A prominent scar reminds him of how much fun it was before he tried to make sure his dad's dog would win!

Jim and Dave had a lot of fun together. Being just fourteen months apart they were almost like twins. One afternoon when Jim and Dave were young lads eleven and twelve years of age, they gave us a good scare too. Dave had a way of playing tricks on us with his delightful sense of humor, so we weren't always sure whether he was to be taken seriously or not.

I was in the office inside our house at Pibor. We lived in what was known then as "Hostetter's house." They had lived there until Paul and his family were expelled, the first missionaries on whom the ax fell, with everyone else still to follow. Missionary houses tended to be identified by the name of the first person who had occupied it.

On that afternoon of which I'm writing, Dave and Jim came into the office and asked if they could chop some wood. We always had to chop dry branches and logs for the wood burning cook-store. Normally, an Anuak or a Murle was engaged to do this, but the boys thought it would be a fun experience to chop a little wood.

I looked at their shorts and bare feet and had a moment of concern as to the wisdom of their doing this without shoes, but gave it no more than a passing thought and gave them my okay to go ahead. My parting words were, "Be sure you boys are careful not to chop yourselves with those bare feet." With that they left, happy with the "permission granted" status under which they could begin.

They weren't gone more than fifteen minutes when Dave came back in alone with the words, "Dad, Jim chopped his foot!"

I thought he was kidding and responded with, "You've got to be kidding."

It was no joke! Jim had already made his way over to the mission hospital and when I arrived, Dr. Mary Smith was busy stitching up a 3" gash running right down the entire length of the foot, just off center. A quarter of an inch on the angle of the gash and he'd have severed the tendon.

Again, our prayers of thanks took on special meaning. We were reminded again of how utterly dependent we were upon the Lord's loving, protecting care. It was a painful experience, but everyone learned important lessons out of it.

Dave and I were reminiscing recently about some of the boy's experiences in Africa. At one point, he said to me, "Dad, do you remember that big Nile perch we picked up that day when we were coming down from Pibor to Akobo with that old launch?" (a three day trip in an old diesel launch that had 4 bunks in it) "Do you remember how we put that huge fish up on the top and how the juice from the fish oozed out and ran all over our jackets? Boy, how they smelled and we couldn't get that terrible, dead fish smell out of them? Dad, that's one of our experiences you've got to include in your book."

Our grandchildren have listened to many a story from our years in the Sudan and Ethiopia. Once, while sitting around the table with Jim's family, I got to talking about some of our fabulous experiences in Africa. At one point, Doug, then about eleven, pipes up and says, "Grandpa, you ought to write a book. It'd be a best seller." Would that this young lad had prophetic blood flowing in his young veins!

Seriously, one of the reasons for writing this book is so that our children and grandchildren will be able to recall some of their incredible experiences and praise God for His marvelous, loving care as we worked together for Him in the heart of Africa. What a privilege it was for our whole family, even though some experiences were painful and threatening. Looking back, we know, beyond the shadow of a doubt, that God who called us mercifully protected us and enabled us to complete the task He had entrusted to us.

CHAPTER SEVEN

CUSTOMS AND CONCEPTS

Almost every day was a learning experience. While trying to understand how the Anuak language was put together, I was constantly grappling with "meaning". If we were to have an accurate translation which expressed what the Bible was saying the way an Anuak would say it had he been there and was writing it to his own people, I needed to know what Anuaks thought and believed about — well, "almost everything." I needed to enter into their "world-view." This was an intriguing, compelling, often baffling pursuit that had to include study time with informants and village time listening and observing. On our discovery-trail we were reminded of the words from the Bible itself when it says, "Even a little child shall lead them."

A letter home tells how it happened for us.

August 22, 1950:

SPITTING TO BLESS

"Our people are so very poor and hungry these days. They are at the door constantly begging for money to buy a little grain that the merchants had gotten a few weeks ago. The grain is more than half the normal price and our people are selling everything to get a little money together to buy it. ...

"The other day Dennis gave a small tin can full of grain to an old woman who comes here quite regularly. She was so happy,

Lavina said, that she took Dennis's head in her hands and spit on the top of it to show her gratitude. Needless to say, Dennis was embarrassed to tears."

I played a little joke on one of our guests from America over this custom of spitting on the head to extend a blessing or to show appreciation. Dr. Ed Fairman who has a good sense of humor (which always helps) was visiting us when we lived at Pokwo. Anuaks had come in from the village to see who the new visitors were and to welcome Ed and Marian and their young son, Tim. We were all having a good time and I was interpreting. I finally said to Ed, "How would you like to receive an Anuak blessing?"

Not knowing the custom, he innocently said, "Well, I guess I can always use an additional blessing." He, of course, couldn't follow the conversation the Anuaks and I were having in the Anuak language, so before he knew it, this village chief put his hands on Ed's head, pushed it slightly down and gently spit on it. This was a blessing, the memory of which stayed with Ed permanently!

On another occasion, in the village, I saw a young Anuak lad who had come in from a distance present himself to a village elder who happened to be his uncle. The old man was so overjoyed to see the young man that he overdid it a bit. He really put a load of saliva on the young man's head. The man sitting next to him even scolded him saying that was not a proper way to bless someone! I learned that the amount of saliva was to be minimal and primarily symbolic rather than for cleansing!

SPITTING WHEN FORGIVING

When we were searching for an Anuak word to use in the translation of "to forgive," they told me what they had used in the language of a neighboring tribe. They said those people express "to forgive" by saying "to spit on the ground." I learned that in that tribe when there was trouble, anger or misunderstanding which had been peacefully resolved and reconciliation followed, the party who had been offended would spit on the ground. The estrangement was ended and harmony had been restored. They said that when God sent His son Jesus to die on the cross, he brought the enmity between God and man to an end. Because of the price that Jesus had paid with his blood on the cross, God forgives those who come to him confessing their wrong. In that language to say, "God forgives us" they expressed it by saying "God spits on the ground." For those people, it was a beautiful, appropriate and normal way to describe what it means "to forgive."

In the Anuak language, one of the ways to express this same concept is to say, "God put His liver down." Anger, hostility, and/or estrangement cause one's liver to jump up. For the Anuak to put the liver down is to forgive. We were learning to express the great truths of the Gospel in ways appropriate to their culture and world view.

JUST TWO COFFEE BEANS

One morning at Pokwo we were just ready to sit down to eat when we heard a clapping of hands at the back door. This is the way Anuaks let it be known that they were outside one's door. Very appropriate for the kind of grass tukls they lived in.

Two middle aged men, wearing a simple pair of shorts, as Anuaks always did, were standing outside to greet me. They said they were about to start fishing and would like to have some coffee. Since our breakfast coffee hadn't been drunk yet, I quickly assured them this would be no problem and invited them in to have a cup of coffee with us. "No, no," they protested, "We don't want coffee to drink, we want dried coffee beans that haven't been roasted yet." So, I obligingly went in and asked Lavina for a little can of coffee beans as the men had requested.

When I went out with the can of coffee beans, the one man reached forward and took just two beans out of the can. Now it was my turn to protest. I said, "Look, you can't make coffee with just two beans. Please take the whole can."

They responded somewhat condescendingly and said, "No, two beans is all we need. We're not making coffee to drink. We need only these two beans to throw into the river because when we do this the fish will really bite." I've never tried it, but my suspicion is that it wouldn't work for this missionary the way they said it worked for them.

GREETING THE CHIEF WHO HAD DIED

One morning an Anuak man from the village and I were hiking together to a distant village. We were visiting and conversing together as we walked. I was in front and he was close behind me. I'd been talking, but when I got no reply, I turned around to look and establish eye contact. The man was no longer there. I turned back and soon found him about 30 feet off the path. He was on his knees talking out loud to no one visible. He was in front of a dilapidated, abandoned Anuak hut. I waited a moment before speaking, somewhat surprised to hear him talking to someone who obviously wasn't there. With no further explanation, my companion said, "I just stopped for a moment to greet our chief who once lived here before he died."

I understood better what it meant for Africans to honor the "living dead." It was important for my friend to keep on the right side of this dead person whose memory was vivid enough to cause his spirit to respond appropriately if he wasn't properly respected. Was this ancestor worship or just respect for someone they believe still to be present through his spirit? I had more food for thought as I pondered the meaning of this. We had a long trail ahead of us and plenty of time to think.

THE MAN WHO COULD
STAY UNDER WATER AND SURVIVE

The Anuaks have many myths and stories that they believe profoundly. One story going around during our stay at Pokwo was about a certain Anuak, still living, who had the ability to go into the river, submerge himself and come out on the river bank at another village miles further down stream. I had a lot of fun kidding and challenging them about that when, sometimes, we sat around under the shade of a tree and traded stories. They would always insist that it was true.

Finally, I thought, "I've got to find a way to make them show me that it actually happened or I will have to prove them to be mistaken." We couldn't both be right. Finally one day I said, "Why don't you bring the man himself to me and we'll talk with him under the tree and hear him tell us how he can do this."

To my surprise one morning right after breakfast a large number, possibly 20 or 25 grown, adult Anuak men appeared outside our kitchen door. They had brought the man himself. I brought out a couple of chairs so that the important men could sit on them and I would have one for my own comfort. They insisted that this was the man. It was interesting how cagey they were. I challenged the man to go into the river in front of the house and stay under for some minutes to prove that he could really do this. "No," they said, "he can't do that for you unless there is a reason for him to do so. If there was something lost in the river, he could go under the water and stay under until he found the missing item and bring it up."

"Well," I said, "I can easily arrange that. I'll go in the house and get my gun and throw it in the river from the canoe. Then I'll come back and fetch your friend and point to the general area and ask him to go under the water and remain under until he finds it and comes to the surface with it."

With that the group turned quite serious and began to debate among themselves, discussing the matter in low, solemn voices which I couldn't fully understand. Finally, the spokesman for the group said, "No, we've told our friend not to do it because this foreigner might kill you under the water."

The meeting ended abruptly. Everyone had had a lot of fun, but nobody proved anything to anybody. Later, I gave them a can of coffee beans which they could use to either brew some coffee or throw in the river, two at a time, and induce the fish to bite. If I hadn't been there, I could never believe that we grown men spent that much time earnestly discussing such a ridiculous possibility. When the group left, they were happy and everyone felt we'd had a great time! Question: How does one communicate the Gospel effectively among people with elements such as this framing their world-view of reality? It reinforced my conviction that this was a task that only the Holy Spirit could accomplish. We'd keep on studying and trying to understand, but, in the end, the miracle to change the mind and to believe was His to do.

ANUAK NAMES

We found the way Anuaks named their babies fascinating. But before I get into that, let me say that we missionaries were all given new names soon after we arrived. I was named, Odola, war Omot (Odola, the son of Omot). I was given the name of one of the ancestors who had lived on land where our house was built. Lavina was given the name, Nyijobi, which means "the offspring of a buffalo." I never did understand why they'd called her that. She was just too pretty and to well proportioned for a name like that. But the Anuaks always insisted that it was a name of honor and great respect. I had no trouble with that and concurred that the Anuaks were very perceptive!

Bob Swart was called Bom. Don McClure was called Odan. That seemed a good adaptation because the Anuaks normally named their boys with names that started with "O." This may be apocryphal, but some of our colleagues suggested Dr. McClure was called Odan because the Anuaks had heard his wife, Lyda, so frequently trying to call Don in to have lunch at noon. She'd have to call him more than once with a long, loud, "Oh, Donnnn! Oh, Donnnn, lunch is ready." How can we ever be sure?

Some missionary names seemed self apparent. Wilma Kats was named, Nyikwach, which means, "the offspring of a cat" (the leopard). Joan Yilek, who was on the heavier side, and a great missionary, was called, Nyilyech, the offspring of an elephant. The Anuaks had done it again!

I heard that Apio had given birth to another child. Late that afternoon when my translation work for the day had been completed and the Anuak informants had left, I said, "I'll take a moment and hike down to Apio's village and see if she and the child are doing okay or not."

When I arrived, Apio was already up and about. She was pounding grain at the pounding hole. Her belly was tightly bound and kept in with a belly band of ropes tightly assembled together. She was happy to see me and glad for the excuse to sit down for a bit as her strength wouldn't be up to par for a few days yet. We had a pleasant conversation, prayed together and talked about God's gift of children. Apio was one of the stronger Christian women and known for her sincere prayer life. It was a joy and blessing to fellowship with her.

Before leaving, I said, "Well now, what name did you give to the baby?"

She responded by saying, "Odola," (that was the African name they had given me, naming me after one of their ancestors who lived on the land on which our house was built) "you know our custom. We haven't named him yet. We have to wait some days first to be sure he will live." I knew that, but had carelessly forgotten to take it into account when I asked her what the name was.

With light hearted bantering, I said, "Well, when was the baby born?"

She, in turn, responded by saying,"He came out yesterday afternoon."

To this I responded by saying, "Well then, I suppose you will call him, 'Afternoon.'" Anuaks often named their children in association with some event that might be associated with the child's birth. For example, if a mother gave birth while travelling on the steamer, she would most likely call the child, "Steamer." If a child was weak and it appeared that he might not live at the time of birth, he would later be called, "Will not live." Normally the first two boys born to Anuak parents, were called "Omot" and "Ojulu." Girls had the same names but their names started with an "A", which mean they were called "Amot" and "Ajulu." You always knew who was the oldest and whether it was a boy or a girl. As children increased in the family, names were less predictable.

Anyway, when I met Apio on the path some ten days later, I asked her, "What did you decide to name that baby?"

With a typical Anuak response, she said, "Didn't you say we should call him, 'Afternoon' (Aboya)? We called him, 'Afternoon.'" Ten years later, when we left, he was still called, "Afternoon." They considered it a good name and I had no regrets!

Our nurse, Lillian Huiskens, ran into this naming of children in an interesting way. She was constantly trying to get the women to use more sanitary methods in caring for their children. Anuak women had some sort of mid-wife system operating whenever they gave birth. This mid-wife, who was either a relative or some older person with experience in these matters, would attend the birth of the baby. They had no instruments, of course, so they just used a sharp blade of dry grass to cut the umbilical cord. Being unsterile, babies sometimes died from infected umbilical cords. The struggle was to help them understand what was happening and to call on Lillian to assist in these births that were not too far out in distant villages.

It took a long time, but eventually one lady called on Lillian when her baby was born. Lillian went out with her sharp scissors and cut that cord with her scissors instead of with a blade of grass as was customary. It was a big event. It had never happened in all of Anuak history. There had been a lot resistance to the idea. A certain amount of superstition was connected with how that umbilical cord should be cut and who was authorized to do it.

Lillian made history. We all talked about it for a long time. Its importance wasn't lost on the Anuaks either. The mother, following tradition, named the baby in association to a significant event. What could be more important than that her baby had had its umbilical cord cut with a scissors. You guessed it! The baby was named "Scissors" (Makath). He grew up with no bad effects from his history making entry into the world. He grew into manhood with everyone calling him "Scissors." Anyone who inquired knew he was the first Anuak baby to have had his umbilical cord cut with a clean, sterile medical scissors. After awhile, the Anuaks forgot all about how he'd gotten his name, and accepted it as normal. But it would be a long time before cutting umbilical cords in Anuak country using sterile instruments was normal procedure.

I'd, of course, known from the anthropologists that Africans frequently named their children with some association to events surrounding the birth. So, we weren't surprised, but found it fascinating. We found people with names like "Won't live," "To be thrown out," "A bad one," "One to be chased," "He will die," "A cursed one" and "One who bites." None of these were very flattering. They didn't want to give babies names accenting the positive and the attractive, lest it draw the attention of the evil spirits who would harm their newborn babies. And they always delayed giving the newborn baby a name of any kind at all until they were sure that the child would live. Being a "non-entity" was the way they perceived a newborn. And, in any case, the low profile was safer with innumerable unseen, evil spirits lurking in the shadows.

THERI
THE INFLUENCE OF A PREGNANT WOMAN

Anuaks believed that a pregnant woman cast an evil shadow on certain things and events. The influence of a pregnant women had to be counteracted. She mustn't be around the cattle or there might be miscarriages of calves. Cows would give less milk when a pregnant woman was among them.

The belief that a pregnant woman could actually cause a newborn baby's umbilical cord to pop out and not heal properly was very strong. Every Anuak believed this to be so. They called this influence *"theri."* This is the way it worked.

When a baby was born, the hut in which the woman and baby were living was surrounded with a thorn fence. Three or four foot thorn branches were cut in the forest and brought home. These were stuck upright in the ground in a circle around the hut. In a small village, sometimes the entire village was circled in this way.

Anyone passing that hut or village would know, immediately, that there was a newborn baby and mother there. Any pregnant woman approaching a tukl or village circled with thorns, would divert widely from the path and proceed around the village keeping a safe distance of at least forty or fifty yards from where the baby and mother were located.

Whenever the navel of a newly born baby failed to heal properly and infection set in, the immediate, burning question was, "What pregnant women caused 'theri?' Who did it?" And, if the baby died, it became a matter of life and death for the suspected person. With the coming of the British colonializers, the "life for a life" with respect to theri was prohibited. However, in their villages, the Anuaks continued to deal with these matters as they always had. As missionaries, when we told what Jesus Christ could do for our people, we frequently told them that He was more powerful than theri, and that they need not fear. Jesus was more powerful than anything that tried to harm those who put their trust in Him. We longed for and waited for the day when Anuak women would no longer have their tukls circled with thorns because of their fear of theri. We prayed for the time when pregnant Anuak women would not need to be ostracized and live in fear that an accusing finger might be pointed at them when babies died for these reasons.

It took a long time, but eventually, it began. Little by little women were being set free from fear because of Jesus. Those were great times of happiness when in the worship services or prayer meeting an Anuak mother would share and say, "I didn't put thorns around my house when my baby was born. I'm no longer afraid of theri because Jesus is stronger. See how healthy my baby is today."

With these kinds of words they were declaring "the mighty acts of God" as they experienced His salvation. We remembered then that Jesus had said, "I am the light of the world. ... He who follows me shall not walk in darkness. ... I am come that they might have life and have it more abundantly." Our hearts were glad. To be a missionary there was totally satisfying. We praised God and worshipped Him!

In many respects, we lived as strangers in a forbidding land among a people whose ways often confounded us. Consider this experience:

I'd gone downstream a couple of miles by boat with several Anuaks to see if we could get an animal for some meat. Several village people joined us as we made our way back of the village toward the swamp area on the edge of the thorn tree forest. Almost immediately we spotted a small herd of waterbuck. We could actually smell them before we saw them because of their strong body odor, which odor tended to carry over into the flavor of the cooked meat as well. Waterbuck was our meat of last resort, but it made good gravy! Eventually, we learned to enjoy it and never really were troubled by the strong flavor.

That morning I brought a nice animal down with my .348, lever action rifle. The men immediately ran to the fallen animal and were proceeding to cut its throat when it suddenly, inexplicably, jumped to its feet and began to run away. The men all followed it in hot pursuit as they disappeared among the trees. I was left standing alone, gun in hand.

After a bit I started to call out to see if someone from among them might answer so I'd know where to follow them. No one responded, but shortly a man came up from the riverbank. He was passing by in his canoe and had heard me. He now joined me and called out himself. I didn't hear anything, but he said, "They're over in that direction."

I followed the man into the forest and when we came upon my hunting party, they were already skinning the animal. They had successfully caught up with it and finished what I had started.

Now, the baffling thing is this. As we stood around while some of the men were dressing the meat out, one of the village people asked me if I knew why that animal had gotten up and run away.

I responded by saying, "Well, I suppose I didn't hit him in the right place."

To this, in a condescending manner, he said to me, "No, Odola" (my African name), "the problem is that one of the men in your party has a wife who is pregnant. And, whenever you hunt with a man whose wife is pregnant the animals run away like this."

Another occasion I recall is when our man who carried up the water from the river to fill our water barrels failed to do so. I went out back where his little house was and found him sitting in the low doorway. He had a bandage on his toe. He explained that he couldn't go into the water because of his bandage and therefore hadn't filled the barrels.

That was a fair explanation, but then I noticed that his house had thorns around it like Anuaks would normally put around a hut in which a mother had recently given birth to a baby.

I said to him, "Deng, I understand about the bandage, but why do you have these thorns around your house?"

He turned his head slightly and pointing with his tongue he said,"Omot's wife over there is pregnant and every time she walks past my house my toe goes like this." And then, he motioned with his hand how his toe throbbed whenever she came past his hut. It was a strange world and we had a lot to learn!

GWITH
A LAST WILL OR TESTAMENT

Anuaks have powerful, pivotal customs that arise out of critical junctures in their lives. One such practice is that of the "final blessing, will or testament"(gwith). When a man knows that the time of his death is near, he will call for a person he trusts to whom he can commit his final blessing.

The man sits on an animal skin beside the dying person and listens intently to each item in the blessing. He has to listen carefully because if he fails to accurately carry out the instructions of the dying person, after that person has died, the curse attached to it is most severe.

It works something like this: The person anticipating death speaks. He says, " I have three cows that are in the village of Ojulu. They belong to me. You must get them after I die and dispose of them in this way ......"

The man listening, repeats the word several times to fix it in his mind. He then takes a dry blade of grass about six or eight inches in length and puts it down in front of him.

Again, the person about to die might say, " I have a string of dimui beads. They were borrowed by my brother for use in his son's marriage. They must never be lost. You must recover these so that my own son can use them for his marriage."

The man listening, similarly repeats the words of the dying man to fix them firmly in his memory. A second blade of grass is laid down which is slightly different in length from the previous one.

This speaking of the testament continues until the five or six items on the dying man's mind have been addressed. Finally, when the last item has been covered and the last blade of grass has been laid down, the dying man pronounces a curse on the man to whom he has entrusted his will and testament. He concludes with the solemn warning, "If you fail to carry out my word or change it in any way, one of your eyes will fall to the ground." This has a powerful way of concentrating the mind, as you can imagine.

The person leaves with the blades of dry grass and when he reaches his own village, carefully puts them away, only to bring them out over and over again to fix permanently in his memory what the blades of dried grass represent. At the appropriate time, after the death of the person who has spoken, the testament is executed. Few, if any, would doubt the word of the man who was under a solemn oath to be truthful less he lose his eye.

SHI-JWOK
AN EVIL EYE

I learned a lot about the Anuak language and customs by visiting their villages and staying overnight. It was great to be under the mosquito net, continuing to listen to their conversations until I fell asleep. I was also amazed at the noise in these villages. Dogs were barking, babies crying and Anuaks were stirring at different times all through the night keeping the fire going or having a smoke. There was a lot of coughing, too, as I recall.

One night in the village of Othil, about four miles from home, I slept under my net inside one of their houses. When I came out in the morning, I discovered the chief and a large group of people sitting around him having an, obviously, important meeting. They all welcomed me profusely, including the chief and the elders sitting near him. I was a bit suspicious when they all decided that the meeting was over, almost as soon as I had sat down to listen in on their deliberations.

Later I learned that I had stumbled unto a meeting in which they were discussing the matter of the evil eye, and what to do about the baby that had been born and would most certainly grow up having the power of the evil eye. Such a person would be called a *"shi-jwok"* and would have the ability to cast evil spells on people, villages, and events. A person suspected of being a shi-jwok was greatly feared and people were always on the lookout for someone who might be a shi- jwok and have caused a misfortune.

They were discussing the fate of a little, newborn baby whose testicle had not come down. A child born with that abnormality among the Anuak was cursed and had to be killed. If allowed to grow to adulthood, this person would have the ability to curse people and cause great harm.

Normally, before the British had come to govern the Sudan, Anuaks would take such a baby, put it in a gourd and either let it float away on the river or they might put it in a swamp in the hot sun to die, in which case the vultures would have the last word.

I understood then why the meeting had ended so abruptly. They were fearful that I would report them to our local district commissioner, a British official.

Our first furlough soon followed that experience. After we returned from the states, I inquired as to the child and was told, "Oh, that baby died." My presence had delayed the inevitable, but had not prevented it. I was reminded again that without Jesus there is darkness, fear and superstition which brings death. Jesus alone can change all of that. That's the heart of the good news from God. Jesus, himself, said, "I am the light of the world." And again, He said, "I am come that they might have life, and have it more abundantly." There is no other Savior! We are entrusted with that good news from God, and are commissioned to take this powerful, saving Gospel to the very ends of the earth and to proclaim it unashamedly to every tribe and people. And, what better way, than to tell them, each in his own language.

JWOK
GOD, SPIRIT, LUCK, ILLNESS ...

Perhaps the most powerful concept affecting the lives of Anuaks was their understanding of jwok. Studying their language and customs, I found the meaning of this word most difficult to fully understand. The word, "*jwok*," was constantly on the lips of Anuaks. God, the creator, was Jwok. A person could be a jwok. An individual who was ill was said to have a jwok. If the fish weren't biting it was because of the word of jwok. This seemed to imply bad luck or fate. When one was ill and dying, his jwoks, called ju in the plural were leaving his body one by one, vacating the vital organs with which they were identified. When all the spirits (ju) had departed, the person was dead. If one was startled, the one word, spontaneous response was, "Jwok."

In trying to understand the wide areas of meaning associated with this word jwok, it became apparent that this reflected a world-view with many unknowns and many things that were fearful and foreboding. The word jwok and its many different meanings suggested a world of unfriendly, harmful spirits. Basically, jwok was associated with the unknown and that which couldn't be explained but had to be treated with respect and kept friendly. Gifts and sacrifices were made to jwok.

It was interesting and significant that when people were learning to read, whenever they guessed how to read the sentence which said, "God (Jwok) is good," they would invariably say, "God (Jwok) is bad." They would consistently guess wrong. For them, Jwok was bad.

You can imagine the problems and concern this raised as to how to be sure we were using the correct word for "God." In the end, we, normally added a descriptive expression so that we'd be saying, "God who made the heavens and the earth."

JWEIY
SPIRIT, BREATH ...

Another baffling linguistic problem arose as to the use of the word for "spirit". Like the Greek, the Anuak word we determined meant "spirit" also meant "breath". The problem was that this word, *jweiy*, which we understood to be akin to "spirit" had to be the jweiy of something or someone else. Whatever the word, jweiy, meant, it had no volition of its own. We always had to use a modifying expression with this word. It was the jweiy of God or the jweiy of a person or animal that had power to do something.

There was also a further complication. When this word was modified with an adjective it required a plural form. This was the word that was used in a descriptive phrase to translate the word, "Holy Spirit." The complication was that when I heard Anuaks praying for the "Holy Spirit who will live within us," I thought I heard them saying, "Give us the "Holy Spirits to live within us." I wondered how they conceptualized this expression. What was going on in their mind. Similarly, they also used a plural adjective to modify water . Surely, they conceived of water as being singular. Were they doing the same thing with the term which meant "spirit?" Was the same thing in their minds as was in mine? These were the kinds of questions we pondered night and day for months, even years as we tried to accurately translate the Biblical concepts.

SHIK
COMMAND OR "GOSPEL"?

I remember the effort to find a way to say, "Gospel." One of the early words used was *shik*, which, in fact, meant "message." However, the word was so strongly associated with a message from a village chief for his people to do something he commanded them to do, that it distorted what we were trying to say when teaching that God has given us His Son to be the "Giver" of our salvation. For example, the chief would send word out for the people to cut the grass off the road at the beginning of each dry season. This was a shik from the chief.

The "message" we had brought, however, was the "good news" about what God had done for us. We had not come, first of all with a shik, that is a message of command to obey in order to be accepted. Using the word shik, in other words, made it more difficult to make clear the central affirmation we had about God's loving mercy and grace made evident in the life and ministry of Jesus Christ, which culminated in His sacrificial, vicarious death on the cross on our behalf.

The word, shik, approximated the expression "to command one to do something" much more closely than the expression "a message about something that had already been done." *Shik-Jwok* meant "God's commandment." To express "good news from God" (gospel of God) we came to use an entirely different expression. Literally translated, the term used for "the gospel" in our translation said, "The new, sweet word from God" (Lum Jwok mana nyan ni met). When Anuaks heard the message about Jesus Christ, they would frequently react to it during those early months with the expression, Lum Jwok met (The word of God is sweet). We had come with the "new sweet word from God." How wonderful it is, indeed!

SHWINY - LIVER
SEAT OF THE EMOTIONS

We struggled with the concept of "forgiveness" for a long while too. Anuaks used *shwiny* (the liver) with modifying expressions to convey their attitudes and moods. We discovered that Anuaks could have many different kinds of livers (shwiny). One's liver could jump up. Meaning: to become angry. A liver could sit down. Meaning: To no longer be upset or angry. A liver could be walking around. Meaning: One was restless, troubled and worrying. A liver might not yet have arrived. Meaning: One was still in thought about something else. A liver could be absent: Meaning: The person wasn't interest or involved. A liver could be hot. Meaning: to be upset and disturbed emotionally. A liver could be cold. Meaning: Not to be that interested or possibly dispassionate about something. A small liver. Meaning: Not greedy. A large liver. Meaning: to be greedy. (just the opposite of big hearted.) We had to be careful how we transferred concepts. A liver could fall down. Meaning: to become saddened. A liver could be sweet. Meaning: to be happy with something, to like or to love. A liver might be black. Meaning: to be very unhappy and unforgiving. A liver could also be white. Meaning: No ulterior motives, innocent, pure. A liver could be destroyed. Meaning: One was extremely displeased and unhappy. A liver could be bad. Meaning: one who was a bad person.

And this list could still go on. We learned to express the gospel and to translate the New Testament in this context. To make a translation which was the dynamic equivalent of the original language was our goal. To achieve it, the task continued night and day and never ended. No challenge could have been more captivating, compelling or satisfying.

TO BELIEVE AND TO TRUST

How to translate "to believe," "to trust" and "to have hope" proved to be extremely difficult. At first we thought the word *yey* meant "to believe." In a sense it did, but when I listened to school boys trying to share the Christian message in the village, it always came across as a response to a shik from God. It fit their world-view. We had to do something to keep the spirits happy so that they would yey us. The idea seemed to be that we had to yey to what God was telling us so that God would yey us in return. It became clear that the primary thrust of the word meant "to accept," "to agree to" or, in some contexts, "to believe that a thing is true."

To try to figure out the range of meanings words and expressions had was a never ending, all consuming quest. One was always on the alert, night and day, for new insights. Nothing, for me, could have been more challenging or satisfying.

There would be long periods when I was baffled and unable to understand what was going on. The word for "to believe" was much more difficult than one would have first suspected. I began hearing them use the word yey as "response." If you called to someone at a distance and this person answered back, they said he answered you. For this they used the word yey. If a girl accepted the advances of a young man and agreed to sleep with him or to marry him, the word used was yey. It was the same word we were trying to use for "to believe." What we meant when we used it and what the Anuaks understood were two different things. What we said made good sense to them because they were hearing our words from within their world-view. But in

117

reality, we had a serious miscommunication of the central message of the gospel about God's grace.

Being a Nilotic language, Anuak has expressions and words which were common to other languages spoken over a very wide area. These included Shullik, Acholli, Alango, Alur and others spoken in the Sudan, Zaire, Uganda and Kenya. I tried to learn what I could from people working in those languages.

During this same period we were wrestling with how to translate "to trust." We first used the Anuak word, ngadho. But we soon became aware that this word, ngadho, was much more akin to our idea of "to hope so." When using that word, they were meaning something more like, "I have been hoping so." To trust or to have faith was much stronger than that. We struggled to understand what was in the Anuak speaker's mind when he used words like that.

In the end, we found it necessary sometimes to use descriptive phrases or to combine terms to express the true meaning of the Biblical terms. By combining yey and ngadho in one expression, we approximated the central thrust of what it means "to believe in" or "to trust" or "to have faith in" in Anuak. An entirely different term was used to express the concept "to love."

There is much more to be said, but this will give you a feel for what was involved. Every Bible translator will know what I've been attempting to describe.

In many respects, the Anuak language was a beautiful work of art. The grammar was extremely complicated, but, for the most part, regular and predictable. Part of the process of understanding the grammar involved making long lists of words that acted in certain ways under similar conditions. We called them "form classes." Some such groupings had a common rationale, but others just seemed to belong in that category with no obvious explanation. They were neither masculine, feminine or neuter!

The Anuak language made extensive use of the subjunctive mood. They used beautiful nuances to express the mood or feeling of what was being said. They also had a propensity for using the passive voice. Instead of saying, "He did it" they often said, "It was done by him."

THE TRANSLATION PROCEDURE ITSELF

Our translation team normally had two persons and myself. They sat across the desk from me. One of the two men knew no English, but was extremely intelligent and alert in Anuak. Having Othow War Adier, a non-English speaking person on the team, forced us to carry on most of our conversation in Anuak as we discussed the verse being translated. It contributed toward our achieving an idiomatic translation which sounded like it would have sounded had an Anuak spoken it originally rather than as a translation from another language. If Othow couldn't understand and repeat the translated verse back to us without stumbling, it needed further refinement. Sometimes it was a tedious, painstaking process requiring huge amounts of time and patience.

Across the years, I had a total of three different full-time, English-speaking informants, Jok Deng, James Buya, and Ocala Alero. None had more than the equivalent of an eighth grade education. Their English usage, especially in the beginning, was limited. Much time and patience was required as we worked together as they tried to understand the meaning of the English text.

To make things convenient, on my desk I always had two book-stands in front of me. One held my Greek New Testament and the other a New Testament in English. Stacked up on the right-hand corner of the desk were copies of as many translations as were available at that time. Among them were the translations by Goodspeed, Moffet, Weymouth, Williams, Phillips and others. These served as instant reference commentaries.

Before every translation session, we earnestly prayed that God would give us understanding and insight. We asked that our translation would have the same quality of inspiration as did the other translations. We asked that what we put on paper would, indeed, be the very word of God. We asked God for help that we not become professionals and become calloused or indifferent to the fact that we were handling the Word of God, written. We asked for the help of the Holy Spirit. Sometimes, when we didn't know how to express it in Anuak, we stopped and prayed again for the Holy Spirit to help us.

It was a demanding, exhausting, exhilarating task. It required discipline and determination to patiently see it through, verse by verse — each on a 3 by 5 card, typed up each day into a growing manuscript to be evaluated, corrected and improved upon. It would take a dozen years to complete it. But for me, every day was a dream coming true. I cannot adequately praise God for that unspeakable challenge and privilege.

During our later years of translating, beside my desk there was an IBM electric typewriter, a lead acid car battery and an invertor to convert 12 volts into 110 volts of power to run the typewriter. A young Anuak man by the name of Stephen Omot Didumu, whom Kitty Crandall had earlier taught to type, took the 3 by 5 cards each day and typed them into the manuscript. At night when the generator was running, the battery was charged up so that Stephen had power to run his typewriter the next day. When the translation was finally ready in its final form, this young man typed every word of it in triplicate so we could send it off to the American Bible Society for printing.

CHECKING THE FINAL TRANSLATION

When the last verse had been translated and all the limited test-printings had been used and reviewed, one essential task remained. We brought together a committee of Anuak speakers from the three different areas where Anuaks lived — the Baro River, Pochala, and Akobo areas. Several of these young men walked over a hundred miles to get to Pibor where the conference was held.

Every day for six weeks we went over the translation, verse by verse. All three areas with their dialectical differences had to be taken into consideration. Sometimes we discovered that words carried slightly different meanings depending on where one lived. For example, the word used in the book of Acts to translate "storm," the storm that destroyed the ship on which Paul was travelling, accented a meaning of "a strong wind" to speakers along the Baro, whereas to people living at Akobo it meant only "very cold weather." By the time the wind had reached Akobo it was minimal, but the "cold" was the main thing this word conveyed. In such cases, additional modifying expressions were added to clarify the meaning so that wherever Anuaks lived they would be able to understand the meaning readily.

And so it went for some six weeks. When the review and modifications required had been completed, the young men returned to their villages. Some of them had a walk of a hundred miles ahead of them. They left, eager for the day when the printed New Testament would be returned from America, when they would have in their hands God's precious word in their very own New Testament in their language.

"If I speak in the tongues of men and of angels, but have not love, I am only a resounding gong or a clanging cymbal."

1 Cor 13:1

CHAPTER EIGHT

OUR FIRST FURLOUGH

We took a shortened, nine-month furlough our first trip back to the states. Two reasons dictated we do that. The mission wanted to stagger furloughs so that everyone from Akobo wouldn't be scheduled to be away in the states at the same time. We were assigned to take an early furlough to get that schedule going and to permit me to return to the Summer Institute of Linguistics in Norman, Oklahoma. This would enable me to check out my analysis of the Anuak language and seek answers to several perplexing questions about which I was still unsure.

CHECKING MY LANGUAGE ANALYSIS

The most basic question that I needed answered was the question of whether or not I had analyzed the language correctly in concluding that we should write it morpho-phonemically. Put in simple terms it was the question of whether or not we would write the words as they sounded when spoken, or whether we should write the basic form of the word before it had been influenced by neighboring sounds. The Anuak words were very short with basically a consonant-vowel-consonant stem. To this basic stem one added suffixes, prefixes and infixes to indicate personal pronouns, tenses for verbs etc.

The problem was complicated in that in Anuak I had observed that tense indicators sometimes seemed to be attached to the particle or word preceding the verb itself. It seemed strange to me that whether something happened in the past or in, let's say, the future would be indicated by adding a vowel to the word preceding the verb rather than that it would be treated as part of the verb. This problem kept me awake many nights at Akobo and I wasn't absolutely certain that I had come to the right conclusion.

It was a tremendous relief when at SIL, they confirmed my analysis as being correct and that this phenomenon was not unknown in some other languages with which the Wycliffe Bible Translators had worked. They confirmed the correctness of writing the basic, unaffected sounds or morphemes because in doing so the graphemics or identity of the word would remain stable and the conditioned sounds would be, as it were, automatic when the words were pronounced in the sentence patterns. To have spelled the words according to the conditioned sounds, would, as I had reasoned, cause readers to sound out words as they read, rather than identifying words in sequence. By writing the basic morphemes making up the individual words, the reader would be able to identify the words without having to sound them out. In reading, the conditioned assimulated sounds would occur automatically as in normal speech.

STUDYING AND SPEAKING

After the summer, we'd moved to New Jersey where we lived in the Reformed Church in America's comfortable missionary residence on the campus of New Brunswick Theological Seminary. The John Muilenbergs were in the other half of the duplex. We enjoyed a good many late night cups of coffee sharing from our overseas experiences. Living in New Brunswick permitted me to take several courses at the Princeton Theological Seminary. One of my joys then was to study Greek under Dr. Bruce Metzger.

Lavina was pretty busy during all of those months with three lively youngsters. She had to hustle to keep her home organized and have us all on the road Sunday mornings and often on week-nights for speaking engagements. There was a lot of interest in what RCA missionaries were doing in our latest and newest mission field. All of this was sheer delight.

I remember one rather frightening and unexpected speaking engagement I had while in the East. I was extremely busy with studying and frequent speaking assignments. Apparently, I didn't always read our mail too carefully.

On this occasion I had spoken in the Albany area of upper New York state on Sunday and had returned on the overnight train to New York City. I slept as best I could in my "Sunday suit." The connection was close. I carried my suitcase with me to the door of the famous 5th Avenue, Marble Collegiate Church where Dr. Norman Vincent Peale ministered.

I was met at the door by Mrs. Weber, Morrie Swart's mother. She said that I'd best hurry because the meeting was about to start. I had assumed I was speaking to a group of women somewhere in the basement. Instead, I was led into a packed church, filled with women from all over the state. It was a statewide RCA women's gathering.

Once on the platform, I learned that there would be two of us speaking. The other guest speaker was Andrew Branch from Brewton, Alabama. As I waited my turn to speak and try to adjust to this unexpected turn of events, I couldn't help but wonder what my dad and mother would have thought could they have seen that little farm boy from Minnesota preaching in Norman Vincent Peale's church. I thought to myself, God certainly has a great sense of humor to have me where I am this morning. It turned out to be a fun experience, even when I sipped tea with a box lunch with ladies who were culturally much more sophisticated than was I from my humble origins and more recent experience of living with mud and grass.

INOCULATIONS NO FUN

Our worst experience that furlough was probably the day we all had our inoculations in preparation for returning to Africa. Lavina and the three boys and I all had one of those "shots" late that afternoon. We stopped in a restaurant for a bite to eat on our way back from New York to New Brunswick. We entered the restaurant feeling just fine. While we were eating, one by one the children and then Lavina and I, also, put our food aside and were feeling too ill to eat. Once home, we all went straight to bed, but for Lavina and me there was to be no sleep. The children were all burning up with fevers and just plain miserable and sick. We learned an important lesson that night, never ever would all of us have our "shots" at the same time. Somebody has to be well enough to take care of the sick! It was all part of being a missionary! And we all survived, none the worse for it today!

ANOTHER PERSON'S OPINION

It was quite a trick to travel from Africa to America with five children ranging in ages from still being in the basket to young teenagers. We always tried to arrange our luggage so that some of the pieces were small enough for everyone except the little guy in the basket to carry something.

We'll never forget the sidewalk experience out in front of the hotel in New York City. Denny, who was already in college at this time, had flown in to meet us. So, in actual fact, we had all six children with us when we left from the hotel for Grand Central Station. We had arranged for two taxis to transport us from the hotel to the station. When the taxis pulled up, we had our twenty two pieces of luggage, large and small, piled up outside and waiting. It took a little juggling of bags to get everything in.

A man was standing on the sidewalk about twenty feet away watching the whole operation. Finally, he wandered over to give us his sage advice, saying, "You know, if I had to travel like that, I think I'd stay home!" I'm sure he meant it!

We had a good laugh over his remark and responded saying, "Well, sir, we've come ten thousand miles so far and we have only a thousand left to go. We think we'll make it."

It was true. Only a missionary would travel like that. But travelling like that was only a small part of the story of things only a missionary would do. Ours was a daunting challenge and a rare privilege. No one ever need feel sorry for us! We might even be "fools for Christ's sake."

But now, all those furlough experiences had swiftly ended and we were heading back for the Sudan. We would soon be back in a different world. We loved them both, but our hearts were in Africa where God had called us.

HEADING BACK TO AFRICA
FEBRUARY 1952

We returned from furlough to Akobo in February, 1952. The trip back was rugged. Just before we left Holland, Michigan, Dennis came down with the measles. He was well enough to travel, but we knew that Jim and Dave would likely get them about the time we reached Khartoum

They surprised us and this complicated our travels considerably. The night before we were to get off the Queen Mary in Southampton, both of the boys developed burning fevers. We knew exactly what it was, but hoped we could unobtrusively board the plane in London the next day and fly on to Khartoum.

During the night before the morning we were to dock, David's fever was so high that he had a frightening convulsion. Never having seen one, we were scared to death. Our only thought was to find the ship's doctor as speedily as possible. Having had no experience with seeing someone have a convulsion, it appeared to us that he was dying.

The doctor examined him and reassured us that this was not uncommon with genuine German measles. He told us what to do, but when the ship docked in the morning, the first thing we saw was an old model, black ambulance at the dock waiting to take our two little boys away from us and put them into quarantine. We were told they'd be well cared for and that we shouldn't plan to travel further for at least two weeks. They said, "Our experience is that it's best if you leave the children to us and not show your faces until it's time to collect them. The children make the adjustment better if the parents don't show up. Go to London and enjoy yourselves since you have to wait anyway."

DELAYED IN ENGLAND

It seemed rough to us, but what could we do? We took their advice and Lavina, Dennis and I took a train to London where we stayed in the Victoria hotel. Sounds much more romantic than it was in fact. No central heating. It was cold. At night they put heated stones under the blankets in the foot-end of our bed to keep us warm.

We chanced to be in London on a very historic occasion. This was the time when King George of England died and his daughter, Elizabeth, then in Kenya, came to the throne. We were on the street when all of London fell totally silent and everything stopped as a token of respect for their departed sovereign.

We visited Westminster Abbey and other historic places, but our hearts were restless for the children. And, this being one of England's coldest winters didn't brighten our spirits either. We couldn't have been happier, when they told us we could fetch the children and be on our way. Two solid weeks had elapsed.

These little tykes hadn't forgotten us either. They were so happy to see us they could hardly contain themselves. Jimmy and David both had blisters on their right thumbs from sobbing and sucking. Jimmy said, "I cried for Daddy and Dave cried for Mommy." We hoped it would never happen again!

FURTHER DELAYS CAIRO TO KHARTOUM

That evening we flew out of London for Khartoum by way of Cairo. When we landed in Cairo, a strong wind was blowing. After refueling, we were on our way, but remembered that it was so windy they had had some difficulty closing the door on the plane. It was about 8:30 in the morning. Khartoum was at least six hours away.

As we flew south toward Khartoum, we were counting the hours until we'd arrive. It'd been a difficult and tiring trip. But our difficulties weren't to go away quite so easily. About one thirty, just after having our lunch on the plane, the steward came through and announced that Khartoum was in the grip of a powerful wind and haboob. If things didn't clear up in the next half hour, we'd have to return to Cairo. Our hearts sank when we felt the plane bank to head back. We said, "What next?"

It was about dark time when we approached Cairo and were diverted to Cyprus. The wind of the morning had developed into a full blown sandstorm in Cairo too. We landed in the darkness in Cyprus on a dimly lighted airstrip they'd used during the war. I'd bought four pounds of apples in London to treat our missionary hosts upon arrival, but these were now taken away from us and confiscated by customs. We were all herded into a gasoline lamp lighted quonset hut to check our papers. The other 25 passengers and we were eventually loaded onto a bus and we struck out for Nicosea some two hours away. It was now eleven o'clock when we reached the hotel and it was cold. In the morning at four o'clock we were all back on the bus and heading back to the plane. The two little boys didn't think they had anything to be really happy about and they made their feelings known! Dennis took it all in stride as he was by then nearly ten years old.

RETURNING TO A HOT COUNTRY

You can scarcely imagine our joy when we finally landed in Khartoum. From there it was on to Akobo and home in the Upper Nile. The change in climate was staggering. We had left my folks in Minnesota with a temperature that day showing twenty degrees below zero. Now it was over 100 degrees night and day. We thought we'd die and started advising other missionaries never to be so foolish as to come back from furlough during the peak of the hot, dry season.

But in just a week or two our bodies adjusted and we were eager to begin where we had left off. Of course, it wouldn't be quite the same because while we were heading for home on furlough our brand new grass-roofed house, built on the mission compound, had burned to the ground. Everything we owned outside of what we had in our suitcases had gone up in smoke and disappeared in ten minutes. They told us how swiftly a grass roof burns. We were starting over again.

We were amazed at how little that supposedly major loss affected us. The initial shock was considerable when Dr. Luman Shafer had asked that first night upon arrival in the states if he and I might take a little walk together. I remember how uncomfortable I felt when he suggested this and wondered, momentarily, if I had done something wrong and was going to be instructed about that in some way. But almost immediately as we walked the hallway in the hotel, while Lavina waited and wondered, he said, "Harvey, I have some bad news to share with you."

My first reaction was, "Somebody has died."

He said, "Your house at Akobo was destroyed by fire. It happened even before you got on the ship in Alexandria, but we didn't want to spoil your trip home with this sad information and, so, we withheld it from you until we could explain what happened to you in person."

It was a terrible shock. The floor seemed to be rocking. I thought, "What will Lavina say?"

My first question was, "What about my books?"

He said, "They are all gone. Everything was burned. Nothing was saved."

I wanted to cry, but held it in. Later we shared with Lavina, and she rightfully cried for us all.

But now we were back at Akobo and eager to resume my work of translating the New Testament into Anuak. Bob Swart had worked desperately hard to rebuild our house and have things as nice as possible for us upon arrival. The old, metal bed frames were still useable and new springs had replaced the burned out ones. The metal chests of drawers were still useable. A little brown paint and they'd be as useable as before. Bethany Reformed Church in Grand Rapids, Michigan had replaced my books with a basic reference library. The New Era Reformed Church had given Lavina a new set of pots and pans. Gifts of money and materials had come from many friends throughout the church.

We soon put the losses from the fire behind us and were none the worse for it. God's grace was more than sufficient. Lee and Kitty Crandall, whose things were also burned in that same fire, testified similarly. We said, "We must learn to travel lightly." The only things we really missed were the burned photographs, the first locks of the children's hair and my college and seminary papers. Fortunately, my language study materials had travelled with me. I was, indeed, ready to resume translating.

"*Even youths grow tired and weary, and young men stumble and fall; but those who hope in the Lord will renew their strength. They will soar on wings like eagles; they will run and not grow weary, they will walk and not be faint.*"

Isaiah 40:30-31

CHAPTER NINE

POKWO - VILLAGE OF LIFE
PART 1

The year was 1953. Pokwo station on the Baro river was now started. The necessary government papers had all been processed and Don McClure and Lyda were already there building the new station. Pokwo was on the Baro river about 140 miles, as the bird flies, east of Akobo. It was situated on the river about 21 miles from a place called Gambela.

This trading post was a mile square enclave given by Ethiopia to the British by treaty for trading purposes. It was as far as Nile steamers could go into Ethiopia itself. Two or three times during the height of the rains this flotilla of some five or seven barges would make its way from Kosti and Malakal into Ethiopia. They brought salt, sugar, cooking oil and other supplies in and went back down stream with coffee. To make it around the bends in the river, barges were dropped off while part of the flotilla continued on up stream. These were then tied up and the steamer would return down stream to bring up the others. Quite a process. Sometimes these barges got stuck on the sand if the river dropped too quickly. I'm sure the captain and crew had some anxious moments sometimes wondering if they might not be stuck for the season until rains returned the following year.

Pokwo station was on a beautiful, strategic location. Bob and I had made the first survey to explore its feasibility. But now Don and Lyda were getting started and a lot of hard work was involved. Starting in tents, moving into grass and finally into a permanent building in a remote area is no small feat. Don was a pioneer at heart and seemed to love it.

But it was furlough time for the McClures and they had to find a way to keep that fledgling work open and going. The pool in which there were possibilities for personnel was the Akobo mission station. Nobody was volunteering. We all loved our work and our location.

So, when Don approached Lavina and me and said, "I think you and Lavina should come to Pokwo and fill in for us while Lyda and I go on furlough" our instinctive response was, "Not if we can help it." We didn't say this to Don, of course, but we both knew that this is how we felt.

LAVINA AT AKOBO — HARVEY IN THE CONGO

About this same time, I was a member of a four person team chosen by the mission to study mission work in eight different missions in the then Belgian Congo, Rwanda and Uganda. The team was made up of Milton and Peggy Thompson, Dotty Rankin and myself. I'd be gone eight weeks, sleep on 31 different cots or beds and cover 4100 miles before the study was completed. It was a tremendous challenge to try to learn how other missions did their work successfully. Our mission was made up of mostly young, inexperienced missionaries. Those who were older wanted us to have the learning experience this would be for each of us, and also to report back to the mission on our findings with recommendations.

Christmas eve the four of us in our party were on the Nile steamer heading toward Juba. It was an eight day journey. On board was the Ford station wagon that would carry our gear and the four of us. We wouldn't be back until the last week in February.

Lavina was left alone at Akobo with Jimmy and David. Dennis was in school in Egypt. I missed them so painfully. I'm sure they had lonely days and nights as well. Many times I thought, "I wish somebody else had been chosen to make this trip. Life is too short to be separated from my family like this." That was real negative thinking! And such thinking is never productive. At times, I would remind myself that God understood. With the Psalmist I'd say, "He knows our frame; He remembers that we are dust." Then again, when the sun was shining, we'd be singing George Beverly Shea's song, "Every step every mile of the way."

We learned so much from other missionaries during those weeks on the road. Some of the lessons affected my entire missionary career. In retrospect, the separation, the work involved in making the study and producing our report, was imminently worth the effort and cost.

GOD GIVES US WILLING HEARTS

But now to get back to the unresolved question about our being reassigned to Pokwo. Lavina and I didn't want to go, but we had agreed before I left on that tour that we'd both keep on praying about it and discuss it further when I returned. We did just that.

Both Lavina and I had had a change of heart. Without being able to discuss the matter because of the great distances that separated us, we had both come to feel that God wanted us to help out at Pokwo. We were at peace with each other and with the Lord. Our hearts were united and both of us were happy.

Don was so pleased that we were ready to come. He made all the arrangement with local officials about our living there. He said, "You don't need a visa. The local governor is willing to let you come and live down here in the country without having to go through the government offices in Addis Ababa." We learned later that this would create problems for us when the government in Addis became aware that we were at Pokwo and Don and Lyda were in America.

We had another slight complication before we'd get settled as a family inside Ethiopia at Pokwo. Lavina was happily expecting our fourth child. Complications with the others suggested she shouldn't live in isolation at Pokwo during those first uncertain weeks. Our mission doctor said she should spend some time in Khartoum near medical facilities and then proceed to Pokwo by way of Addis Ababa.

This was done. At the same time, I want on ahead with Dennis, Jimmy and David to overlap with Don and Lyda for a few weeks before they took off. The station was so new that I helped Don screen his house and did other jobs to help them get away on schedule for furlough. When they left, I was there alone with the children batching it. Our closest medical facility was about 50 miles as the crow flies over the mountains toward Addis Ababa. In Gambela was the British government officer living in the enclave, a one mile square territory under British rule. Two or three Greek merchants and traders also lived there. We got our groceries and supplies through them and our mail came in via Gambela. To get there, we normally used an outboard, but during the short dry season the road was just barely passable for three or four months.

When Don left for furlough my parting words were, "Be sure to come back on time now." Don had a reputation for taking long furloughs. He was such a popular speaker that he just couldn't seem to get away. I wanted him back so we could return to Akobo.

The boys and I were alone for about six weeks. Lavina was cleared to travel and did so by flying to Addis Ababa. I had previously been in Addis and with a herculean effort had secured a one time permit for Mission Aviation to cross the border from Malakal in the Sudan to land in Dembidollo to fly Lavina over the mountain to Gambela.

All the missionaries said we'd made history that happy day when the old Rapide, twin engined bi-plane landed inside Ethiopia. The children and I had travelled to Dembidollo a few days earlier on one of those big, ten ton, diesel trucks that hauled salt up the mountain and coffee back down. We were there to welcome Lavina off the plane. She looked so beautiful and it was like a little bit of heaven had come to earth to have her back. The children and I were all equally excited and thrilled.

We flew to Gambela where there was a grassy, government airstrip, as most of the airstrips in that part of the world were then. We travelled home the 21 miles by outboard. The MAF pilot and engineer spent the night at Pokwo and I drove them back in the outboard the next morning. The Hoekstra family was together again. We would spend some 21 months at Pokwo before Don and Lyda returned. These would be among the happiest, most productive years of our ministry among the Anuak. We had surrendered to the Lord's leading. He never failed to keep His promises. Our hearts were supremely happy.

THE CHALLENGE AND EXCITEMENT OF POKWO

Pokwo station was an exciting challenge and responsibility. I wanted to carry Don's work forward in such a way that he'd be proud of us when he returned. I respected and admired Don and had some qualms as to whether or not I could come near filling his shoes.

We had some marvelous experiences and a wide variety of them during those 21 months at Pokwo. We soon discovered that the Anuaks living along the Barro were wilder than the Anuaks with whom we'd been working at Akobo. The men all had both guns and spears. The Ethiopian authorities didn't exercise the same authority over them as the British did in the Sudan. More killings and beatings occurred. Stick fights between different age sets was common. It reminded us the what it may have been like in the days of Robin Hood. Rivalry and killings between the younger age sets and the older men were not uncommon. The Anuaks along the Barro were more prosperous, the soil was fertile and beer parties were held in connection with all their social events. Their drumming and singing went on into the night and we would fall asleep with these distant drums beating rhythmically in our ears. There was both danger and romance.

We lived in the new McClure house with its round tukls and large connecting, screened-in verandas. Lavina's wood burning stove was out under the big tamarind tree located about 25 feet from the back door. Once when she was sterilizing milk on that outside stove, the horse came along, and without our knowing it, pushed off the lid and drained the kettle. That same day, my office door to the tukl on one end of the house accidently stood ajar. When I returned to my desk, a freshly laid egg was there in the middle of it. A hen had wandered in and done her thing right then and there!

Snakes sometimes sneaked in also. One night I was in Gambela overnight and Lavina and the two boys were home alone. They were all in their beds on the veranda when Lavina heard the dog's tin eating dish swishing around on the floor. She had a flashlight with nearly dead batteries beside the bed and decided, out of curiosity, to find out what was going on. To her amazement, she made out the form of a six- foot red cobra beside the dog's dish. Quickly, she ran back to bed and jumped up on it safely out of reach. She began to call and both Anuaks and the single lady missionary, Joan Yilek, approached the house to see what was going on. Lavina alerted them about the snake. Joan went back home and returned with her 16 gauge shot-gun. She was hesitant as to what to do. Lavina said the Anuaks kept saying, "Shoot, shoot it so that it doesn't get away." Joan heeded their advice, took careful aim and pulled the trigger. The snake was cut in half by the blast. The McClure's refrigerator carried the pocked shell indentations from the ricocheted pellets ever afterward! Lavina and the kids slept peacefully and couldn't wait until I returned to share the excitement with me.

There were only ten or eleven believers on the station and none in the surrounding villages when we arrived. The believers were all workmen engaged to help open the station. Several of them had been brought along from Akobo. Having help that knew what was expected was extremely useful in a pioneer situation.

On that trip to the Belgian Congo I had determined that if I ever had the opportunity, I'd try to put some of the things I'd learned there into practice. I wanted to have a mission station that was first of all a teaching center. The workmen should be given the opportunity to learn to read and have in-depth Bible teaching as part of their daily schedule. It wasn't right to have workmen spending all their time working and being viewed as a burden rather than seeing them as an opportunity for teaching.

Being at Pokwo provided that chance. We had a program with a daily schedule of time for Bible study, learning to read, of working on mission jobs or working in small fields of land we designated for them to grow their own corn from which they could supplement their meager income. It was marvelous to see how God was blessing that. But first, let me tell you about Akway, war Achudhi.

THE FIRST ANUAK EVANGELIST

Very soon after I arrived at Pokwo, I met a young Anuak on the compound sitting under a tree. He was reading from a green-covered mimeographed copy of the First Epistle of John. He looked up at me and said, "You don't remember me. But I remember you. When you were in Gambela several years ago with another man you called, 'Bomb' you ate supper at the home of the man I was working for" (it was a young Norwegian, living in Ethiopia at that time and serving with the Bank of Ethiopia). "Before you left, you a gave a little book to this man. With that book, he taught me to read. When Odan came here, I learned more about Jesus and was baptized."

I was overjoyed to hear his story. Bob and I had been in Gambela nearly three years earlier. We had come into the area from Akobo to survey the possibility of opening a station on the Barro river. At that time, we were totally frustrated by the local Ethiopian officials. Although we had proper papers, including a paper signed by his majesty, emperor Haili Sellasie himself, the local official said, "Where is my name?"

We were refused permission. Bob and I had spent ten days, hoping and waiting, but very frustrated. We wondered how we could have missed the Lord's leading.

Finally, on that last night, this young Norwegian, a committed Christian, had invited us to his bachelor home to eat with him. It was then that he had asked for a primer as he wanted to teach his servant how to read. Bob had remained behind then to proceed to Addis to see if he could get the coveted paper. I drove the jeep back to Akobo, going some 200 miles down along the one side of the river, then crossing over on the only ferry near Doleib Hill and going back an additional 175 miles on the opposite side of the river to Akobo. Little did either of us know how God was at work in and through our frustration. I have often reflected on those days and praised God for the way He turns apparent defeat into victory to those who try to do His will.

Some weeks later when we called the small little band of Christian workmen together, we challenged them as to whether or not there wasn't someone among them who could do the work of an evangelist in the many unreached Anuak villages. I explained how my task was to translate the Bible and that I needed to be near my family as well as needing to be around to care for the sick who came into the clinic we were holding under the tree each morning.

To that question about an evangelist they responded with a typical Anuak reply by asking, "Is there anyone besides Akway War Achudi?" This Anuak response meant that Akway was their choice. He could do it. He was the young man who had been the servant of that Norwegian banker. He was the one who was reading under the tree.

The next question was, "But how can he do this? He will be among people who are not his relatives. He will need a mosquito net, a blanket and a way to get his food."

TEACHING ANUAK BELIEVERS HOW TO TITHE

It was then that I again remembered from my experience in the Congo. There was one station in the Presbyterian mission that everyone talked about. Missionaries in different stations would say, "Wait until you get to Bulape (a Presbyterian mission station). There is a station that taught its people to tithe!" And it was so.

As I met with our few believers at Pokwo, my heart burned within me to challenge them to learn how to give the tithe. There was still no offering of any kind in the worship services. I explained how the tithe worked. I said,"Each of you earns 30 piasters a week. Three of those piasters belong to the Lord. If each of you would give three piasters every week from what you get, Akway, the Lord's servant, could go and be your evangelist in the villages."

They weren't at all sure about doing this. In fact, they would have preferred not to. I spoke to them a second time and suggested that they try it just for one month. If at the end of one month they found they were becoming poor, we could meet again and discuss it.

To this they agreed. To help them get started, I took small pieces of paper and stapled them in the shape of an envelope. When they received their pay on Saturday, 3 piasters were in each envelope and 27 piasters were outside the envelope. It was a crude way to do it, but the object lesson was clear.

On Wednesday evenings, the group met on our sitting veranda for prayer, Bible study and worship. One of the Anuaks had a record book. The names of the tithers were recorded along with the three piaster amount. Everyone was excited to be doing this. We sensed that it was pleasing to the Lord.

The Lord has a marvelous way of giving us an object lesson at just the right moment. During that following month, a group of Christian workers and I took the truck to an Anuak chief's village, Itang, about ten or twelve miles in the down stream direction from the mission. I had hoped to return early. Instead, we were forced to wait a couple of hours before the chief returned to the village. Consequently, on our return to the mission as we were passing through the large swamp where the animals frequently came down near the end of the day for water, it was the exact, right moment. As we approached, we saw a large herd of waterbuck. I stepped out of the truck and moved cautiously forward, put the gun to my shoulder, took careful aim and pulled the trigger. When we ran over to the fallen animal, David Okwier looked at the other fellows, stretched his arms out and up and said in Anuak, "Look how God is blessing us." He related the provision of meat in abundance to their decision to tithe.

The question of whether or not they would continue tithing at the end of the month was never raised. Later as new believers were added to the flock, all became tithers from the moment they made their profession, even before they were baptized. The paper envelopes gave way to small cloth envelopes sewed by one of the women believers. Each envelope had the name of the person who was tithing written on it in bold black letters. The Wednesday evening prayer times became times of great blessing and joy as the tithes increased, were recorded and they decided what to do with the extra money. God's blessing was upon us. Our hearts were glad. Incidentally, the horns of the waterbuck measured 27 inches from their tip to the base at the head.

GOD BLESSED THE WORK AT POKWO

We had a neat program going during our months at Pokwo. I looked on the station as being an adult, non-formal education institution. The boys' school would wait until Don returned from furlough. Meanwhile, we'd try out what I'd learned on that tour. Young men came in from the Gila river area and other distant villages seeking employment. We took about 25 into the program at a time. Each young man was given a plot of land along the river on mission property for growing his own corn. These young men spent part of each day in their own fields, part of the day in working on the compound, and part of the day in literacy and Bible teaching classes. Each day began at six a.m. with a time of worship, singing and Bible study. God blessed with visitors from the nearby village frequently attending. When the challenge was given to turn away from the old ways and commit their lives to Jesus Christ, some would stand and profess faith right then and there. I often came home to breakfast with happy experiences to share with Lavina. By then she had the oatmeal or dura porridge cooked and the coffee pot was always enticing. Jimmy and David were waiting for Daddy so they could eat.

During that period, we taught the first 51 Anuaks how to read. From this group of young men came several of the first Anuak evangelists like Akway and David Okwier. When the men returned to their villages they spread the good news about Jesus to others.

OLOK OMOL — ONE TIN FOR THE LORD

Several incidents stand out in my memory. I recall a Sunday when we had been worshipping under the huge Tamarind tree on the compound. I'd preached the sermon that morning flanked by a goat that had wandered in. Several dogs were lying around among us also. Babies cried until the mother gave the child another "sip" which was always available upon demand.

The service had ended and most everyone had gone. Still standing there was a five gallon, empty gasoline tin now full of shelled corn. I asked Olok Omol, who also took care of our mission cows, what the corn was for.

He looked at me with a quizzical smile and said, "Odola, didn't you tell us that if we got ten tins of corn that one of them belonged to the Lord. I had ten tins and this one belongs to Him."

I was chagrined and ashamed. I had taught them how to tithe and when the evidence was in front of me I was spiritually too insensitive to recognize it.

I'll never forget our last Wednesday night prayer meeting at Pokwo. We were to return to Akobo as Don was expected back from America any day. Meanwhile, Joan Yilek would bridge the gap until the McClures returned.

A SECOND ANUAK EVANGELIST

On the last such meeting in which Lavina and I participated, we challenged them to be faithful in their tithing and to pray for and encourage Akway who was evangelizing in the villages. I remember saying, "Isn't there someone from among you who could join Akway for just two months to encourage his heart?"

A tall, handsome, muscular young man stood up. He arranged his cloth carefully as they would often do when one had something important to say. It was David Okwier. This is what he said. "I have been here nearly two years. The first summer when I went home to my village, I still hadn't learned to read. People wanted to know what I had learned and I was unable to tell them accurately. This time, when I came back, I determined to learn how to read well. I've done that, but I've never really witnessed to my people. I will help Akway for two months just as you have suggested."

David Okwier was that same David who had stretched his arms out when that animal fell and said, "Look see how God is blessing us." David never stopped helping Akway. When the two months ended, he just kept right on doing the work of an evangelist. As the Christian group grew, they began to support David Okwier financially along with Akway. Instead of one evangelist they had two.

David became known for his eloquent and forceful preaching. People talked about him with pride. But David fell ill with tuberculosis and before long his strong body was weakened and he was a skeleton of his former self. Everyone knew that his time was short.

DAVID OKWIER GOES TO BE WITH JESUS

To conclude our account about David, we need to move ahead five years to 1960. We were now back in the Sudan living at Pibor. One morning, we heard a clap outside our door. A young Anuak called Ochan Cham was at our door. He had walked nearly a hundred miles to tell us. David Okwier had died.

This was his story. The night before David died, he called his Anuak brothers to his bedside in that little African hut.

He could hardly speak because of his weakness and terrible cough. But this is what he told them. "When Okwier dies please don't wail and mourn like the Anuaks do in the villages. Rather, be glad. Tell them that Okwier has gone to be with Jesus. Please go through the villages and say that Okwier has gone to be with Jesus." Before morning, he did just that.

Ochan Cham had been on the way for more than a month. He was going through the villages as David had asked. The message travelled with Ochan from Pokwo to Pibor. God be praised! Ochan, himself, was suffering from tuberculosis. While we were on furlough in 1961, Ochan, too, went to be with Jesus and was there with Okwier. When we heard it, we wanted to cry and sing praises to God all at the same time.

OBEDIENCE BRINGS BLESSING AND JOY

Our years at Pokwo were among our best. And to think that we might have missed it, had we refused to obey the Lord's leading by stubbornly insisting on remaining at Akobo. We saw the Lord pour out his blessing upon us and on our ministry. It was challenging and satisfying to be laying solid foundations for the future development of the Anuak church. The real foundation was Jesus Christ, Himself. We were co-laborers with God and He alone could give the increase.

Our experience confirmed the truth of God's word. The Gospel was God's power to bring salvation to all who had a chance to hear and would believe. We knew that something was happening in the lives of Anuaks in Pokwo because we were there. It fit in with a basic point of view that has rather shaped our lives and various "missions" all through the years of our life. We have wanted to make an essential difference for Christ. We have wanted to be somewhere doing something essential for Him that wouldn't happen unless we did it. We have wanted to be available to Him for whatever He might have in mind. I hope we will, by His grace and mercy, never see things differently.

Our experience is that when we hold nothing back and are truly available to Him, everything changes. Burdens become lighter. Sacrifices fade into insignificance. We find ourselves echoing the words of the Apostle, "Indeed I count everything as loss because of the surpassing worth of knowing Christ Jesus my Lord ... That I might know Him and the power of His resurrection." And again, no matter how forbidding the moment we can say, "I can do all things in Him who strengthens me." And, yes, "I have learned in whatsoever state I am, therewith, to be content." O, to be sure, we stub our toe and fall miserably short, but in our best moments, these are the springs of our motivation and strength.

JIMMY AND DAVID HAVE SCARLET FEVER

We lived at Pokwo from April in 1953 until February, 1955. Sometimes things were pretty rough living alone, down stream 21 miles from the nearest contact with the outside world. Without medical care, we were on our own trusting the Lord to care for us and our little children. Jimmy and David were four and five years when we moved there.

I remember one Sunday noon when Jimmy came in from playing and flopped on his bed. He had a raging fever. Within half an hour, David did the same thing. We treated them for malaria. The rule of thumb was always treat for malaria first.

This time, the malaria medicine did nothing. The fevers kept right on burning their little bodies night and day. We were worried about polio because only a few months earlier a little missionary child, Chris Arnold, had died at Akobo from that dreadful disease. At that same time, another missionary child, Phil Roode, our doctor's son, had also had it and came out of it with a limp arm and shoulder. Could this be polio striking at Pokwo?

Finally, on Wednesday, in the middle of the night at 2:30 in the morning, I went out where our young men were sleeping and called in a young, trustworthy Anuak to carry an urgent note cross country, across the mountain to Dr. John Cremer, stationed in Dembidollo. We asked the doctor to come. I would meet him on Friday at four in the afternoon on the river bank in Gambela. We knew he'd be there. No question about it.

Meanwhile, we began searching the "Worldbook" encyclopedia that the McClures had on their shelves to try to discover what the children might have. We also started giving them penicillin injections. The fever began to break. I told Lavina, "I think these boys have scarlet fever." I had noticed that their tongues had a strawberry like appearance.

The doctor was there sitting on the riverbank waiting for me with his medical kit in hand when I pulled up on schedule with the boat. He asked how the boys were doing and then we were speeding downstream toward Pokwo. In an hour we were there. Immediately, he took each child and had them say, "aah," while he looked into their mouths. When he'd completed his investigation, he turned to us and said, "These boys have scarlet fever. They'll get along alright now. Just keep up with the penicillin a few more days."

Lavina and I looked at each other with a sigh of relief. The tension broke and I light-heartedly said, "I think the "Worldbook" people ought to give us a free set for being able to diagnose accurately what these boys had from what was written in the "Worldbook!"

The next morning, I took Dr. Cremer back to Gambela. It took a little longer going against the current. He got in his Jeep and returned the 46 miles on the "staircase" mountain road to his family and hospital. I picked up the mail and a few supplies and was home by noon. The crisis was over. We felt relieved and gave thanks to God.

"All scripture is inspired by God and profitable for teaching, for reproof, for correction, and for training in righteousness, that the man of God may be complete, equipped for every good work."

II Timothy 3:16-17

PART 2

FRIGHTENING EXPERIENCES AT POKWO

We had some good scares during our time at Pokwo. The Anuaks in that area were pretty rough at times.

LAVINA AND THE ANGRY MAN WITH THE GUN

I often hunted for our meat. I'd normally go out late in the afternoon on horseback a number of miles back from the river in the flat grassland near what we described as saddle mountain. I'd carry my heavy rifle with me and get down to shoot. A young Anuak would hold the bridle. Sometimes, if an animal was wounded I'd pursue it on horseback at a fast clip. Once, I jumped off the horse and pursued the wounded animal on foot. It would run, turn around and threaten to charge me. The adrenalin flowed freely. When this animal, a medium sized hartebeest turned and ran again, I pulled out my hunting knife, eventually got hold of its tail, slowed it to a walk and while still holding the tail was able to knife it and bring it down. Once, while chasing the animal with the horse, I lost my pith helmet and only stumbled onto it some weeks later on another such trip.

This particular afternoon, I had left home around three o'clock. When I returned after dark, the compound was humming with excited voices. I sensed, immediately, that something unusual had happened. Lavina had quite a story to share with me.

She said that soon after I left, Ateng, who helped us in the clinic came in and speaking in English said, "Madam, there is going to be a big trouble. A man has come from the village and is looking for his wife who he says ran away from him. He thinks she's on the compound but hasn't found her. He just left to go back to the village to get his gun and says he's coming back to find either his wife or kill the man who is hiding her."

Lavina said she and the children were in the back yard and Ateng advised them to get into the house so they wouldn't be hurt. She said that's what they did and kept an eye on the path toward the village. It wasn't long and this man was on the compound with his old Italian, heavy rifle, which most adult Anuak men owned and used in marriage talks. The man slipped shells into his gun as Ateng went toward him and tried to persuade him not to come on the compound with a loaded gun. At that moment, the man raised his gun and pointed it straight at Ateng. He pulled the trigger, but fortunately it was a faulty shell and didn't go off.

As the man began dashing in and out of huts on the mission compound, Lavina discovered that her house was full of women. They had come around the down side of the house and entered by the front door. The woman the man was looking for was inside our house in the toilet room on the far end hiding. Meanwhile, on the other end, Lavina discovered that several of our young people had gone into my office where Don McClure also kept his gun case. They had gotten the door of the gun case open, guns out, and were proceeding to load them. Lavina persuaded them otherwise and managed to get the guns back where they belonged.

In the middle of all of that, she heard a vehicle in the distance. Now, trucks almost never came down that rarely used, ill kept road. God's timing was perfect. Someone ran out to the road, hailed the truck, and on it was the captain of the Ethiopian police post at Itang, some 15 miles down river from the mission. He was quickly told what was taking place. As the truck turned into the compound, the angry Anuak with the gun ran off the compound to escape, calling over his shoulder that he'd be back that night to kill everyone, including these foreigners (missionaries).

The Ethiopian police captain went to the village itself, down stream from us about a fourth of a mile. They took the chief from the village hostage and announced he'd be held at Itang until the village turned over the culprit.

Once the truck had gone, other men from the village came and found the woman in question. They tied her hands and led her off to the village. "Her crying and screaming were so pitiful," Lavina said, "and there was nothing I could do to help her."

That's what all the humming conversation was about when I returned from hunting. Lavina and been through a terrifying experience with the little boys and I hadn't even been aware nor was I available to assist.

We were plenty afraid that night. It was nearly ten o'clock before the Anuaks and we stopped talking about it just outside our back door. When finally, we crawled into our beds on the veranda, sleep was long in coming and when it did, we had only little "sleeps" and then we'd be awake. We expected someone to come sneaking out of the nearby papaya grove or out of the bananas any moment. Never was daylight more welcome!

Before the week was out, the guilty man was located and turned over to the police. He paid a fine of a young cow, the chief was back home, and we were back to normal. Every such experience threw us upon the mercy of God and we knew that He had to keep us safe if we were to make it. Looking back, we praise Him for doing just that.

STOPPING A REVENGE KILLING AFTER DARK

Lavina and I had just finished our Bible story time with the children and had concluded our prayers. It was about eight o'clock in the evening. Four men came out of the darkness and were at our front door. They were from the village of Pokwo, downstream about a quarter of a mile. Standing outside in the light from our Alladin lamp, we could recognize them and subsequently invited them in.

There was uproar in the village. A messenger had just arrived from the down-river village over which their chief also had jurisdiction. The messenger alarmed and angered the older men in our village by his report telling how the younger men, the "jo lwak," had killed one of their older men's age set, a person from the "jo bworo" group. Tempers were high and they wanted to kill a young man from the "jo lwak" living among them in revenge. They wanted to do so before daylight.

The men at the door each had an old Italian army rifle in his hands. They had come because they were not in favor of doing what the hot-heads were proposing. So they had come to ask if I'd accompany them back to the village and try to persuade the men in the village to calm down.

Their chief was away in Gambela and had stopped by before leaving, as he often did, and had asked me to "watch his village" while he was away.

I looked at Lavina and could tell she was uneasy about my going. I wasn't that comfortable with the idea either but felt I should do so. So, I pumped up the gasoline lantern, lit it, and stepped out into the darkness with the four Anuak men. We had barely started when we spotted two young men, presumebly from the jo lwak, barely distinguishable, in the darkness. I could make out that they each had a heavy rifle in their hands. It didn't make me feel any more secure with those fellows in the dark and we in the bright light of the lantern. Such were my thoughts as I left the compound and started down the trail beside the river. My Anuak men had already put bullets into the chambers of their guns.

The river was on one side and tall, ten-foot grass on the other the entire distance. The lantern made it hard to see anyone in the darkness. I was truly afraid that someone might take a shot at us before we reached the village.

Once there, it was immediately apparent that the entire village was stirred up with anger. Loud voices and a steady murmuring of conversations came from all directions. I was taken to the area where some fifteen or twenty of the older age set, the "jo bworo," had collected themselves. I greeted them in Anuak, but said nothing for some little while. Finally, I found the words to speak and said, "I have heard from the men what has happened to one of your people. I understand why you are angry. But it is not good that you do something in haste or in anger. It will be much better for you to do nothing until you have all slept and the sun begins to shine in the morning." I was hoping that by morning better judgment would prevail. I continued, "You know that your chief is gone. You also know that your chief came to see me before he left for Gambela. These were his words to me, 'Odola, watch my people until I return. Don't let them fight or kill someone.' " With that, I said, "Because of the word of your chief, I forbid anyone to leave the village or to kill a young man before morning. Tomorrow, I will return and we can decide together what should be done."

With that nearly everyone agreed and said, "Odola, that is good talk. We agree that we will do nothing before the sun shines tomorrow."

Only one person disagreed and said loudly so that all could hear him, "Why should we listen to the voice of this foreigner? He has no power over us."

But God was in it and this man was rebuffed and overruled. I immediately left and headed for home, lantern in hand brightening the path. Few women were ever happier to welcome home their husbands than was Lavina that night. At our bedside, we thanked God that He had used us to save a life and that He had protected ours. We prayed for the day when the Anuak would have surrendered their lives to Jesus Christ and the drunkenness that led to fighting and the anger which followed with killings would have stopped. We thanked God for the privilege of being there to tell them that through Jesus Christ their lives could be made whole. We slept peacefully. In the morning good sense prevailed. Tempers calmed and, hopefully, the village would remain at peace until their chief returned. Looking back to those days, I fear that eventually some young man, perhaps totally innocent of wrong doing, paid the supreme price. Revenge killings are no respecter of persons! However long it took, normally someone paid the price.

TRANSLATOR - DOCTOR - DENTIST

We maintained a heavy work load at Pokwo. Besides early morning prayers, Bible teaching and literacy classes, helping in the clinic and translating until one o'clock when we had our noon meal, after a short siesta, we had another go at it in the afternoon. Lavina had sewing classes with the Anuak girls and was teaching them to read. I'd be at the desk with two informants directly across from me six days a week. The translation work continued along with other station programs.

While we were busy translating, people were coming in from the villages to be treated in the clinic. I had a good helper, but reserved the matter of giving needed injections and seeing the more complicated cases for myself. Sometimes I could hear them grumbling as folks waited for this missionary to come out. The sun was hot and they couldn't figure out why he spent so much time in the house with his wife. Normally, I tried to stick to the desk until eleven o'clock, but if the pressure became unbearable, I'd give in, dismiss the informants until later in the day, and go out to see the sick.

Once we had the captain of the Ethiopian police down at Itang come in with pneumonia. Lavina invited him and his a wife to stay in our spare bedroom until he was better. They were with us for the entire week. Every day I gave him the needed penicillin injections. It was a privilege to serve the Lord, meeting the needs of the sick, even as Jesus had done. When first in the Sudan, I had seriously considered returning to the states to qualify as a missionary doctor. That lasted only a few weeks and disappeared completely once I got into the work of translation. Even so, I always enjoyed "playing doctor" and in doing so was able to help a lot of hurting people.

My "medical practice" included being the local dentist. These poor folks had no way of dealing with painful, decaying teeth other than to knock them out or dig them out, sometimes using a fish spear. Before I had proper dental tools, we used a pliers out of the truck without anesthesia. I hate to think of it now! Two or three would restrain the patient while I extracted the tooth. Sometimes, it took a couple of weeks before the victim felt like blessing me, Anuak style — just a gentle spitting on the head with a minimum of saliva. Just enough to make it authentic!

LEOPARD INTERFERES WITH THE TRANSLATING

Once when I was translating, a couple of men came to the window and begged me to come with them to help them kill the leopard that had been in their village during the night. This leopard had taken one of their goats and they were afraid for their dogs and children. Leopards were said to be especially fond of dog meat.

I agreed to go and saddled up the horse, taking with me my heavy .348 calibre rifle, a canteen of water and a book to read. We went together to the village and tied the horse there. They took me back of the village about an eighth of a mile to a big, dry swamp where the grass was more than ten feet tall. There I found a man sitting with his heavy rifle on his lap. About fifteen feet away was a dead dog which he was using to allure the leopard. I sat down beside him. In about a half hour, he began complaining about the hot sun. He doubted the leopard would come anyway and decided he had had enough of it. I was just new and told him I was going to stay.

After they all left to go back to the village, I was alone with the dead dog. I dragged the dog a little farther from where I was sitting and waited. I had my gun across my knees with the bullet in the chamber. I started reading but kept wondering whether that leopard might come from behind me out of the tall grass. It was scary and I don't remember a thing I read. You'll never believe this, but within fifteen minutes of the other man leaving, a huge male leopard came out of the grass about sixty feet away from me and started coming toward where I was sitting. I don't believe he ever saw me. I remained sitting, raised my gun to my shoulder, took careful aim and pulled the trigger. The leopard fell over dead in its tracks. I had shot it through the heart.

In less time than it takes to tell you, it seemed that the whole village was out there. They looked at the leopard. They looked at me and then, again, at the leopard. Their joy was boundless. They could sleep in peace and not be afraid for their children and dogs. I felt like someone probably feels who pitches a "no- hitter" in the big leagues. It was great sport and a far cry from sitting behind the desk translating the Bible into Anuak.

They soon brought the horse and we draped this huge leopard over the horse just in front of the saddle. I went riding home like a great white hunter. Anuaks were singing and dancing for joy as we came onto the compound. Lavina and the boys came out to welcome us back. She had heard the shot from our back yard. Who knows, in protecting the Anuak village, perhaps we had also protected ourselves. The skin was so large that when we hung it on the wall, the head came close to the top of the wall and the tail was nearly touching the floor. In the afternoon I was back at the desk.

·········

You'll recall that during our first weeks at Pokwo Lavina was in Khartoum and the three boys and I missed her terribly. When she finally reached us, it was so wonderful to have her with us again. We'd had a great summer with our three boys, Dennis, now eleven and Jimmy and David. Jimmy was five and Dave was just fourteen months younger.

When the summer was over and Dennis had to go back to school, he would be going to the Bingham Academy in Addis Ababa. He cried hard when he left and so did his mother. From Dembidollo where they stopped for a day enroute, he wrote such a pathetic letter home. I can still see it as if it were yesterday. He wrote,*"Please watch Jimmy and Dave that they don't fall into the river. I want to come home, please, please, please ..."* Christmas couldn't come soon enough!

EXPECTING A BABY AT POKWO
NO SIMPLE MATTER

D-day was approaching. Lavina was great with child. Less than a month remained before the big event. We had looked at some books just in case! But we knew we had to get to the hospital in Dembidollo if at all possible.

On the appointed day in November, we started for Gambela in the outboard. It was a rough trip because an unanticipated shower overtook us on the way and we also had trouble with spark plugs leading up. It took us most of the afternoon to reach Gambela. Once there, we were warmly cared for by a Greek bachelor merchant.

In the morning four young Anuak fellows, Lavina, the two children and I started up the mountain. We had 46 miles to go. The road was so rough, we called it a "staircase" leading to Dembidollo. Sometimes, Lavina would get out and walk up the steep hill because of the discomfort in riding. We thought, "This baby will come before we ever get there!"

As it turned out, we still had to wait another month for God's surprise Christmas gift, our "Carol Joy."

Once in Dembidollo, the doctor did his examination and made his predictions. He said, "I can only suggest that it's going to be another boy." I don't know if he knew anything about it or not, but he said, "The heart tones indicate that it'll be a boy." We didn't want to hear that because we already had three boys and really wanted a girl this time around. We talked about it quite a bit, rather lamenting that we'd likely have another boy. Even Jimmy and Dave sensed what we were talking about. We talked about those 'heart tones' and wondered if they could really tell. Jimmy, who was only five and a half, had questions we couldn't answer.

When the moment came, the tension of that special event was shattered when Dr. Cremer excitedly and joyfully exclaimed, "We've got a girl here!"

I was right there and could scarcely believe my ears and eyes. All the lights seemed, suddenly, to be shining more brightly. Our hope and dream had become reality. We had a little girl! Both the doctor and we talked about that unforgettable moment many times in the years that lay ahead. The boys were excited too.

Soon afterwards Mary Nell Harper, one of the nurses at Dembidollo, was saying to Jimmy, "So you've got a baby sister!"

Quick as a flash, Jimmy responded by saying, "Yep, my dad changed the heartbeats." Our conversation about the heart tones had taken on added dimensions. Jimmy was as excited as his mom and dad with a baby girl in the family. Born three days before Christmas, we named her, "Carol Joy." She has never disappointed us and we know she was appropriately named. God's Christmas gift to us!

Eight days later, we put Carol Joy in a small cardboard box which served as a bassinet and put her on the front seat between us in the International pick-up truck. We started down the mountain, with Dr. Cremer and two of his sons traveling behind us in their Jeep. They didn't want us to make the journey alone.

By mid-afternoon we were at the Sako river. It was getting hotter and hotter. Under a tree there, Lavina took all of Carol Joy's clothes off, laid her on a blanket and cooled her off. By the time we reached Gambela on the river, darkness had already fallen. We learned that the river had fallen to a point where we couldn't safely reach home by outboard.

The only thing to do was to attempt it by road. The two vehicles gave us confidence we could make it. Everything went well until, a little over halfway home, we came upon a swamp of water that had not receded back far enough for us to pass through between it and the river bank.

Perhaps with the four- wheeled Jeep we could make it through, but not with the International which had only a two-wheel drive. We loaded what we could on the Jeep and made it. It was eleven o'clock when we stopped by the deep ditch that surrounded the mission compound. The last 150 yards would be on foot. Anuaks living on the compound had heard us coming. They were so excited to have us back.

They immediately wanted to know what God had given us. Was it a boy or a girl? When they learned that it was a girl, on the spot, they named her "Awile," the one who changed the pattern from boys to girls. With wild joy and excitement they created and sang songs fitting to the occasion. It was a night for thanksgiving to God. The house was dirty and dusty. We'd been gone for more than a month. It could have been depressing, except that we came home with our bundle of love. But we were all tired and hungry and needed to eat.

Here's where Lavina shone. On the eighth day, she made that arduous trip, and at the end of the journey, prepared a meal from scratch and fed the hungry travellers. We fetched water from the river and boiled it so we'd have cool drinking water the next day. Everything was difficult and tedious. How Lavina ever did it I'll never know other than that God gave her special strength during those days. In our prayers we told the Lord how much we recognized this and how unspeakably grateful we were. We were glad to be His missionaries at what seemed then to be "the ends of the earth." We had experienced again that He keeps His promises. He had said it again in our hearts. "I will be with you always, even to the ends of the earth." This gave us the strength and courage we needed. It was one o'clock in the morning before we all lay down for the balance of the night.

Breakfast in the morning! Then it was to fetch the International from where we'd abandoned it the night before. By late afternoon the Cremers were making their way back over the mountain. Again, we were alone. This time we had a tiny, precious, 10 day old baby to love and protect. We'd prepared for it by getting film. Few babies had more pictures taken. Her grandparents were glad!

WE RETURN TO AKOBO

Except for the six or seven months that Joan Yilek was with us following her furlough, we were alone at Pokwo. In February of '55 Don and Lyda were back in Addis and expected at Pokwo soon. Joan said she could easily cope until they arrived. We should leave as earlier scheduled.

The MAF plane flew Lavina, Jimmy, David and Carol back to Akobo. Dennis and I went cross country on horseback and with carriers. It was a journey of some 140 miles and took us 8 days. We crossed several rivers and swam the horses beside the canoe. While crossing, we knocked against the side of the canoe to keep the crocodiles away. This was dry season and it was hot. Dennis and I would start out each day before the sun was shining, cook our breakfast around ten thirty and then wait until later in the afternoon before starting out again. It was just too hot to move in the middle of the day. What a marvelous experience for a thirteen year old boy and his dad. Precious times for both of us. Little did we know then that one day Dennis would be back flying over this same route as a missionary pilot with MAF. His many long treks as a boy, I'm sure, gave him an early appreciation for what a plane might do to make missionaries' lives more pleasant and productive.

Before leaving that long trekking experience, I need to share a couple of interesting experiences we had along the way. The first day out, Denny and I were feeling sorry for the horses and when we stopped to rest, decided we'd remove their bridles so they could eat the grass a little more comfortably. The horses, however, took advantage of our generous hearts and soon headed down the trail in the direction of Pokwo from where we had started five hours earlier. Heading in that direction, they no longer seemed tired as before and we had a very fast run to outflank them and head them off. I can assure you they ate grass with bridles on the rest of the way unless we tethered them down securely.

On our last afternoon, the horses were showing signs of fatigue. We stopped in this village and discovered they had been making Anuak beer. The left-over mash from the beer making process had been dumped on the edge of the village. We took the horses over to that mash and I wish you could have seen them. They, literally, pushed their noses deep into it and gorged themselves on it. For the rest of the journey to Akobo that afternoon, we were riding on horses that had all the energy we could control. Had there been a horse officer, I suspect the horses might have been given a ticket for drunk driving. For us, it was a relief to speed on and gain an hour on reaching Akobo before dark. We laughed about our drunken horses more than once! It was good to be back at Akobo after an absence of 21 months. I would now have more time for my beloved translation work.

Moving the Hoekstra's personal belongings 150 miles by
river from Pokwo to Akobo - 1955

Church Drum at the Anuak church in Akobo, the Sudan

CHAPTER TEN

BACK AT AKOBO
A NEW MAF PLANE

Lavina had flown with MAF from Gambela to Akobo with Carol, Jim, and Dave. We were expecting our fifth child and the new little Hoekstra would be arriving in a few short weeks.

DISAPPOINTMENT UPON ARRIVAL AT AKOBO

We had lived at Pokwo without a doctor until the day Lavina flew back to Akobo. She was eager to get home and into her own house. But it wasn't to be! Folks at Akobo had arranged for the plane to fly her and the children to the mission station in Nasir, 90 miles down-river, where there was a doctor. Lavina and the children stayed in Nasir ten days with other missionaries until they all flew into Akobo together to attend the annual mission meeting, scheduled to be held there for the first time ever.

Eight days after we'd left Pokwo, Dennis and I rode up on the opposite side of the river just across from our house in Akobo. We'd made the 140 mile trek, cross-country, from Pokwo on horseback. We quickly swam the horses across the river and were home at last. I could scarcely believe my ears when I was told that Lavina and the children were in Nasir. I was so eager to see them and so very disappointed not to find them there. Fortunately, we had only the night to wait because the next morning folks began arriving for our annual mission meeting and Lavina and the doctor from Nasir would be among them.

With that initial disappointment, home sweet home didn't seem quite that sweet. This was dry season and everything seemed dried up and barren looking besides. Pokwo was always lush and green, but here things looked rather dead and uninspiring. It'd take a little adjusting to settle in again.

I remember straightening things up around the yard and in the house that afternoon yet. We were really tired from the long trek but there was work to be done if we were to be ready for the influx of missionaries and their families the next day.

MISSION MEETING HELD AT AKOBO
1956

We had no time to think of the "flesh pots" of Pokwo as missionaries came from the other stations. Some came by truck or Jeep and others flew in with MAF. Lavina was so thrilled to be home that morning and immediately plunged into getting the house ready for guests. The kids were all excited with their new surroundings and were soon exploring the place, inside and out. Other mission children were there for them to get acquainted with. They had so many exciting things to share and to learn from each other. They were happy with their new home.

The entire station was a bee-hive of activity getting ready for the mission meeting. Some real logistical matters had to be considered. Where would all these people sleep? How would they be fed? They'd shot an animal the day before so there should be plenty of meat. But now they were beginning to have some doubts about being able to preserve it. It couldn't all be refrigerated. Would it keep? Regrettably, the answer proved to be "no." After the mission meeting, we talked about the catastrophe of the spoiled meat and the awful smelling gravy on numerous occasions. Folks involved were given an "A" for effort but an "F" on results. It was just one of the problems that was inevitable in trying to cope with so many people with so few houses and facilities.

Our house was on the north end of the compound, separated from the other residences by the school, library and the banana grove. The old McClure house, where the Sikkemas, lived came next. Between it and the Swart house was the fruit orchard. Beyond the Swarts at the end stood the single missionaries ladies' house. These houses came to be identified with the first family who lived there and seemed to carry that name all through the years. In practice, we had other folks living in them at different times. The Crandalls, the Arnolds, the Roodes and the Sikkemas as well as the Jordans were all part of the Anuak missionary family at some time or other during our years in the Sudan. Things changed a lot from those first years when just the McClures, Swarts, Wilma Kats and we started out there. Bob and Morrie had arrived in April of '48 along with Wilma Kats. They had joined the McClures when returning from furlough. We had caught up with them three months later and always felt that we had been part of it from the beginning.

We'd never had an annual mission meeting at Akobo. Normally, these were held in Doleib Hill or Malakal, a day's trip to the north of us. We were always excited about going there for the mission meeting to meet folks we hadn't seen for a year. For the ladies it was a treat just to get out of the station. They loved the opportunity to get into those two Greek shops in Malakal and replenish their dwindling supplies. They'd shop for the year ahead and had to plan rather carefully.

One thing I remember about those mission meetings is that many of us would be ill with diarrhea before the week ended. Temporary pit holes, food prepared in abundance, and masses of flies made it almost inevitable. We, who had been so eager to come, now could scarcely wait to get home and become well again.

This year the Akobo folks had bravely invited their colleagues to meet in our station. We knew it was planned, but just arriving from Pokwo made the hustle and bustle of getting ready with last minute contingencies and unforeseen problems popping up demanding a solution seem more taxing.

They had a master plan showing where everyone would be housed. We'd all eat together in the McClure house where the Crandalls were then living. Our house was to have the following people. Gordon and Jean Marshall, the MAF couple, would occupy the middle tukl on the front. Dr. Bob and Vi Gordon and their three children and Bob's father would sleep in my office and the attached storage room. Out in the back, we had a two room, thatched roof, mud floor storeroom. Lowrie and Margaret Anderson and Milton and Peggy Thompson slept there. In front of the tukl in which the Gordons were sleeping, was a tent for our overseas special guests and speaker for the conference, Dr. Ed Fairman, his wife, Marian, and their young four year old son, Timmy. The place was full. There was no more room in the inn! We, ourselves, would sleep on the sleeping veranda on the bathroom end of the house.

MARK STEPHEN BORN WHILE MISSION MEETS

And then, guess what? During the middle of the conference, about 3 a.m. in the morning, Lavina says, "This is the night. Maybe you'd better go get the doctor."

What a time to decide to have a baby! But it was out of our control! I quickly dressed and ran down to the mission to crank up the generator. When I did so, every light on the compound came on. The generator always shut itself down with the help of an alarm clock turning a spool on the back to shut off the flow of diesel fuel.

Immediately, of course, everyone was awake and knew that "the party" was about to begin.

What a setting in which to have a baby. Lavina was terrific and took it all in good humor. We didn't have just one doctor, we had three doctors and two nurses in attendance.

Here's the picture. Guests in our back yard. Guests in our end tukl. Guests in the middle tukl. Guests in a tent in the front yard. Our four children asleep on their beds on the sleeping veranda. In the end tukl, just off the bathroom and bedroom, Lavina is having the baby.

At twenty minutes to five in the morning, the party is over. Mark Stephen has been born. The children slept through it all. How kind and merciful is the Lord!

When I went down to join the others for breakfast, they all wanted to know what the big idea was of waking everyone up in the middle of the night with those lights. They had a great time "pulling my leg." It was celebration time. God had given us a beautiful, perfect little boy. After breakfast, all the mission kids wanted to come down and see what a brand new baby looked like. They stood in awe as they looked at this red faced little guy in the basket. Gayle Swart commented, "Boy, he sure has big hands." In that basket, unknown then, God had placed another missionary. What a cause for celebration and thanks to God.

Lavina joined the crowd in no time. Even Mark was soon on display in his little basket on the edges of the mission meeting. Later in the week, the business sessions gave way to fun and games. That night, our "party" came in for a lot of good ribbing. Mark was number five for us. The Treasurer of our RCA board at that time was Dr. Henry Bovenkerk. He was great but missionaries joked about how he "pinched pennies" for the Board. We all had the impression that he didn't like missionaries having large families because it cost the Board too much money for children's allowances. Our salaries varied those years according to the number of children one had.

That evening during the charades, a faked telegram, purportedly to us from Dr. Bovenkerk was read out — "Congratulations ... stop ... repeat .... stop ... signed Bovenkerk." Missionaries have a great sense of humor and we were having fun!

GOOD TIMES AT AKOBO

Lavina and I had a promising ministry underway at Pokwo. We loved it there and had there been a need for us to continue, we'd have been happy to do so. It wasn't until we had again settled in at Akobo that we realized what blessings and joys we had missed out on at Akobo.

God gave us a wonderfully compatible group in our station and in the Presbyterian mission. It was a joy and a privilege to be members of the team. Each of us knew why we were there and what was expected of each of us. Over the years, we had many fantastic times together. In our work, we complemented each other's contributions. In our social relationships, we played and prayed and worshipped together. A variety of activities brought us together.

The weekly teas followed by volley-ball were a sheer delight. We had our mid-week evening prayer meeting, taking turns in the different homes. Sunday afternoons in the hour before dusk we had an English worship service in either the McClure's or Swart's home. English-speaking teachers and school boys, our British district commissioner, Dick Lythe, and his wife, Nora, with their children and missionary colleagues made up the congregations. Wilma Kats, Joan Yilek or Morrie Swart played the small portable organ. Sometimes Morrie and Bob sang us a beautiful duet or Bob played his trombone. We took turns preaching. One of the sermons by Don McClure has always stuck in my memory; it was based on Revelation where it says, "Let no man steal thy crown." We missionaries loved each other worked well together and upheld each other in our prayers. At Akobo we were greatly blessed by being joined together with colleagues we found compatible and supportive. We were a family. Our children called the adults "Uncle" and "Aunt." These ties became so strong that they vied with blood relatives in attraction. On furloughs our children sometimes had difficulty sorting out who was a "real uncle and aunt" from who was a mission "uncle and aunt." We were truly an extended family straight out of Africa.

FURLOUGH - A NEW PLANE FOR MAF

It would soon be time for our regular furlough. I was pressing hard with the translation effort. You might say that we were burning the candle at both ends! I was more tired than normal. My heart was beating irregularly. Doctors weren't sure whether I had a serious heart condition or not.

Once in America, it was determined that a little more relaxation and a little more recreation and rest was all that was required. A change of pace, better food and living conditions and I was back to normal.

Two things of significance occurred during that furlough. During the first months in the states, we lived in the missionary residence in Grand Rapids. It was during that time that we began dreaming of the possibility of raising funds for a plane for MAF to use in the Sudan. They were flying an old Rapide aircraft, a somewhat ancient bi-plane with canvas covering. It wasn't ideally suited for Sudan conditions and they were praying for the Lord to provide them with something smaller, more efficient and suited for their ministry.

I had never raised large amounts of money and had no idea as to how to go about it. But the Lord has marvelous surprises and he had one for me that was full of excitement.

"NOW DON'T YOU GO BUYING ANY AIRPLANES!"

I'd been thinking a good bit about MAF's need for a different plane. It was a need I wanted to help meet. But the man who came up to me after the service in Bethany Reformed Church in Grand Rapids, Michigan, said, "I think my partner and I can get you that Jeep you need." I was most surprised and responded by saying, "That Jeep may not be our highest priority. Why don't you let me think it over and get back to you." After going over it together, the next time we met, the man handed me a check for $3,500. I had never seen a check that large in all my life. It could be used toward that new MAF plane. Lavina and I talked about it all the way to the mission house.

That same week I learned of a used Cessna 180 airplane that a local manufacturer was planning to sell. I made an appointment and we talked about how we might purchase his plane. He was Charles Werner of Werner Manufacturing. He wanted $8,500. I knew I couldn't find that kind of money, but I wanted that plane for MAF so badly that I was bold to suggest that if he could let us have it for $5,000 we'd find a way to pay for it. After a moment's hesitation, he said, "Well, let me talk to the boss and we'll let you know." He was referring to his wife! In fact, both of them were great people!

The next morning, by agreement, at exactly nine o'clock the phone rang. This was to be his answer. I'm walking toward the phone, when Lavina (probably meaning it besides) says, "Now, don't you go buying any airplanes!"

I picked up the phone. The voice on the other end of the line says, "If you want that plane you can have it for $5,000 dollars." With Lavina's words still fresh on my mind, I didn't know what to say. There was an awkward silence. This time, Mr. Werner said,"Well, do you want it, or don't you?"

Without a moments hesitation, I said, "We'll take it." I had bought an airplane with only $3,500 on hand. I quickly made a call to a dear friend in Grand Haven, Michigan, Mr. Franklin Kieft, and told him what I had done. He said he'd see what he could do. That afternoon he came to the house with a check for the remaining $1500. He'd gone to the bank and borrowed the money. Together, we went to examine the plane. We were both thrilled with what we saw. We had bought a beautiful, hardly used Cessna 180 for MAF.

Twenty years later, Ed Stouten, the man from Bethany who had given the $3,500, shared with me how his partner and he had cleaned themselves out to make that gift. He told me how grateful he was to have been challenged then. He said, "It taught me how to give and to trust the Lord. If I hadn't done it then, I'd never have had the joy of giving over $200,000 since then for the Lord's work. It was your challenging me that the Lord used to teach me how to give." He was so grateful and so was I. We praised the Lord together.

Now that I had the plane, I didn't know what to do with it. In my excitement, I decided to call Stewart King, head of MAF in London. We knew Stewart well from our times together in the Sudan and I was itching to tell him. For ordinary people like me, making an overseas call in those days was a major event!

Stewart could scarcely believe what I was telling him. This was beyond his wildest dreams. More good news would follow, but I couldn't tell him yet. It was our hope to send this plane to the Sudan with floats as well. Then MAF would be able to operate rain or shine!

Stewart suggested I call Grady Parrot, president of MAF in Fullerton, California. The day before Christmas, Grady picked up the plane and flew it to their hanger for modifications making it suitable for use in the Sudan.

Lavina, the children, and I were in Minnesota that Christmas with my folks on the farm. We were just ready to step out the door to go to our little country church for its Sunday School Christmas program when the phone rang. It was long distance. My cousin, Dick Hoekstra, was calling from Chicago. I shall never forget his words. He said, "Harvey, are you still wanting to put pontoons on that plane for the Sudan?" He always liked to kid around and before I could respond, he said, "I'll put a pontoon on one side for you. Which side do you want?" He continued,"You'll probably be getting in on the right side most of the time, how about if I put one on that side for you?" Four days later, there was a check in the mailbox for $2,100.

God had better things in mind with respect to that plane than we had dared to dream. MAF actually sold that plane to a group of sheep ranchers in Australia for only a little less than the cost of a brand new one. God's people kept giving us help. When the project was completed, churches and individuals had provided funds for a brand new Cessna 180, equipped with pontoons, with a spare engine and whatever modifications were required to fit it for the Sudan. This plane made a dramatic difference in MAF's ability to serve the Lord and His missionaries with safety and efficiency that amazed us all. It changed the way we lived and worked! This was God's gracious gift and we gave Him our overflowing thanks.

GRADUATE STUDY

That furlough we moved to Hartford, Connecticut in January for graduate study. I was enrolled in the Kennedy School of Missions for their second semester.

I concentrated in linguistic studies under Dr. William Welmers, a specialist in African languages. While there I completed the necessary class-room work to qualify for their PHD field degree program. When I completed the translation of the Anuak New Testament, I hoped to pursue a field degree program doing a study of "The religious vocabulary of the Anuak language as it relates to communicating the essential Christian message among animistic peoples." But this was not to be, because during the final year of work on the Anuak New Testament, our dear friends and colleagues, Paul and Winifred Hostetter, were to become the first missionaries to be expelled from the Sudan. They had only just gotten into their linguistic work among the Murle. Paul had worked out a writing system and a set of primers, but hadn't gotten into the translation of the New Testament.

Within days of the Hostetters leaving the Sudan, I received a letter from Bob Swart who was then on furlough. He wanted us to move to Pibor to complete the Anuak New Testament there and to begin work on the Murle as soon as this was finished. Any thoughts of earning a field degree were put aside. Translating the New Testament into Murle was of infinitely greater importance. I did not know then that seventeen years later, the Lord would give me the opportunity to earn a doctorate in the science of missions at Fuller's prestigious School of World Missions. I am reminded of the words of Jeremiah, "I know the plans that I have for you," says the Lord, "plans for welfare and not for evil, to give you a future and a hope."

CHAPTER ELEVEN

POCHALA

Pochala was a government administrative post off in the direction of Ethiopia. To get there, we waited for the dry season when the dirt roads were passable. There was just one road. It was ninety miles straight south from Akobo to Pibor. Another ninety miles directly East would take us to Pochala. The country in between these places was flat savannah land with tall grass, thousands of wild animals and very few trees. Only occasionally when we came near the river were there villages. About twenty-five miles from Pibor, on the way from Akobo, was a small cluster of Arab merchants' shops. Between Pibor and Pochala there were a few more trees and we passed through a number of sizeable Anuak villages, including where the main Anuak king, Adonga, lived. Low areas made the road impassable very early when the rains began.

My assignment and deepest longing was to translate the New Testament into the Anuak language. I worked at it night and day. But I also loved to do the work of an evangelist and to preach in the villages. I always felt that this also had a side benefit of contributing to the quality of my translation effort. Off the compound, most of my preaching was in nearby native villages. Once a year we'd travel greater distances from home.

We tried to get to Pochala every dry season for a week or ten days of evangelistic meetings there and in neighboring Anuak villages. Eventually, an Anuak evangelist was stationed in that area. Years later when the civil war heated up between the North and the South, this young evangelist was murdered because of his working for Jesus Christ and the church.

We had some very good times in Pochala. I remember arriving there, travelling on an Arab merchant's truck. It was Easter Sunday morning. The only Christians in this little mud-walled, thatched roof town were members of the police and their families who had become Christians in another province under the influence of British missionaries. They were known for their strong Christian commitment.

We had a communion service that Easter Sunday morning in the house of one of these families. We used plain tea and a homemade, pancake-like bread for elements. In that service, Jesus was as powerfully present with us as I have ever experienced him in any of our beautiful, liturgically correct services in America. We experienced in a moving way the truth he had promised when he said, "I will be with you always even to the end of the age." And again, we experienced, as we did so many times during our years in Africa, that where two or three are gathered together, there He was in the midst of us.

Once, after Mission Aviation had begun to fly us missionaries around, we flew into Pochala with our stateside guest, Dr. Louis Benes, editor of the Church Herald. It was great fun to have him there with us. We could see things as they appeared to people from the outside. It made us realize how we had changed. Things that were novel and surprising to Dr. Benes had already become commonplace to us. A visitor helped us realize the danger of almost making too complete an adjustment to things that were different and even inconvenient.

One night we were having our service with just the light of an old fashioned, wick, kerosene lantern. It hung from a post helping support the grass fence around these few huts. It's a wonder we didn't burn the place down. With that dim light, we'd been singing and singing Anuak hymns from our first Anuak hymn book. Bob and Morrie Swart had put that together. Finally, when we had nearly exhausted ourselves,

Dr. Benes says, "Let's sing number" (and I've forgotten the number) "and then we will have sung every hymn in the book."

REBEKKA

On one of those visits to Pochala, I had a shocking surprise. Earlier in the afternoon, I'd met with the family of one of the police stationed there. They'd had a new baby and were wanting me to baptize the baby before I left the next day, going back on that merchant's truck. Arrangements were made for the baby to be baptized that evening. We met that night in the moonlight aided by a dimly burning flashlight.

When it came time for the baptism, I suddenly realized I had forgotten to ask for the name. So I said, "And what did you name this child?"

The father, without a moment's hesitation, said, "You name her."

No question about it. I had to do it. The name that popped into my mind was, "Rebekka." On the spot, then and there, I baptized her as "Rebekka." The name took!

The following year when I returned they couldn't wait to show me "Rebekka." They said, "Come, you must see how Rebekka has grown." God's good hand was upon her!

BAPTIZING A KING WHO HAD FOUR WIVES

Another year, three of us missionaries went together to spend a week in Pochala. We were Bob Swart from Pibor, Tal Wilson from Obel, and myself. The Anuak evangelist had come in from the village to share with us in these meetings. Every day we had several services out in the open with people sitting on the ground, some trying to find whatever shade they could. This was dry season and it was hot. When we slept at night the little sand flies nearly killed us. I never understood how people could live there permanently.

On our last afternoon, one of the Anuak kings who came from the same village where the evangelist had been working all year, asked us if he might be baptized. I shall never forget his words. He said, "I've been listening to all that you missionaries have been preaching all week. These are the same words I have been hearing from the Anuak evangelist whom you sent to my village. I believe all that I have heard. I want to become a person of this Jesus. I want to be baptized, but I have four wives in my village. May I be baptized?"

Bob, Tal and I looked at each other as to who would answer. There was an uncomfortable silence. Finally, because I spoke the Anuak language (Bob knew a good bit of it from his period at Akobo, but Tal was totally dependent upon an interpreter), I told him what I thought.

I said, "What you did before you heard about Jesus Christ cannot always be undone. You have four wives and children. I believe God wants you to continue to be their husband and father. You must not send them away. Rather you must show them the love that you have learned about in God's book. I, personally, think you should be baptized. The only thing is that you must make a commitment before the Lord not to marry additional wives, now that you have become a person of Jesus Christ."

We missionaries then discussed it further. Bob and Tal agreed with what I had said. In speaking up, I felt myself vulnerable. Did Bob and Tal feel as I did about this or would I be embarrassed by their contrary opinions? I recall the relief I felt when they both concurred. That evening, along with many others, this Anuak king was baptized.

We left the next day and the king and the Anuak evangelist returned to the king's village. We reported the incident, according to the rules laid down by the church when a person caught up in a plural marriage had been baptized. The Presbytery, upon hearing what we had done, sent a senior pastor, Adwok, from the Shullik church to investigate and report back.

When he returned from there, Adwok told how he had arrived at Pochala, crossed the crocodile infested river and walked many miles on the trail through the tall grass where lion were known to be hungry. He shared his fears, but he said, "When I arrived in the king's village, one of the first huts I saw, was a hut with a large cross made from poles, extending upward out of the center." He said, "I knew then that the Gospel had been preached there." Before he left, Adwok baptized 35 people, including the four wives of the king.

This never would have happened, had we not baptized that Anuak king the last night we were in Pochala. It was a right decision and we believed that God had given us the courage to make it.

PREACHING THE GOSPEL TO POLYGAMISTS

What to do about plural marriages had been a hot item for discussion in the various missions in Africa, including the Presbyterian Mission in which we Reformed Church missionaries were serving. Our colleagues in the Anglican church further south in the Sudan had, like most missions in Africa, taken a rigid stand against baptizing men who had more than one wife. Rules varied, which sometimes allowed women to be baptized or under which men could choose which wife to keep and which wives to send away or be cared for in some other fashion. But generally speaking, baptizing polygamists was forbidden. Our Anglican colleagues held those views, and at one stage made it rather clear to our mission that if we began baptizing people involved in plural marriages our cooperative efforts in places like Bishop Gwynne Divinity College might be jeopardized.

So our mission moved on these matters cautiously and responsibly. That's why Pastor Adwok made his trip and reported back. His report did a lot to persuade those who had remained unconvinced that we were moving in the right direction.

Missionaries had pretty strong views on this subject. One missionary I respected highly flatly said, "If they love the Lord, they'll give up their wives." I found it hard to believe that Jesus would want these women who were mothers with children to be cast adrift like that. These children needed the strong hand of their father, which would be denied if a believer's polygamous family was destroyed. Then, too, the women would likely have to turn to prostitution of some sort to cope. It just didn't seem to be the kind of thing that Jesus would have done had he been there with us in the flesh. It sounded more like something the pharisees and religious leaders with whom Jesus so frequently argued might have felt comfortable doing.

We sometimes quoted Scripture to support our different perspectives on the subject. Paul's word to the Corinthian believers was one of my favorites. "Let each of you remain in the condition in which you were called." I Corinthians 7:20. There were some situations and relationships that couldn't be untangled without doing more harm than good. We are saved by grace not by fulfilling the requirements of a law. I felt strongly on the subject and comfortable that Jesus was pleased with it.

Personally, I always pictured myself preaching the grand and glorious good news about Jesus Christ in Anuak villages where everyone would come to listen. In front of me would be the village chief, his several wives and children, village elders, many of whom had at least two wives. And there were others who, more because of economics than conviction, remained monogamous — all of these and their children were there listening..

I would urge the people to put their trust in this Jesus who had loved the world so much that he had come from heaven to earth to live among us. He had shown us what is in the heart of God. We knew that God was not far away, but that He was near because He had visited us and, while living among us in that distant land, had healed our sick, driven out the demons and even raised the dead.

I'd finish my message by telling them of the perfect sacrifice, Jesus, the Lamb of God. And then I would tell them, how God had accepted that sacrifice made on our behalf, and how He had honored Jesus for what he had done by raising Him from the dead. And there was no doubt about it because he had met his friends again after rising from the dead and had showed them his hands and his side proving that he was that same Jesus they had been with during those three years. I told them how this Jesus had gone back to heaven and how, before he left, he had told his followers to go into every country to the most distant places and tell this good news so that people might turn away from their wrong ways and turn back to God. I told them how Jesus has given his followers power to do this and how Jesus had said that they must keep on telling this good news until one day when he would again return back to earth. Finally, I would tell them that Jesus hadn't come back yet, and that his followers were still doing what he told them to do.

I felt a little ashamed when I told them it took so long to come to where my Anuak friends lived because it was a long way and a very difficult place to reach. A poor excuse! But aside from that, the climactic moment would come when I could invite all who were listening to believe and be baptized. I just could not imagine that I had to have any reservations about that at all. The Bible says so clearly that the time was coming when "whoever calls upon the name of the Lord will be saved." That moment was now.

I couldn't imagine that if the village chief stood and said, "I believe this good news, want to be baptized and become a person of your Jesus" that I would have to say, "Oh, I'm sorry. I didn't realize ... I didn't mean this for you." I could never imagine that I would have to find some inadequate substitute way to permit him to be sort of a half-way Christian because of wives he'd married before he'd heard this good news from God.

These are some of the thoughts that lay behind my response to the Anuak king that day in Pochala.

*"...Believe in the Lord Jesus, and you will be saved
— you and your household."*

Acts 16:31

CHAPTER TWELVE

PIBOR AND THE MURLE BECKON

We returned to the Sudan during the first part of 1957. We didn't know then that before our term was finished, we, like most of the other missionaries would be expelled from the Sudan on short notice. The civil war, pitting black Southern tribes-people, now either Christian or animist, against the Arab Muslim Northerner was gaining momentum. In their efforts to forcibly Arabicize and Islamize the south, the Arab north would bring the country to disaster. When it happened, we recalled the prophetic words of Dr. Glenn Reed, the wise missionary statesman of the United Presbyterian Church who had predicted that the time was short and that at best we might have fifteen years to work. We would be given less than fourteen!

In 1959 the Hostetters left the Sudan, the first to be expelled. The following year, Lavina and our family moved into the vacant Hostetter house in Pibor. We completed the Anuak translation there. We had scarcely finished when we began work on the Murle. Paul had done the basic spade work in the language. We could build on his foundation. Even while Paul was still in the Sudan, he and I had collaborated on developing a writing system using Arabic symbols. Murle would be written using the Arabic script.

Way back in 1954 while we were at Pokwo, more or less academic discussions were underway in the mission as to whether or not we might one day want to consider writing these Nilotic languages using the Arabic script. Arguments pro and con were common among us. Some thought we should actively pursue this possibility in view of the fact that one day most of the children in the schools would likely be reading and writing in Arabic. Why not build on that foundation? But could these Nilotic languages be written accurately using Arabic letters when in Arabic the consonants were accented while in the tribal languages the accent was on the vowel?

A FUN EXPERIENCE WITH ARABIC SCRIPT

Years earlier in my free time at Pokwo, I had done a little experimenting on the side. What I did was rather crude, but it proved a point. Anuak, which was one of the Nilotic languages, could, indeed, be written using Arabic letters. In my experiment, I used the Arabic consonants, and simply used numerals from the Arabic for the various vowels. I had three young Anuak men who were my guinea pigs. Before too long I was able to write unknown words in Anuak on the blackboard, using Arabic letters. As I wrote the words on the board, they were able to call them back to me. We were having great fun.

I decided at that time to ask the mission leaders for permission to prove my point at the mission meeting in Nasir in 1954. It was agreed and I had these three men row downstream in a wooden canoe nearly 150 miles to the Nasir station located on the Sobat river into which the Baro flowed from Gambela.

They gave me a half hour one afternoon for my presentation. The young men sat in the front row and I was at the blackboard. I'd write an Anuak word on the board using the Arabic script. My young men could read virtually anything I wrote. After a half an hour, I had proved my point beyond dispute. The Anuak language, at least, could be written in Arabic script with a degree of accuracy that made reading as easy as when using the Roman alphabet.

It was a fun afternoon. I felt that a number of my colleagues had been quite favorably impressed. When the young men left, and made their way to the river to begin the tough rowing upstream toward home in Pokwo, the business meeting resumed. As we began, one of my colleagues who didn't like the idea of using the Arabic script no matter what, acknowledged, "Harvey has certainly demonstrated that these languages can be read using Arabic letters, but I remain unconvinced. The meeting will please come to order!"

It was all in a missionary's day and we had a great, good time with it. Years later at Pibor, the Murle would be written using Arabic letters.

The only school for the Murle was run by the government. Because it was taught in Arabic, the Arabic script was the script the students knew. It made good sense to build on that foundation. Anyone already able to read Arabic could go on and learn to read in the vernacular written with these same Arabic symbols and a few modifications with relative ease. The argument against using Arabic letters because of Arabic's close association with the Koran remained. At Pibor, however, there was no choice. Murle would be written in Arabic script or it would not be written at all. The decision had been made. It was for Arabic script. We purchased an Arabic typewriter, modified two or three keys, learned to type from right to left and voweled it by hand.

I made rapid progress with the Murle translation. My informant was completely bi-lingual in Murle and Anuak. We were using the Anuak translation as our basic text. Admittedly, this first translation was more of a "living Bible" type translation. It seemed possible that the entire New Testament might be completed in less than five years. Our hopes were high.

ASSIGNED TO BISHOP GWYNNE

The mission, however, was again short of personnel. Someone had to fill in at Bishop Gwynne Divinity College where students for the ministry were being trained. The mission had wanted to assign us there on previous occasions but we had always successfully escaped their threatened "draft." The need to complete the Anuak translation always prevailed. This time, however, the Anuak New Testament was finished and being printed by the American Bible Society. Now was the perfect opportunity for the mission to send us to Bishop Gwynne. And it happened just as we had feared.

We found ourselves on the staff at Bishop Gwynne College. The Murle translation was put in "cold storage." We were told that our assignment was temporary until the need at Mundri could be met. We were not unduly unhappy. I felt it an honor to be teaching in this theological seminary. I worked night and day as I had no old lectures on which I could rely. It was a great experience and I suspect I could have been happy with a long term assignment if the need for the Murle translation didn't exist.

RETURN TO PIBOR - MISSIONARY EXPULSIONS

My career as a professor in a theological seminary was to be short-lived. At Mundri we always had an early morning chapel hour, after which Lavina and I had our breakfast. This particular morning in December of 1961, I had no sooner opened the back door, when Lavina shushed me with upraised hand, saying excitedly, "Quiet, quiet! The Swarts and the Sikkemas have been expelled from the Sudan."

She had her head close to the shortwave Zenith radio on which we could pick up the mission broadcasts. We couldn't talk, but we could listen in and keep in touch.

We were shocked and dismayed. The ax had fallen. We had known this could happen at any time, but when the moment came we could hardly believe it.

Within the week, the mission asked us to return to Pibor to take up where Bob and Morrie would leave off. Just before we left Mundri, our dear friend, Bishop Oliver Allison, bishop of the Sudan who was visiting Bishop Gwynne at the time, stood between Lavina and me, and putting his long arms around us, lovingly committed us to the Lord for whatever He had for us in His tomorrow. We headed for Pibor.

Bob and Morrie had already disposed of most of their things among the Arab merchants across the river. Bob and I spent as much time as possible together so that I could learn from him all I could. We wanted to have good continuity with anything he had going at Pibor. We were overwhelmed with the responsibilities that would soon fall on our shoulders. The Swarts and the Sikkemas had been given 30 days to leave. Their time was nearly up.

SEVEN DAYS TO LEAVE THE SUDAN

Bob and Morrie still had one more day with us at Pibor when the entire picture changed. The MAF plane had flown into Pibor this particular morning. At noon I was on the radio talking to Malakal. Milton Thompson was on the radio for the mission. He inquired, "Did you get my letter which I sent to you on the plane?"

I responded that I hadn't opened the mail yet and wasn't sure whether his letter had come or not.

With that, Milton said,"Well, then I better give you the bad news now. You have just seven days to pack your bags."

I could scarcely believe my ears. We, too, were being expelled from the Sudan. As soon as we'd returned to Pibor, the government officials realized that we had been missed because of our being at Mundri in another province. In no time, they corrected their oversight!

The words were hardly out of Milton's mouth, when I came back with, "Milt, there's no market for used furniture here at Pibor. Bob has flooded the market."

I'll never understand why I said that. I suspect it was an effort to ease the searing pain with a light hearted, attempted joke. Putting all jokes aside, we knew that our ministry in the Sudan was finished. Night had fallen! We wanted to cry, but there was no time.

Even before we ate, Lavina and I started moving boxes out of the attic. Sorting and packing had begun. We had our meal in near silence. What did the Lord have in mind? What did the future hold? It would be months before some of the answers were in. During those months, we would learn what it is to lean on the Lord in a new way and to "wait" and then "wait" again with patience!

During those few remaining, rushing days at Pibor there was one agonizing question that kept surfacing over and over in our conversations. It lay heavily upon our hearts. The Anuak New Testaments! How would we ever get them into the hands of the Anuak people? We knew that the American Bible Society had printed them and that they were supposed to have been shipped. But we knew nothing as to their actual whereabouts. Where were they? How would they ever reach the Anuak people? With all the missionaries leaving, how could it happen? This was the constant, recurring cry of our hearts to the Lord. Our hearts were burdened and heavy!

Milton Thompson and Robb McLaughlin came down to help us sort out our things, get rid of what we could and start closing down the station. We carried out with us what two small MAF planes could carry. Milton and Robb packed up what would fit in an outboard and aluminum canoe to go out by steamer. A paddle wheel steamer was coming from Malakal but it could get only as far as the village of Likwangili about 25 miles north of Pibor.

John Ducker, an MAF pilot, and Milton Thompson made the run with the two boats from Pibor to meet the steamer coming in from Malakal. The river was falling fast. This would be the last steamer before the dry season.

But alas, on the trip down-stream to where the steamer was expected, the canoe got in the wake of the outboard and capsized in about five feet of water. The men fished the things out of the river, but by the time they arrived in Likwangali, the steamer had already come and gone. The only thing they could do was park our things on the river bank near one of the Arab merchant's shops. There they cooked and steamed in the hot sun until the roads became passable and a merchant's truck collected them to deliver them to the single ladies who were still working at Akobo.

It was three months later before our water-soaked goods arrived in Akobo. The dear ladies did all they could, but the damage was done. They dried out and aired out what they could and repacked the whole lot for eventual transporting to Ethiopia. In October that same year they arrived in Addis Ababa where Lavina and I were now living and studying Amharic in preparation, hopefully, for use in Ethiopia if we could get a resident visa.

Sometimes, with a bit of humor, we reminded ourselves that the Lord was teaching us to "travel light." It was only ten years earlier that we had lost everything when our house burned at Akobo. This time, we left most everything behind at Pibor. In less than fifteen years, we'd again leave everything behind in Ethiopia. We were reminded that our citizenship is in heaven and that here we have no abiding city.

A LAST MINUTE BAPTISM AT PIBOR

The last morning was hectic. Last minute packing! People from the Arab shops across the river coming out of curiosity to see what was happening. A few wanting to buy small items thought useful to them. Friends among the Murle and Anuak just wanting to be near us for a little while yet before we'd be gone forever.

Lavina's letter to our home church in Silver Creek, Minnesota, dated January 5, 1962 beautifully describes the unforgettable impromptu baptismal service that took place during our last hours at Pibor:

"It was with tears in our eyes and aching hearts that we left our home, our work and the people whom we had learned to love. As the little MAF plane flew us over the mission compound, it was hard to realize that we would never again return. It makes me sad to think of it. I guess I am like many other people that look so long at the door that is closed behind them, they fail to see the door the Lord is opening before them. ...

"*The morning we left Pibor, I had to get away from the business and relax a bit. So I walked out to the village to say good-bye to some of my friends. I stopped to see Bur, Ocan's wife. She had come to Pibor this spring knowing nothing of the Lord and with a mother who is very much opposed to her son-in-law's new religion. Ocan, her husband, is a very dear Christian man. He is an Anuak and a tuberculosis patient at the hospital. Under Ocan's teaching Bur came to love the Lord.*

"*While we were at Mundri, she stood up in church and said she believed in Jesus and wanted to be baptized. At that time Bob Swart told her that when Harvey returned to Pibor she would be baptised.*

"*I could see she was sad about something. When I asked what was making her sad, this is what she told me: 'When you were away at Mundri, I told the people I believed in Jesus. Bomb (Bob) told me that when Odola (Harvey's African name) returned I would be baptized.' She went on, 'Now you have come back, but today you are leaving and you will never return and I am not baptized.*"

"*I went home and told Harvey. When he heard this, he said, "We'll stop everything and have a service right now."*

"*So we beat the church drum, called the people together and had a most wonderful time of fellowship with the people that last morning. It was well worth the time it took. How I wish you could have seen Bur's face when she left the church following her baptism. It was radiant — so different from when I saw her an hour earlier. It was a great joy to all of us. It is experiences like this that make it well worth the investment of our lives in a land like Africa. I praise God for the privilege that has been ours to serve in the Sudan these fourteen years.*"

In this same letter, Lavina tells of the sadness felt at Pibor by the Murle that their New Testament hadn't been completed before we had to leave. She tells of Ocan's joy that the Anuak New Testament was finished and then she says:

"*As he praised God for this, a cloud came over his face and he said, ' If only the Murle had it too.' *"

Lavina's letter continued:

"Yes, that has been our dream and prayer to give the Murle people the New Testament also. ... Konyi, a Murle elder, pleaded with Harvey to go somewhere, 'anywhere,' he said, 'and translate the Bible for us too.' ..."

Lavina's letter tells us of those precious, last hallowed moments at Pibor. The service of which she writes had barely finished when it was time to go across the river and fly out.

GOD'S PERFECT TIMING

It was mid-day, January 10, 1962. The two small MAF planes had just landed at Pibor. A number of our Anuak and Murle friends were there with us at the door of the plane when it opened. The pilot handed me a small package. He said, "You'll probably want to open this before you leave."

When I opened that package, inside it were the first five printed, beautifully bound copies of the Anuak New Testament. We handed them out to the Anuaks who were there and could read. We will never forget the words of one of the men as he said, "Our hearts (livers) are heavy as you go away, but you are leaving behind God's best gift. You have given us His Word in our language."

There were an additional thousand copies in Khartoum, printed and shipped out by the American Bible Society.

MAF had flown in to fetch us. We took with us what we could. We had an hour and a half from when we took off until we'd make our first stop in Malakal.

Alone with our thoughts, one side of the heart was heavy, and the other was light with God's joy and peace. I thought of the verse from Isaiah, "Thou wilt keep him in perfect peace, whose mind is stayed on thee." This was God's promise and our challenge to trust Him for His tomorrow. We had long since learned that God keeps His promises.

We were over Malakal now and would soon be landing. Our hearts were still in Pibor with the Murle and the Anuak savoring those last moments at the door of the plane. Over and over their words kept coming back: "You are leaving behind God's best gift. You have given us His Word in our language." To God be all glory, honor and praise forever and ever!

FINDING THE MESENGOS

Harvey and Livina, their first trek into the rain forest to reach the Mesengo.

Hoekstra's first stick house being built at Godare.

Lavina cooking on three stones
during first weeks at Godare.

It took 25 workmen 17 days to bring the Landrover 52
miles through the forest from Teppi to the Godare River.

Harvey and Balti the Chief.

Clearing the airstrip in the rainforest.

Removing a huge log from the future airstrip.

Air-drops by mission plane before the strip was ready.

Hoekstra family, less Denny, who was away in college.

Denny was then flying for MAF in Ethopia.

Women using large baskets
to carry edible roots from the forest.

Mesengo men collect honey
from behives placed high in trees.

CHAPTER THIRTEEN

A NEW CHALLENGE IN ETHIOPIA

It was January, 1963. The door for us to continue working in the Sudan had slammed shut. Harvey and Lavina were marking time in Alexandria, Egypt at Schutz, the school for missionary children. Our children, Jim, Dave, Carol and Mark were students there.

Dr. Glenn Reed, the United Presbyterians' Regional Secretary for Africa flew in from Asmara in Eritrea to meet with the Sudan expellies. Our numbers were increasing. Those with children at Schutz gravitated to Egypt. The number of missionaries still in the Sudan was dwindling rapidly. Some were given a month's notice, others were given a week to get out while several were told to pack their bags and be out in twenty four hours. We'd been given a week.

It was agreed that we and several other families should apply for visas to work in the mission in Ethiopia. Harvey and Lavina should plan to locate on the Gila River where the McClures were. We should continue our Murle translation, having the people I'd been working with at Pibor cross over from the Sudan into Ethiopia on foot and work with us there. Pibor was probably a little over a hundred miles away using their trails. Walking this distance was not that difficult for people who had been walking wherever they went since birth. Such were our plans!

But it was not to be! The coveted visa permitting us to live in Ethiopia and continue the Murle translation at the Gila River was denied by the government. We, along with the Adairs, who had worked on the Shullik translation in the Sudan were denied visas into Ethiopia. We had been classified as linguists, which at that time was anathema to the Ethiopian government which was opposed to work being done on vernacular languages. It would take another eighteen months before we'd be granted a resident visa. This would be our "wilderness wandering" before entering the promised land of Ethiopia. The task the Lord would entrust to us would be difficult and sometimes dangerous. God knew what lessons we must first learn before we'd be "fit and meet for the Master's service." Eighteen eventful but trying months went by, months of anxious waiting and uncertainty about the final outcome, before the coveted visa was granted.

During those months, we worked in Egypt on the Murle manuscripts, getting them ready for the British and Foreign Bible Society for printing. We spent months in other African countries as well as in Addis Ababa on an extended tourist visa. Confident that we'd eventually be granted a resident visa, we spent our time in Ethiopia studying Amharic.

Dr. Don McClure worked tirelessly with government officials trying by every means to secure that elusive visa. In the end, it was the royal family's interest in the Mesengo people, that resulted in our being granted a visa on the condition that we open a new work among the people living in the rain forest in Southwest Ethiopia. The personal intervention of the Crown Princess on our behalf opened the door and gave us a new opportunity and tremendous challenge to believe and trust God for the unknowns of His tomorrow. We were to open a new work among a "hidden" people who had yet to hear the precious, powerful saving name of Jesus Christ.

GETTING READY FOR THE
RAIN FOREST

An enormous burden was lifted when our resident visa was finally in hand. Boundless energy was released. All thoughts and prayers now centered on plans and preparations to facilitate our moving into the forest to live among the Mesengo. It would be no easy task.

From my letter, dated November 15th, 1964, we recall some of the many details of preparation required before we could begin our ministry in that forbidding place.

"The day was beautiful again as is every day here in Addis at this time of the year. It'll be quite different in a couple of weeks when we go to our new post, to be known as the 'Godare River Post'.

"What busy days these are. The entire house is in a mess now and we have only straight chairs left to sit on. Most everything has been sacked or boxed. I bought thirty six 10 foot by 12 inch boards for boxing things and they're nearly gone. The saws and hammers have been working overtime.

"This past week we ordered our year's food supply, four local saddles, 2 pack saddles, 8 axes, 8 shovels, 40 grass knives, 6 pick axes, three files, an umbrella tent, two folding chairs, 20 sacks, 12 smaller sacks, 40 yards of sacking, 5 bolts of unbleached cotton cloth, a used umbrella tent... Fortunately, we can go to the office and get money and put it on our account. I guess they know that once we get started the drain on funds will be over.

"It is interesting when you buy a saddle in the native market. You buy the basic seat and then add parts of straps to it until you finally have a complete unit. All of this takes a terrific amount of time and bargaining. ... I just remembered some other items purchased this week. On Monday I spent more than half the day in the junk yard getting an old jeep rear end axle, wheel and tire assembly. This had to be shipped to Mizan Tefari (Ghimmera) later to be put under the "tumble bug", that is, the dirt remover which will go to the Godare for work on the airstrip. I also bought

a used water tank and three small barrels, plus some plastic hose and a gas pump. What a world!

"There is so much to remember. We have check lists which are constantly being revised. Yesterday, while getting hinges and hasps, I suddenly remembered we'd forgotten springs for the screen doors. Remember the time, Pa, when we ordered that Land-O-Lakes powdered milk in Mpls. Well, this time we bought it all right here in Addis ... 8 cases of it. Enough for a year!

"Other activities of the week included two conferences with the Crown Princess and the Crown Prince. The land for our site is being given to us by the Crown Prince. We get a lot of kidding from our colleagues about being so close to the Royal family. The Crown Prince is the oldest son of His majesty, Emperor Haile Selassie I, and next in line for the throne. Mr. Hanna, the mission representative, and I went together. His Highness asked many questions about the Mesengo and then offered to help if we had need, and finally he called in his secretary and asked him to draft a letter to the Minister of the Interior granting us permission for the land and to start work immediately. He's arranging a conference for this Wednesday with himself, the Governor General of the Province and ourselves. It is all quite thrilling for us."

Three weeks after this letter was sent, Lavina, our little boy, Paul, and I were on our way! We had done what we could to be ready. We were trusting God to guide us and protect us from every evil thing. The adventure of what He was calling us to thrilled our hearts. The certainty that He had opened the door and that He finishes well what He begins, gave us courage and strength as we moved ahead leaning heavily upon Him!

CHAPTER FOURTEEN

FINDING THE MESENGO

Before we could open the work, an essential, fact finding survey had to first be made. Letters home to the family told of what the ground survey hoped to find. The partial account of what happened when we actually went in on foot was well reported in the Fall - 1964 issue of the mission's publication, "Ethio-Echo." Here's how the trek was described.

"A rugged journey through heavy undergrowth, forbidding rivers and streams, slippery, moss covered rocks and sloshing mud and rain into the jungle rain forest of Southwest Ethiopia began on October 6, 1964. Four missionaries, a guide, three mules, a donkey and a dozen carriers for tents and food started into the forest. The trip ended two weeks later with a mule abandoned from exhaustion in the forest, and the missionary doctor carried shoulder high on a stretcher by some Mesengo men, concerned for his recovery. The team of missionaries - Dr. Campbell Millar, Ralph Borgeson, Ted Pollock and Harvey Hoekstra - had walked 150 miles in search of a suitable site for the new mission post among the Mesengo people.

"The survey team returned on October 17th wearied by the rigors of the trip but glowing with reports of God's provision and leading. A good site on the Godare River, some fifty miles beyond the last Ethiopian Airlines airfield was chosen. Local officials had offered every assistance and encouragement. The Mesengo people were responsive and friendly. In its report, the survey team made recommendations which the Mission speedily acted upon. These have now been forwarded to the supporting church in America for their approval and implementation.

"As early as 1960 the Mission had its first aerial survey of this area. Now nearly four years later the work will begin. God's leading and provision in the intervening years has been unmistakable. Permissions have been granted. The missionaries are available. The door is open and all the signals read, 'Go, Go, Go'. Yes, He said, 'Go into all the world and preach the Gospel.'

"Every member of the team spoke with grateful appreciation for the privilege of visiting this unique, rain forest area. The journey was made more pleasant by the cool shade of the dense jungle. Hundreds of monkeys greeted the men along the way with angry cries, and often the stillness of the jungle was broken by the sweet melody of an unseen bird deep in the forest.

"The journey was not without its problems. The team soon learned that it isn't easy to change the mind of a mule! The story frequently came to mind of the old mountaineer who said while beating his mule, 'You may be smarter than I am, but you're not stronger!' In the end the team learned that the mule had them licked on both counts! One of the mules refused to move another inch. Nothing could persuade it. With no alternative, it was abandoned in the forest.

"More seriously, on the last day of the trip, Dr. Millar became dangerously ill with an infection that got into his blood stream. Three days earlier he had struck his shin on a hidden rock while crossing a swift stream. Now in a matter of hours he was desperately sick and unable to walk. To go further seemed impossible. And still it was imperative to press on to reach the airstrip some 25 miles ahead. The plane was due in the next morning. As Campbell was lifted from his mule that morning and placed on a cot in a clearing in the forest, we gathered around and knelt in prayer, committing him to God. Perhaps the Mesengos who watched us saw in this simple act a new dimension of life.

"It was midnight when the balance of the party eventually reached the airstrip, for Ted Pollock had walked on ahead to get help and medicine. The journey had been made with carriers and stretcher, and when Campbell grew stronger in late afternoon he was able to again ride the mule. A local official somewhere along the way volunteered his bed for an hour's sleep for the patient. And a medical dresser hurried to meet the party, offering his penicillin. The word had spread quickly and during the night runners came from the little town near the airstrip, wanting to help. When the team arrived that night, a doxology of praise from very tired men was spoken to God. We had learned afresh how utterly dependent upon God we all are. ...

"The survey completed, the missionary family is now moving into the forest where the Mesengo live. The destination is the east bank of the Godare River, some fifty miles from the last airstrip from which supplies will have to be brought in. To be very specific, the exact location for the new mission post is 35 degrees and 3 minutes East longitude and 7 degrees and 27 minutes North latitude, and it is to be called, 'The Godare River Post.'

"The Hoekstras (Harvey, Lavina and their three-year old son, Paul) will travel with five mules and carriers. Paul will ride in a chair on the back of a Mesengo carrier. They'll make quite an impressive safari with their ten chickens for eggs, three rabbits for meat, bush knives, axes, chain saw, boxes of food shaped to be useable for temporary furnishings, and other assorted supplies.

"One of the most precious items will be the little Misavia transceiver. With it the missionary family will be in daily contact with the base station from which supplies can be ordered. Until the Missionary Aviation Fellowship airstrip is ready the small plane will be dropping food from the air along with whatever supplies may be needed. It all calls for a good bit of planning and coordination. One of the first air drops will include two sacks of corn for the fifty Mesengo workmen who will be helping to clear the airstrip Has anyone a bright idea on how one might drop fresh eggs from the air without damage? Someone suggested dropping the hen and letting her produce the eggs later. Both would seem to involve considerable hazards!

"It is hoped that the MAF strip can be completed in six weeks and that by the first of April a strip capable of handling a Dakota plane will be ready. Cutting an airfield out of a jungle forest is no small assignment.

"After the Hoekstras arrive at the site, they will be sending a radio message about the trail which is to be prepared through the forest for the Jeep. When all is ready, Ed Pollock, Jr. and Ralph Borgeson plan to come in with the vehicle and a scraper for use on the airstrip. Ed will continue with the Hoekstras for six or seven months putting up the first buildings. Ralph will return to the base station after surveying the new mission post and marking it."

SERVICES TO BE OFFERED

"The missionaries will spend their first months in tents and temporary stick and grass buildings. From the beginning medical care will be offered, and a trained Ethiopian dresser will be working. The missionary doctor from the base station is to make visits every second month. The following dry season the mission builder, Ted Pollock Sr., (Ed's father) expects to come in to complete the buildings for the post. A school will be opened as soon as buildings and staff are available. It is also hoped to develop agricultural work that will be of benefit in raising the standard of living for the people.

"The Mesengo appeared to be eager for the new mission post to be established for the local chiefs offered the help of their people in clearing a road and airstrip.

'The Mesengo are an intelligent, semi-nomadic people dwelling in clearings they have made in the rain forest. They are widely scattered over an area of 100 miles by 50 miles. They live in simple stick and grass houses, planting and cultivating roughly prepared fields of maize and durra. The soil appears to be productive, but new methods to conserve its fertility and increase its harvests are needed. The Mesengo make extensive use of honey from the wild bees in the forest.

It is their one 'cash crop.' A single Mesengo may have as many as a hundred hives placed high in the trees. The hives are carved from four to five foot lengths of log and hoisted into the trees with vine ropes. Many hives are at least 100 feet high overhead.

"They appear to be a musically inclined people. Many were seen walking on the trails, keeping time with a small stringed instrument they had fashioned with wood and thin metal staves. At their dance, numerous tube-like instruments, made from branches of varying diameters and lengths, were blown upon as one would blow across the neck of a bottle. The music produced was different than anything the team members had previously heard!

"The Mesengo were obviously fond of beads and bright colors. Many were attractively decorated. The men wore leaves and a loin cloth, while the women wore grass and skins or the bark of a tree.

"The survey team was impressed with the apparent friendliness of the Mesengo toward one another. It was not uncommon for carriers who were carrying lighter loads to volunteer to exchange loads with one who had the heavier burden. Men of all age levels shared equally in the work. The team was impressed, too, with the intelligence and resourcefulness the Mesengo showed in coping with the problems they face in living in a rain forest with its lush growth. They have learned how to slash their way through the jungle in an efficient manner which will always be beyond the ability of their foreign guests."

THE NEEDS ARE MANY

"The needs of the Mesengo were apparent. One could not help but remember over and over again the words of Jesus when He said, 'I am come that they may have life and have it more abundantly.' The Mesengo are still waiting to share in that abundant life. We saw many persons suffering from huge tropical ulcers. Apparently shin bone injuries are common in the forest, and with the lack of medical care the slightest injury easily becomes an incurable wound. An improvement in agricultural methods will make for a better diet and better general health. Surely this is part of the abundant life of which Jesus spoke. The needs are genuine and the opportunities and challenges facing the missionary are self-evident. Medical care, education, improvements in agricultural methods, the message of God's love in Christ ... all of these bring the mission to the Mesengo people. Fifteen thousand persons (possibly many more than that) shall have the opportunity to learn of Christ and to share in the abundant life He came to give.

"The challenge facing the Hoekstras is not theirs alone. It comes inescapably to the whole family of God's people. There is a task for each of us in giving, in praying and caring. So, together we shall one day hear a mighty hymn of praise ascend from deep in the rain forests of Southwest Ethiopia. May God grant that none of us shall fail to do his part!"

THE JOURNEY TO THE GODARE BEGINS IN TEPPI

Such was our understanding when Lavina, Paul and I started out from Teppi for the Godare River. On D-day, we flew into Teppi on an Ethiopian Airlines Dakota aircraft. With us were twenty or twenty-five cartons and boxes of supplies. Behind a nearby mud house were our six mules and two horses. They'd been sent over with two mule men by our missionaries in Ghimeera. I'd worked with horses as a farm boy and I'd done a good bit of riding on horses we owned in the Sudan. But to work with mules was something different. I kept remembering the sage advice of an SIM missionary who had a keen sense of humor, George Middleton. He had offered his advice before we left Jimma. He said, "Harvey, be careful for those mules. They are dangerous on both ends and very uncomfortable in the middle." I learned that he spoke as a prophet. Interestingly, we had to teach the Mesengo people to be careful for the rear rather than the front end of the mule. They were fearful of the mouth but had no sense of danger about the rear feet. Their understanding had been shaped by their encounters with leopards, wild boars and baboons!

206

With the help of the mule men, we began loading the cartons. I discovered that those men knew a lot more about mules than I did. A mule has a deceptive way of expanding its girth when the belly band is being tightened. Once finished, the mule relaxes and the band is too lose and the load wants to slip to an unbalanced position. This is never pleasant, but its worse than unpleasant when one has just balanced two baskets of a hundred eggs individually wrapped in papers for protection on the way.

Here's what happened. We'd just about finished loading this one mule with the precious and fragile eggs when the animal looked around at us with a glazed eye, kicked up his heels and caused the load to suddenly tip upside down on opposite sides from what we had intended. Because it was already getting late in the afternoon we didn't examine for damage, but pressed on with the process and then started out. Along with the mules for transport and the horses for riding where we could, we had at least fifteen carriers for the first ten miles down to Metti.

It wasn't until the third morning out that we realized the extent of the damage done to our eggs. Just outside our pup tent the baskets with the eggs were covered with army ants having a feast. Lavina had a painful, painstaking job cleaning up the mess and repackaging the good ones for the rest of the journey. We were learning as we went!

It was after dark when we finally arrived ten miles down the road and found ourselves in Metti. I put up our tent in the dark. It was my first experience in doing so and I paid dearly for my carelessness. About four in the morning a colossal, tropical rain storm descended on us. I had neglected to be sure I knew how to raise and lower the back flap which was designed to cover the small opening with the mosquito covering for fresh air in good weather. The rain came in terribly and I finally had to face it, get out of the tent in my pajamas and forcibly close this opening from the outside. I was drenched and it seemed extremely cold. This was a mistake I didn't make twice!

In the morning, we realized that we'd have to leave some

of our supplies and gear behind in Metti where there were several merchant shops and their families. This would be the last Oromo/Amhara settlement before we went into the forest proper. We arranged to rent an empty room in a decrepit old mud-walled, dirt-floor building. Except for termites and rats, our things could be locked in here safely and the mule men could collect from here for their second trip to Godare. To be sure they brought priority items, I was careful to point out to them the carton with cooking utensils and dishes.

It was well into the morning before we finally pushed off with our motley caravan of mules, horses and carriers. We eventually rounded up twenty men and young boys to each shoulder or put on their head one of the cartons, water tank, radio, live battery and charger or whatever had to go.

UNCUT TRAILS DELAY TREK

We soon discovered that the trail had not been cut. Mesengo promises to have the trail cut for us had been forgotten as soon as our survey team left town! Because the trails were unkempt with low hanging vines, we had to wait for the worst places to be cut back by our men carrying machetes. We learned that Mesengos kept their trails uncut because of their fear that people from neighboring tribes would raid their villages and steal their children.

Because the trails were uncut, we'd be on the way ten days instead of the four or five we'd planned on. There were other surprises too. In fact, we were in the dark about 'most everything going on around us. And we didn't have the advantage of an interpreter guide like on the survey trip. Now we were totally on our own. The only thing the Mesengos knew about us was the word that our survey guide had given them. He'd explained to them that a white missionary, his wife and little boy would be coming in a few weeks to live among them at the Godare. They had promised to welcome us and help us get there. That's just about it! I spoke only two words of Mesengo and we didn't meet anyone who spoke Anuak until several weeks after we'd arrived at the Godare. The Mesengo words I knew weren't all that helpful either. They were "agur gur"—do it quickly! We soon discovered that Mesengos weren't about to be rushed and would do things in their own way at their own pace when they wanted to! But it was great sport and a great challenge. Our hearts were glad and we knew that the Lord was with us and that we were highly privileged to take the good news about Jesus Christ with us. We often wondered how long it would be before we could communicate this fantastic good news.

At the end of this section, I'll quote from a letter I wrote soon after this trip in. When I reread it after thirty years, I was astonished to realize how difficult it had really been. I've always been proud of Lavina for making that trek in there with me. The mission tried to talk her out of it saying she should wait until I had the airstrip finished and we had a shack to live in. She wouldn't hear of it. She wanted to be part of our ministry to the Mesengo from the very beginning. She never once complained about inconveniences except for complaining once or twice about my huge appetite.

Here's the background. In the Sudan I was sedentary, sitting behind a desk translating, using very few calories. My appetite was small and no threat to the food supply available. In the rain forest, I was putting out enormous amounts of energy doing hard, physical work from morning until after dark. I was burning up calories and was always hungry. It was tough to keep enough food on hand and on the table. We depended on airdrops and food was scarce as well as being difficult to prepare because of a lack of cooking utensils or a proper stove on which to prepare the meals. I'll not fault her for chiding me with "tongue in cheek" for eating so much. I remember hearing her say once, "Honey, you never ate this way in the Sudan. Now when we don't have any food you're hungry all the time."

We both lost a lot of weight during those first months before the airstrip was finished. We knew what real hunger pangs are.

MESENGO CARRIERS - SHORT DISTANCES ONLY

But I'm ahead of my story. I told you that we started out from Metti with some 20 carriers. When we started out I had no idea that they'd only carry for a couple of hours and then be returning to Metti. The first time this happened I was dumbfounded.

We had come out of the forest proper and were at a Mesengo clearing where there were scattered stick and grass shacks. Our procession stopped and everyone put their loads down. Lavina and I found some roasting ears of field corn and munched on these while we took the situation in. After what seemed to be a considerable period of time, I gathered that one of the Mesengos there was a local chief or headman and was taking charge. One of our carriers was carrying a heavy 10" by 10" metal box with a padlock on it with hundreds of copper five cent pieces inside. Mesengos wouldn't accept anything other than these five cent pieces for pay. We eventually paid the carriers from Metti each eight or ten of these coins and they left us to return home.

Gradually, people began to pick up pieces of our gear. Men, along with the women, took the larger, heavier pieces. Smaller children would carry something light like an empty water container. Once everything had been picked up, we were on our way. This whole process could take an hour or two.

And that's just the way it went all the way to the Godare. Ten days of it! Only twice did we have some fright. The first time was when the carriers all put their loads down and we saw no other Mesengos or a village in sight. Our thought was — what will we do if they refuse to go further? I don't know what we'd have done. One assurance we had was that our mule men were trustworthy, having come from the Ghimeera mission station.

Well, as you can see, they eventually picked up their loads and took us to where other carriers were available to go on from there.

The trip was challenging and rewarding. Very few people have had such experiences. Looking back I wonder how we dared to do what we did, striking out into the unknown in a forbidding forest with a pretty wife and a three- year-old child. God surely was with us, giving us courage and wisdom to cope.

We'd prepared a special seat for Paul which would fit comfortably on the back of a carrier. The only problem, which he soon discovered, was that Paul would be making the trip looking backward rather than ahead. It didn't take this little three-and-a-half year old guy long to figure out that this was less than satisfactory from his perspective. He had a way to make his feelings evident and it wasn't long before the whole idea was abandoned and Paul was taking turns with me in the saddle looking ahead rather than backwards. Eventually, I found myself walking more than riding and Paul enjoyed the saddle to himself. This was inevitable and as it should be!

DIFFICULT RIVER CROSSINGS AND STEEP HILLS

Crossing the rivers and swift streams was always a challenge. Being dry season most of the rivers were less than hip deep. Even so, occasionally one had to cross over crawling on hands and knees on a log which spanned the swift stream. One river was so treacherous with fast water and slippery, mossy stones that we could barely keep our footing. A Mesengo man carried Paul across and another took Lavina's arm as we both clung to a vine stretched across from bank to bank while we struggled to remain upright.

Sometimes we were able to ride the horses across, but then there was always the steep hill on the other side. Once Lavina questioned whether the horse might make it out of the river and up the hill with her on its back. I suggested she give him a chance, which she did. Unfortunately, the horse became unwilling partway up and gradually backed down into the water, stumbled and sat down with Lavina slipping off into the water. My popularity was at an all time low for some time after that until her wet clothes dried on her body. Wet clothes or not, we kept on moving up one hill and down another toward Godare. Even the monkeys, cautiously sneaking a look as they scampered for safety, were surprised!

The trails were tough to navigate. Often, even in the clearings where growth and brush were always in abundance, hidden stumps knocked one's feet and ankles as the horses made their way through these narrow openings between two stumps. Lavina's legs were badly scarred and black and blue before the ten-day journey ended.

Our last night on the trail we were at a place the Mesengos' called Konkon. There were only a few houses there and people seemed to be scarce. Our carriers insisted that they would go no further. So, using some sort of sign language with someone who appeared to be the head man, we deposited a number of our pieces in a Mesengo stick hut and carried what we could with the few available carriers. We left behind our tent and some other things which we thought we might be able to get along without until, hopefully, our things could be retrieved. To the Mesengos credit, within a few days of our arriving at the Godare, one by one people began showing up, each carrying one of the cartons we'd left behind. Not one piece was lost.

MAF'S FIRST AIR DROPS AT GODARE

That last morning on the trail, I strung up the aerial in the bushes and hooked up our Misavia transceiver to contact MAF in Jimma where they were based 140 miles away. By previous arrangement, they were scheduled to make an air drop or two at Godare that afternoon. I was doubtful that we could make it on time because we estimated it would take another seven or eight hours from Konkon to Godare. Unfortunately, MAF had a heavy schedule and said they had to come in the afternoon or it'd be days before they could make it again. I had no choice but to go on ahead as quickly as possible and leave Lavina and Ed Pollock to come on more leisurely behind me.

I was at the Godare by early afternoon and Lavina caught up within an hour of my arrival. We again strung up the aerial and made contact with MAF. They said they were on the way and that we should listen for the engine of the plane and let them know when we heard it. They were flying up the Godare River from the Bako River and were looking for us. Can you imagine the thrill when we told them on the radio that we heard the plane and when they responded by saying, "We have you in sight and will be making our first drop!"

Mesengos were gathering around rapidly by now and we were concerned that one of the sacks being dropped might fall on one of them. They made two drops, picking up a second load in Teppi. One of the sacks struck the little extension attached to the back of a Mesengo hut where a hen was sitting on its eggs. It was almost too ludicrous to describe! The hen went flying and the eggs were scattered and broken. The woman who owned the chicken was in tears and more than a little upset. So, here I am, a missionary bringing good news, having to comfort a Mesengo woman in a language I cannot speak because of uninvited damage we had inflicted on her.

MAF finished its second drop just after four in the afternoon. A huge tropical rain storm was closing in rapidly as the plane sped away. We searched for the sacks, missed one, and quickly dragged the others into the shelter of a Mesengo grass-roofed hut. The rain came down with a vengeance as we huddled inside trying to keep dry and warm.

When the rain stopped, we still had another eighth of a mile to go to where we'd sleep and begin the clearing for our house in the morning. By the time we covered this distance, it was already becoming dark, as darkness falls swiftly in the tropics. Not only was it getting dark but we were soaking wet from the bushes and brush.

We had no tent because of having to leave it in Konkon for lack of carriers. After the simplest meal you can imagine, we stretched out our sleeping bags on the wet ground, put a single mosquito net up cross-ways over the upper part of our bodies and heads and tried to sleep. A man whose name was Jokjok lit a fire and we eventually fell asleep on the open hillside with the fire burning just off to the side and behind our heads. We were glad that the rain was finished and the night was dry except for the heavy dampness of the hillside and the air itself.

OUR FIRST HOUSE OF STICKS AND GRASS

In the morning at the crack of dawn Mesengos began gathering in sizeable numbers. There must have been fifty or sixty men who showed up. We indicated on our arms that we needed poles for our house so that we could sleep there. Balti, the most powerful Mesengo chief and ritual expert, spoke the word and it was done. Mesengos began carrying in bundles of poles the size of one's arm and about eight or nine feet long. They selected a three foot stump and began constructing our first house. The poles were anchored to the stump which served as a "cornerstone." The poles were laced together with vines. Not a nail was used — there were no nails, in any case. By nightfall a crude, simple but adequate shell of sticks, vines and poles had been put together to become our first house at the Godare. The following day they brought in bundles of grass and roofed it. Unfortunately, the house, although only about 8 by 10 feet, was larger than normal Mesengo huts. Consequently, the roof was a bit too flat and later when the rain fell it leaked like a sieve.

Using the shortwave radio, we requested the mission to purchase a canvas tarp to cover the house. This was eventually gotten in on mules and the problem was solved. I recall, also, that within a few days our small tent arrived from Konkon and we began sleeping at night where it was dry. Our larger tent from Sears arrived much later by mule, but it was there in time for the children to use when they came home from school.

We couldn't speak the language but somehow communicated our needs. One problem was to have a container large enough to hold water for household chores. Balti the chief sent over a huge crock container that held at least 20 or 25 gallons. Normally they used this kind to make beer. Balti not only sent this huge crock over but assigned three young girls to fill it with water every day from the nearby spring.

EARLY DIFFICULTIES CONFIRMED BY LETTER

Before continuing our account of how things went during the early days at Godare, let me share with you a letter written in unvarnished prose less than three weeks after we arrived. It corroborates and confirms the accuracy of my recollection of what we encountered on the trek in.

From a letter written December 18, 1964:

"Dear Dad and Mother,

"Forgive the scrawl. I'm writing this on a small cardboard box on my lap in Teppi. Lavina, Paul and Ed Pollock, Jr. are back there on the Godare River and I'm here waiting for the children. I arrived at 1 a.m. this morning by moonlight and rain — all at the same time! I left home on Tuesday a.m. in the rain and spent 3 1/2 days on the way — got lost in the forest for several hours or I'd have been here earlier. That forest is treacherous.

"The journey out took us five days (travel time not counting the five days waiting as they cut the trail ahead of us). What a trip! About eight or nine rivers to cross — waded them and crossed one on a log. At night the army ants attacked us. Once in a pouring rain I had to get out and lower the back flap on the tent. The trail had not been cut and it was slow going. Vines and ants everywhere. Paul got caught around the neck once and really screamed — poor kid. He got a good neck burn out of it, but it's healed again. Lavina had her legs all scratched and swollen from thorns and hidden stumps. We walked a good bit of the way because the vines were too low. With tennis shoes on we waded the rivers and walked in wet feet and legs most of the way. The worst part of that was to sleep in wet sleeping bags and then dress into wet trouser legs and socks in the morning! Brrr!

"We expected it to be difficult, but it is even more difficult than we had figured. It has rained every night since we arrived. We put up two small shacks with sticks, but they have no roofs. Lavina was cooking in the mud inside the house when I left and bearing up real well. We've been sitting on boxes to eat and using metal camp cooking utensils. Paul manages real well. The chickens survived and the four rabbits. Rex (our dog) became mad after we arrived and I had to destroy him. Rabies are so bad here in Ethiopia. We lost a mule in the river at Godare for 24 hours — too swift for a tired mule!

"The day we arrived, we hooked up the radio. MAF dropped two loads of blankets, sugar, salt, flour, clothes etc. ... a load of corn, also fresh meat and mail. We arrived one hour before MAF came. At 4:30 p.m. we had a mammoth rain. The first days have been difficult and somewhat discouraging, but the worst is now past. The Lord has helped us and we continue looking to Him.

"At night the army ants often attack us. Fortunately, we have Gamexene powder and it drives them off. Boy are they hot! They'll eat you alive if you allow them to. In the forest itself little hot black ants keep falling into the neck. ...

"I should be home two days before Christmas. Carol will be eleven on the 21st on the trail. The trails are now being cut and this makes it easier.

"On our trip in we used over 100 different carriers, six mules and two horses. Paul had a long, long ride and travelled real well after he got used to it. Food is a problem, but I ate fresh roasting ears in the fire most of the way back. Also found an egg in one village and made pancakes. One night I had a cold can of green beans and six wieners from a can. Sorry page is full. Hope to give further picture later. Don't worry about us. The Lord is near and will keep and help. Write soon again. Love, Harvey and family."

CHAPTER FIFTEEN

ON THE
GODARE - TEPPI TRAIL

We'd been at the Godare less than ten days when I had to leave to trek back to Teppi to meet Carol and Mark. Their school vacation from Good Shepherd was beginning and both they and we wanted to be together for Christmas.

I could safely leave Lavina and Paul because Ed Pollock, Jr. was at the Godare. He'd kindly trekked in with us and would be helping us during those first few weeks. Ed was the son of Ted and Dolly, the mission builder family, a sharp, capable young man educated to become an engineer.

During those first days at the Godare, we needed to deal with the basics of how to cook, have water on hand and we needed a way to shower and have a toilet. We were surrounded by twisted vines, bushes and trees. It was a tangled, jumbled mass of ten to fifteen foot growth with hidden stumps which, every day, we kept trying to cut back from the center. Until the mules left for another load from Metti, they were right on top of us. When we pushed out into the entangled mess to dig our pit latrine, it seemed that we were way out there where we wanted it. Later, however, as we kept on clearing back we discovered that the toilet was right in the center of things! We also put up an outside shower by hoisting up an old tank which someone had once used for gasoline to which we attached a sprinkle head. We put a grass enclosure around both the toilet and shower for privacy. A white cloth hanging on the opening indicated that it was occupied. In the shower we laced one inch sticks together for a small platform so that we wouldn't be standing in the mud and so that the water could get away.

Our house had been built on a side hill. The Mesengos never bothered to level the floor. It turned out to be a blessing in disguise because when the heavy rains came and the roof leaked, the water that came through the roof or that came cascading down the hillside went in one side and out the other. Even so, I saw Lavina walking around in the house with tennis shoes sticky with mud more than once those first mornings when she prepared our breakfast.

At first we had no table or chairs, but simply sat on our wooden trek boxes and ate our meals from our laps. When Carol and Mark joined us, we dragged in a 12-inch four-foot log to serve as our sofa. I made a shelf in the kitchen by rail splitting a small 6-inch log. It was all pretty simple living. The floor didn't need to be swept at first because the chickens came in to find whatever might have fallen to the ground when we ate. They never found much but always felt it was worth their effort! Before making breakfast Lavina often had to go around with a small tin can to collect the huge night crawlers which came in overnight. I'd never seen such beautiful bait for fishermen go to waste!

During those first days Lavina cooked on three stones the way the Mesengos did. There wasn't a lot to cook, but what there was had to be done that way. Later we learned to make our own charcoal and she often cooked on a small grill that fit into an empty gasoline tin from which the end had been removed and in which there was a small opening in the side for ventilation.

That was sort of what I left them with when I took off for Teppi. This was supposed to be dry season, but it seemed to rain every night and frequently during the morning and late afternoon hours. It took me three and a half days to return to Teppi. On the way I nearly met with disaster and sudden death or, at best, paralysis.

CAROL AND MARK HOME FOR CHRISTMAS

Carol and Mark were in school in Addis Ababa and itching to see what living in the forest was all about. Carol was eleven and Mark was ten. They flew from Addis to Teppi, about 350 miles, on the Ethiopian Airlines DC3. They were excited to get on their horses and head off toward Godare. It was a fun trip to see their reaction to this new adventure. They were great travelers and explorers along the way. In a few places we discovered wild gooseberries which we enjoyed eating. The baboons and several different kinds of monkeys captivated them.

On our last night out from Godare, we stopped in the village of Konkon. There we made a foolish mistake when we put our tent up in the green grass on the edge of which was a Mesengo chicken cage. Mesengos make cylindrical drums from small stripling sticks which they tie together with vines. These are about the size of a fifty gallon drum. They hang them about five or six feet from the ground, have a pole down from the opening on the end to the ground on which the chickens can walk to get up into this protective cage. Once the chickens are in, the pole is removed and the trap door is fastened. It's a safe place from the wild animals and relatively safe from army ants.

Unknown to us, the grass was infested with lice. We scratched and scratched into the night. And then, to make matters worse, we had a powerful electrical and rain storm. What thunder and lightning! We thought of home at the Godare and wished we were there. This, too, was a mistake we didn't make twice!

The next afternoon Lavina was eagerly anticipating our arrival and had pretty well calculated that we'd arrive when we did. What excitement for all of us to be together in our new forest surroundings. We were overjoyed to have Carol and Mark with us. It was a Christmas vacation that neither they nor we would soon forget. Jim and Dave were in school at Schutz in Egypt and were greatly missed.

Lavina and Paul had done just fine while I was away. There were many new sights and sounds to reckon with. Once Ed, the young man helping us, came running up the hill all excited, exclaiming that he had just seen a gorilla as big as a person. Actually, it was probably one of the big baboons that lived there. Lavina also had an interesting comment to share which Paul had made.

One night she and Paul were in the tent each on a cot listening to the various strange sounds of monkeys and the hooting of a nearby owl. Paul wasn't so sure he liked it there. Finally, he said, "Mommy, do you like living in the forest? Do you like the Mesengo people? Why did we come here? What are we doing here, anyway?"

She said this gave her a good opportunity to explain that we were there because Jesus loved the Mesengo and had sent us there to help them. She told Paul how nobody had ever come to tell them about Jesus. We were going to learn to speak their language and one day we'd begin telling them that God loved them, too, just like He loves us.

She said it seemed to satisfy him and he soon drifted off into a peaceful sleep. Quite an adjustment for a little guy just three and a half years old. True to form for children, he'd learn that Mesengo language quicker than his dad and mom!

BACK ON THE TRAIL TO TEPPI AND SCHOOL

It was so wonderful to be home again and to have Mark and Carol with us for three weeks, but, alas, the days sped by and before we knew it, departure time had come. They'd savored every moment of their short stay exploring and experimenting. With new Mesengo friends they'd had the thrill of swinging across the sharp ravine on thirty-foot rope-like vines securely entangled high in a tree. It only became risky when this cut vine began to dry out and lost its elasticity and strength.

But for Mark and Carol, the vacation was over and it was back to school in Addis. No way to get there except to mount those horses and strike out for Teppi.

The morning we left it was raining and we had to wait until mid-morning before pushing off. We had several Mesengo carriers with us. Around four thirty in the afternoon, we reached a village where we could and probably should have stopped for the night. But we wanted to make up for time lost in the morning and decided to press ahead. Before long we were again in the forest proper. Darkness, inky darkness soon enveloped us. We had to go in single file. Carol and Mark and I were up ahead of the carriers as we could make better time with the animals. In order to encourage the children in the darkness, I suggested we say the "A,B,C's." It was eerie to hear us calling out "A — B — C," each having a turn calling the next letter. (Carol still playfully teases about having to be the last in the procession because she was older than Mark!)

Everything was going along fine in the inky darkness until we came to a river we hadn't reckoned on. It was too deep to wade and the only way across was by crawling over on the log which Mesengos used as their bridge to either side. I fastened the horses and crawled Carol and Mark over, one at a time. It was scary for them alone on the other side of the river. Then I tried to get the horses into the water to have them swim across. I couldn't persuade them to venture it, so I crawled back across on the log to fetch Carol to help me, leaving Mark alone in the darkness. Carol and I tried. She pulled on the bridle and I persuaded from the other end. Nothing worked. Finally, the horse jerked away, kicked Carol in the elbow and started down the trail toward Godare. Carol began sobbing hysterically, "I want my mommy. I want my mommy." I tried to comfort and reassure her. Then Mark, alone in the darkness on the other side of the river, became frightened and was calling me to come and fetch him. Eventually, I had crawled Mark back to the Godare side of the river and had both Carol and Mark with arms around them speaking words of assurance. Carol feared the horse would go all the way back home, but I was confident our carriers who were still behind us would intercept it.

In fact, within fifteen or twenty minutes they appeared with the horse in tow. With their help we all safely crossed the river and by ten o'clock we were at a village where we could spend the night.

Like a typical Mesengo village at this time in the night, it appeared to have no one in it. But an open sided Mesengo shack had warm ashes in it and when I blew on it there was even a live ember or two. We were so exhausted that I let the children lie right on the ground beside the fire where they quickly fell asleep. Around eleven the carriers arrived and I zipped the children in their sleeping bags and we all fell sound asleep. At six thirty in the morning, we cooked a pan of oatmeal for our breakfast and were soon on our way.

We arrived in Metti around eight in the evening. Our hopes were high that we'd be fetched in the morning by Bob Swart who, with Ralph Borgeson, was in Teppi preparing to start out for Godare with the new Landrover. Much to our regret, in the morning we listened to the mission transmission and were told that the Landrover wasn't reassembled yet in Teppi following its transportation by air from Jimma. We were told we'd have to continue on into Teppi with our horses.

This was a real disappointment for weary travelers. We finally reached Teppi, which is about ten miles from Metti and had a reasonably good trail over which vehicles passed occasionally.

We were exhausted, dirty and tired. The children's clothes were hardly what one would like to be seen wearing upon arrival in Addis and at the school. But there was no choice. Ralph Borgeson still talks about how bedraggled we all looked when we arrived after three and a half days on the trail. But our hope was that by the time the children next returned from school for their Easter vacation, we'd have the airstrip ready and they could fly in from Teppi in less than fifteen minutes!

BRINGING IN THE LANDROVER

Bob Swart and Ralph Borgeson agreed to help bring the Landrover into the Godare. When we walked in the first time, we used old Mesengo trails which meandered an estimated distance of some 70 miles. This time, we were going to set our compass and attempt to head straight for the Godare from somewhere near Metti.

Once the vehicle had been put back together, we started out pulling an old two-wheeled trailer on which there was a barrel of fuel, flour for the workmen, a chain saw, axes, shovels, drinking water and food.

The trip to Metti was a breeze. The next morning, we assembled a crew of 25 Amhara-speaking workmen who were hired to help cut our way through the forest and get us across the rivers into Godare. The entire journey would add up to fifty-two miles in seventeen days with 25 men working from sunrise to sunset. It was no small task.

Bob and Ralph and I started out together from Metti. On the second or third day out, we agreed on the direction they were to go. I left them and, taking eight or nine men with me, started out for Godare to begin working on river crossings from that end.

The workmen and I had gone a couple of hours when I began to worry that perhaps Bob and Ralph might not be absolutely sure as to the exact direction they were to take. I decided to leave my men at a clearing in the forest and return to Bob and Ralph to make absolutely certain that we all knew what we were supposed to be doing. They were, of course, surprised to see me, and after our conversations, since it was already getting late in the afternoon, they suggested I have a bite to eat and then start out. The temptation was too great and I agreed. While eating our "picnic" supper, darkness fell and the man who had agreed to accompany me back to my men had disappeared. So, I was on my own.

Before starting out, I cut a three foot stick to have in my hand as I rode my horse. I was soon in the forest proper and it was total darkness. The horse made his way ahead, but I couldn't see a thing. To protect my head I held the stick in front of me to ward off unseen branches. This went on for nearly two hours. I began to fear that I might have bypassed my men so I started shouting like one might call out in the forest, hoping for a response from one of my men. After ten or fifteen minutes of this, I heard what I thought was a faint response. It proved to be from my men. When finally, I emerged from the forest in the clearing where the men had stopped, they were astounded that I had emerged safely out of the darkness. They literally helped me out of the saddle and kept on repeating, "Gobuz sao new (a brave man)." We were soon lying in a row, like cordwood, sleeping. In the morning, I awakened first and when I called them, they all sat up in unison like robots triggered by some hidden switch. It was humorous and too weird to forget readily. Again, my heart was full of praise and thanks to God for protecting me and providing for my every need.

Earlier in the day before Bob and Ralph and I parted company, MAF had flown low over us and dropped a sack of flour. Bob had requested a special drop because it was going to take longer than anticipated. We could see that the trailer didn't have enough food along for twenty five hungry men to sustain them until they reached the Godare. We had worried that MAF might not be able to find us but everything worked out perfectly.

Back at Godare, on the seventeenth day, we had word from the Mesengos that the Landrover was stuck in the mud about five miles from home.

My letter home tells how difficult it was - Feb. 7, 1965:

"The last night we were stuck in the mud, but in the morning with 35 men pushing and pulling and an apron of poles spanning 100 yards of mud we made it. We walked home the last night and Lavina had a nice supper for us. We pulled a heavily loaded trailer through the forest and up and down incredible river banks. It about gives us nightmares to think about it. Bob and Ralph stuck with the car and I came on ahead on the horse and by foot to take care of the air drops. After a night at home, I went back to meet them. We used compasses and met in the middle of the shortcut. In places the forest was so thick I had to crawl on hands and knees to follow the path of the baboons. It was a happy afternoon when I

met the men. *Fortunately, we had rain only two nights out. But that forest was so thick that it took 25 men to cut through it. You simply cannot imagine it.*

"Lavina was home alone here for ten days and did well, but found it plenty difficult ... unable to talk to anyone except Paul and lots of curious people peering in. It wasn't easy, but I admire her for her courage. Few women would do that!"

REMINISCING

As work on the station progressed, I often thought of that night when we four men had arrived at the Godare on that first survey trip. We had gone as far as our government permission allowed, to the banks of the Godare River. We had seen at least two other favorable possibilities for a mission station, but here at the Godare the need seemed greatest. There was no medical care available. There was no school. And this was where the most important Mesengo, chief Balti, lived. Preliminary conversations that first afternoon indicated he was friendly and would not be hostile to our coming.

I thought often of that fateful night at the Godare. We four men were sitting in the darkness under the leaking roof of that open-sided, dilapidated long house in which Mesengo men would gather. We had a flickering candle and were listing the pros and cons about opening our work at Godare. The leaking roof and falling rain along with sheer exhaustion didn't make me overly optimistic that it could be done. I argued that to be at Godare we'd have to have an airstrip for MAF. I asked how an airstrip could be built in so dense a forest area. The other sites closer to Metti seemed much more desirable. But it was Ted Pollock who said, "Harvey, you can do it. You can bring a Landrover in here to help with the buildings and the construction of the airstrip. We can cut our way through the forest and bring it in safely. It's not impossible."

Eventually, we agreed to think about it again in the daylight. We prayed together, blew out the candle and tried to sleep, but no decision had been made. We didn't know then what we'd be recommending to the mission upon our return.

Daylight soon arrived. The sky was clear and the sun was shining. My mood was much more confident now, it seemed. Soon twenty-five or thirty Mesengos came, and we asked them to cut their way into the forest going down the slight incline toward the south from where we had slept. These men had short, razor-sharp, two-bladed knives which they carried at their waist in a protective leather shield. They could cut their way through the dense foliage and vines like cutting butter. They moved straight ahead and every fifty feet or so they'd cut off to the side for twenty-five or thirty feet from the center line. They did this until they had gone into the forest about 700 yards. It was apparent that if the vines, trees and stumps could be dealt with, the land was such that a plane would be able to land. The task would be stupendous, but it could be done.

With that promising information in hand, the decision was unanimous. Godare was the place God would have us open up the new work for Him among the Mesengo.

It was a wise decision, confirmed by the mission and never doubted during our years in Ethiopia.

CHAPTER SIXTEEN

EARLY DAYS AT GODARE

Almost from the moment we arrived, we began treating sick people and bandaging their wounds. People came in with huge, painful tropical ulcers on their shins or almost anywhere on their lower legs. Some struggled to make it leaning on a walking stick, and others, unable to make it on their own, were carried. Even before one looked up, you knew that someone with a longstanding ulcer was approaching. The stench was nauseating. These poor people had had no medical care. Simple wounds frequently became tropical ulcers. They covered these with leaves tied by thin vines, but the pus just oozed out.

We soon ran out of bandages and requested women's societies in our churches for rolled bandages. Before long, the word spread and folks came from considerable distances. You could tell who had been at our back door by the clean, white bandages they were sporting. What a relief it must have been to them to have the pain eased and the putrefying sore gradually becoming smaller and smaller. Some, however, were so large and of such long standing that they had become incurable. One young lad named Ojatiin, the first Mesengo to be baptised, was still wearing a bandage fifteen years after we'd started with him.

At first we treated people right outside the opening to our stick house. Flies and the danger of infections for ourselves dictated that we put up a small shack to be our first clinic. We dubbed it "Godare Medical Arts Building."

People came from great distances as well as from nearby villages. Early one morning, we heard someone coming down the hill to our house wailing and crying. She was one of chief Balti's wives. He'd beaten her over the head with a stick and she had a nasty wound that I attempted to stitch shut with a straight needle. This woman became quite friendly and appreciative and when we began having gatherings for worship, she came frequently. She knew hardship and sorrow. Perhaps her most devastating experience was when Balti, in a drunken rage, picked up his heavy rifle and shot and killed her son, already a young man, right in front of her eyes. The Mesengos could be cruel when under the influence of their fermented honey water.

SEWING ON A FINGER

One morning only a few weeks after we'd arrived, just as we were finishing our breakfast, Balti came in with a real medical emergency. He had brought a young boy in his early teens whose finger had been nearly severed. They were working on the airstrip that morning and this young lad was innocently standing with his hand on the stump on which a couple of men were digging and chopping out the roots with pick axes. Mesengos weren't accustomed to these long handled instruments and miscalculated. The young boy's forefinger was chopped right through the bone with only a little flesh and skin holding it on. We couldn't speak the language yet so I indicated that we'd have to throw the finger away. The old chief shook his head and moved the finger to the position it had before the accident.

At that stage, I called to Lavina and said, "Honey, bring me a pan of water, a darning needle and some thread." I took the needle and fished out the crushed pieces of bone from this terrible injury and proceeded to sew the finger back on. No anesthesia was available but, stoically, he withstood the pain and never cried. Then we needed a splint of some sort to stabilize the finger. We had nothing. The only suitable board out of which to cut a splint was the plywood cover of the rabbit box in which we'd brought our three rabbits. I cleaned this up, positioned it under his hand and forearm. We bandaged it carefully, leaving a small opening for air, gave the boy an injection of penicillin, prayed (in English) for him and sent them home. When they next returned, it looked just terrible. My stitches had all putrefied and the finger was deadly pale. I pinched the fingernail and found that there was still blood there indicating the finger was still alive. I re-bandaged it, continued to give penicillin and prayed for God's miracle. In about six weeks, the gaping wound had closed, the severed bones had fused and the last bandage was removed. The finger was stiff, but it was where they wanted it. I later realized that Mesengos have a strong aversion to deformities of any kind. That was why the chief wanted the finger saved if at all possible.

This story has a marvelous conclusion. That young man became interested in the Gospel, became a believer and was baptized. He attended classes in school and learned to read the Bible, albeit haltingly, in Amharic. As a young man he loved to preach in the villages. I can still picture him holding his hand with that finger which never bent again in the air and calling out, "Gopan omo mo!" (There's just one way)

Years later this same young man, named Roket, by now a married man with three children, was selected by the Mesengo Christians to be ordained with authority to baptize. When I fell ill with severe hepatitis, Roket was chosen to minister to those who were coming to faith and needed to be baptized and nurtured in their newfound faith in Christ.

During the first months before the airstrip was completed, I had to be the doctor, nurse, dentist and midwife! Lavina was a great help as we tried to minister to human need. We were surprised at how proficient we became at recognizing the various kinds of diseases and what kind of treatment or medicine was required. We prayed much to the Lord for wisdom and that He not allow us to make serious errors in judgment. We were consciously aware of our total dependence upon God and trusting Him was our joy and comfort.

WORKING ON THE AIRSTRIP

Ed Pollock, Jr., was a tremendous help to us during those first weeks. He was strong, energetic, and intelligent with an engineer's perspective. He was able to take charge of the work on the airstrip during the times I was trekking between Godare and Teppi.

It was a source of encouragement and assurance for Lavina to have him there when I was away.

We began the work on the airstrip with considerable enthusiasm. Mesengos began clearing back the brush from their old clearing in what was to become the center of the airstrip. As the brush was cut back it became apparent that these former clearings were alive with stumps, both large and small. Every stump had to be dug out at the roots, dragged away and the hole filled in with dirt. For the first ten days, everything looked promising, but then the Mesengos began to show up late and, eventually, they just didn't appear. Having no idea of what an airstrip would look like and with no realization of its importance, the incentive to work wasn't there. Mesengos felt no need for the money we offered them as they felt no need for things money could buy.

It became apparent that we'd never build an airstrip depending on Mesengo labor. What to do?

How relieved I was when the workmen from Teppi and Metti who had helped bring in the Landrover, offered to help build the airstrip for hire. With this crew things began to look much more promising. What a joy to see the daily progress. Compared to work put out by Mesengos, these men were light years ahead!

It was an enormous task. Other huge trees were also being worked on. Stumps of every size were dug out. We'd pay children a few copper five cent pieces for small stumps the size a child might tackle. I sometimes felt that the children had it over the Mesengo men on jobs like that. They let us down occasionally too. I remember one little guy asked for an axe so that he could cut out a stump which we had identified along the airstrip the day before. He disappeared with his axe and in about an hour came back to collect his three coins. That afternoon, riding along that side of the strip with the Landrover, I discovered the stump was still there. He made amends by cutting out an additional stump in due course. He and I both learned something useful that day!

The young men loved to ride in the Landrover and they were a great help volunteering to help drag logs and stumps off the airstrip for the thrill of the ride. They were a great help too in digging out and removing the stones from the central area of the strip where the incline also had an undulation. We dug out hundreds of tons of rock. Interestingly, they were hexagonal in shape and lay on the slant in clusters of eight or ten as if they had been placed there. They made excellent stones later for the foundations of our permanent buildings. When professional builders eventually arrived at Godare they said they had never worked with nicer stone.

I should mention, too, that we learned which trees were worth saving for their lumber. The dampay tree was the one of choice. It was soft, dark-colored wood with a beautiful grain to it. We cut hundreds of logs from trees we felled, planning eventually to have a saw mill and make them into lumber.

My chain-saw was the largest that Sears sold at that time. It was roaring every day. I always had a Mesengo with me to watch and warn me which way a tree or trees might fall. He stood right beside me and would tap me on the shoulder if he thought there was something I should be aware of. Sometimes trees were entangled in vines and before a tree could be persuaded to fall all four or five had to be cut. It was only when the last, key tree was sawed off that they all fell together. The tangled mass of trees and vines on the ground became impenetrable. Sometimes we'd have to tackle these from the lower end of the airstrip to get at them. I marvel and often praised God then and even now that we never had a serious, close call. I wore out three chains to a point where they couldn't be resharpened. The metal part one would normally resharpen was gone! This represents an enormous amount of work and exposure to possible accidents. But the Lord who mercifully heard our prayers was watching over us daily and blessing as He prospered our efforts.

But there was more to do than build the airstrip and run a small clinic. The Mesengos were hungry. It was a bad year for them. The rains had come early and rotted out the roots they'd normally dig out in the forest for food. They depended on these as the amount of corn and dura (sorghum) they grew was minimal. The year we arrived, we found many of them hungry and some of them would likely have starved had we not been there. I recall Raanki coming to me one morning with his four little children, lining them up in front of me and saying that they'd all starve to death if I didn't help him. Their stomachs were distended and bloated from eating grass. He was obviously telling the truth.

We began having shelled corn dropped to us by MAF. Like everything else dropped, the contents were double sacked in burlap bags. If the out sack broke, it was hoped that the inner sack would do what was intended. We flew in many sacks of shelled corn to feed the hungry as well as food for ourselves. Normally, we tried to get the Mesengos to provide some work or service for the small tins of corn we gave out to ward off their hunger. To them it must have indicated something of the love of Jesus Christ that we were concerned for them in this way.

THE MULE MEN RETURN WITH SUPPLIES

You'll remember that we had to leave some of our supplies behind in Metti and that I had pointed out to the mule men which cartons were most important for them to bring on their next trip in. Once the mules were a bit rested, they had returned to Metti for a second load. The two horses stayed behind with us at Godare. With six mules they should be able to bring in most of the essentials.

After a week had passed, we began hoping every day that the mules would arrive with our things. You can imagine our disappointment when finally they showed up with only two mules rather than six. The other four had been left behind in Metti and were either sick or dying. And, instead of bringing the carton with the urgently needed cooking utensils and dishes, they came with two folding chairs, which we discovered we really didn't need, a couple of copper *tishes* (water tubs for washing clothes by hand) and some other things which I've long since forgotten. We were dismayed! Lavina would have to get along with just that boyscout camp cooking set another two weeks at least.

Eventually, when the third trip was completed, we had the things we needed including the cooking utensils, dishes, a portable oven and some flour. You would have laughed to see how happy we were. That very day, Lavina mixed up some bread and the next morning, I assembled the oven, lit a fire, arranged for the oven to hang from some sticks so that it was positioned correctly over the fire and watched the bread bake through the glass window in the door. We didn't have bread tins, so Lavina put the dough in the tin cups of the boyscout set. There we were, grown missionaries, on our hands and knees watching the bread bake in our new, little portable oven. When finally it had baked and was cooled sufficiently for us to eat it, we had the most tasty cup of morning coffee with snacks that anyone can possible imagine. Never had bread tasted so good. Far better than the choicest ice-cream cone, or so it seemed to us that memorable day!

Our letter home, dated February 19, 1965 provides the backdrop on why we were so excited at that time:

"Things are improving steadily. When we look back on the nightmare of those first weeks, we shudder. I don't think folks will ever really understand how difficult it has been. Lavina was telling me last night that during the period I was gone she went to bed hungry many nights. There just was no food here. Then too,

without meat, we felt that empty spot even after we had eaten rice or beans. Now with the garden giving us beans, lettuce, radishes and spinach things are much better. We really lost weight these past weeks. Lavina grabs at least 5 inches of extra dress in the middle and I have 5 inches of extra belt. I guess that means we were both too heavy before too! ...

"Our view here is really tremendous. We overlook the rain forest in the valley and then up a mountain range about six or eight miles off. The scene changes constantly with smoke and haze. During the night the valley fills with fog and in the morning the fog slowly lifts with a beauty all its own. One day this will be a beautiful place.

"The Mesengo people are friendly, but more like Nuer in the Sudan than Anuak. They are fiercely independent and happy to live without help from the foreigner. They do not like to work yet either. We are reminded that only the miracle of the Holy Spirit will ever cause them to believe. The power of heathenism reigns here, but Christ, I am sure, will conquer one day.

"The main chief of the tribe is a mile from our home. He also functions as the main witchdoctor. I saw him sacrifice a chicken and sprinkle a whole family with its blood a week ago. The message of Christ's atonement should be easily understood here."

Lavina had many unique and interesting experiences trying to provide under less than ideal conditions. On another occasion when I was away, she'd boiled a pan of coffee on her three stones and was just waiting for it to settle so she could enjoy it. About that same time, Odi, a Mesengo neighbor lady that we later got to know quite well and who lived just above us on the hill, came sauntering down, smelled the coffee and said, "Uum, smells good" and proceeded to take a good drink from the pan that Lavina had been patiently waiting to cool! We often laughed about that one.

A letter written home, dated March 14, 1965 tells us about my experience trying to build our interim house:

"These last weeks we have been busy rebuilding our house. The old shacks have been torn down, and in their place we have two nice stick and grass roof houses. They seem palatial to us, but, actually, they are just straight 3 to 4 inch sticks with a 6 foot 3 inch wall and a grass roof. We plan to put grass around the outside too to make it more fly and mosquito proof. The floor is still loose dirt, but we will soak it down and then try to pack it. The one building is 22 by 13 feet and the other is 13 feet square. We have the living room and the dining room planned for the long one and the other one will be kitchen. I made a nice board table in the kitchen with three legs down into the dirt about 18 inches. Around our dining room table we have some new furniture. I cut four 18 inch logs yesterday, sawed them into 17 inch lengths and they are gracing our table now serving as dinner stools. We have the two aluminum chairs in the living room, and I cut 20 inch logs into 26 inch lengths for tables in front of each window opening. For our book case, I have two boards on four logs in which we cut grooves to make them fit like a single log. Things are looking up now. And with the strip ready soon we'll be getting our refrigerator in and will be able to have meat regularly. ...

"Well, we just finished a nice supper with hot dogs from a tin and buns and beans with nice chocolate cake for dessert. Not bad!"

MAF MAKES FIRST LANDING GODARE

It was the 16th of March, 1965, when MAF made its first landing. We were so eager for them to come, but I felt uneasy and nervous about the responsibility to say that we felt the strip was ready for inspection and landing. What if we were still some days away from being ready when MAF's pilot would arrive on foot to check it out prior to okaying it? If the strip should prove to be needing a lot more work on it, we wouldn't want him to waste his time while we did work that should have been done before he arrived. We discussed these matters on the mission radio. Tom Frank, a MAF pilot, and Hugh Beck, a MAF engineer/mechanic trekked in from Teppi and gave their approval. I was greatly relieved. The next day, Bob Hutchins flew in from Jimma to make the first landing.

What a day of celebration and apprehension it was. We were excited that the moment had arrived, but we were worried about the safety of our strip for that very first landing. Tall trees still surrounded the strip. The approach on the lower end had tall, forbidding trees that would make a landing tricky and perhaps make it impossible to take off. These were some of the thoughts when the fateful moment arrived. Mesengos had heard the plane and several hundred were racing to get to the airstrip to see it happen. We were worried that someone might run across the strip not knowing the danger involved.

Bob circled the field several times testing it from either end. Once he touched down softly in the direction he would be going when he'd have to take off. He was in the air again and for a moment we wondered, would he return and make the landing or fly back to Jimma because more work was required. What joy to see him make the big circle and head back for the field. He made a perfect landing, but when he opened the door of the small plane, I could tell that he, too, was nervous and glad he'd made it safely. Our prayers thanking God for safety in all things had special significance for all of us that milestone day!

After Bob landed we all walked the strip from one end to the other. Bob felt he needed more clearing on the lower end before he could safely take off. Almost immediately Balti ordered every available man to go down to the lower end and cut as many trees in the clearing as the pilot asked for. That day the Mesengos worked as they may never have worked before. Trees were falling left and right. By late afternoon Bob said he could now fly out safely and that the men could quit. We all tried to make it abundantly clear how happy and thankful we were for the crucial help the Mesengos gave us that day.

In the morning, Bob made several trips to Teppi to fly in supplies. Highest priority was a wood burning cook stove! And he flew in food supplies to cook on it. We were beginning to live. He even flew in our kerosene burning refrigerator. Bending the side panels we could just fit it into the plane. A new day had dawned. We knew also that we could now get out in case of illness or danger. The essential requirement for the success of our mission had been accomplished. We were in touch with the outside world. MAF could fly us to Teppi in less than fifteen minutes and all the way to Jimma in a little over an hour. How we thanked God for MAF. Without their services, the work among the Mesengos could not have been done from Godare. They were God's provision to make our ministry feasible.

Our letter home dated May 2, 1965 tells of the difference MAF was making:

"Our airstrip is completed and is a first class strip, 45 yards by 600 yards of smooth surface. The plane has been in here more than a dozen times since it opened on the 16th of March.

"We hauled four loads from Teppi this week, including barrels of stuff, kerosene, cement etc. It is hard to realize that it took us ten days of fighting thorns, ants and rivers coming in, when we can now make four trips in less than three hours, including loading and unloading. We never cease being thankful for MAF."

FRANK AND GLADYS KIEFT ARRIVE AT THE GODARE

Within a few days, MAF flew in Franklin and Gladys Kieft, our dear friends from Grand Haven Michigan. They'd been helping at Ghimeera for several months while waiting for our airstrip to be completed. We met them at the plane and willing Mesengos helped transport their luggage and other supplies to the back opening of our house. I shall never forget our joy when Lavina and I joined hands with theirs under the tree and lifted our hearts in praise and thanks to God.

Almost immediately we cleared a spot just below our grass house and put up their tent. They lived in that little tent until they left early in June. They not only brought willing hands to work, but Frank brought with him a tremendous testimony of God's leading. Wherever he travelled, Frank shared his story. I have heard it in many countries and in many different settings. It's a marvelous testimony.

*****

Frank was born in 1906 on a farm in Michigan. He was the oldest of ten children. They went to Sunday school and church occasionally, but it wasn't a regular thing. They went to school in the country. Frank says that when he'd finished the sixth grade, his teacher said, "You don't need to come back next year. *We cant learn you anything, anymore.*" That's all the formal education Frank ever had. Spelling and writing were always difficult for him, but he was extremely intelligent and had the mind of an engineer. I discovered there was almost nothing that he couldn't do, improvise or figure out when a need arose. He was a tremendous person to have as a volunteer.

His testimony was so genuine and honoring to God. Basically, this was how he expressed it:

FRANK KIEFT'S TESTIMONY

"I was the oldest of ten children. When I was twenty years old I planned to build my own house and get married. I was strong and ambitious and didn't feel any need for God's help. I didn't want any preachers shouting at me. I could make it on my own.

"About that time, my mother was desperately ill and taken to the Muskegon hospital for surgery. She had a bowel obstruction and was full of poison. After the surgery, my dad called home and said that if we wanted to see mother alive once more, I should bring all the children with me and come to the hospital. The doctor had said she wouldn't make it through the night.

"With the help of a neighbor woman, the kids were dressed up and I took them all in our 1926 touring Ford to the hospital. I remember walking past my mother's bed and feeling as if a powerful hand was on my neck saying, 'Take a look and go home.'

"The neighbor lady again helped get the children to bed. The youngest one was only two years of age. I found myself unable to climb the stairs to go to bed. Instead, I found myself circling the old pot-bellied stove. I went around it three times and went out into the kitchen, fell on my knees at this wooden chair and cried like a baby. At that chair I promised God that if he'd bring my mother home from the hospital so that she could raise her children, I'd do anything He asked me to do the rest of my life.

"In the morning, the phone rang. My dad called from the hospital and said, 'Ma made it through the night'.

"She lived another 35 years and raised her children.

"I'd promised God I'd do anything he asked me to for the rest of my life if He'd bring my mother home alive. At that time, I had thought that meant I'd have to stay out of trouble and attend church on Sundays. I had no idea of how God would challenge me to trust Him and the blessings He had in store for me. ... I often felt overwhelmed when asked to do something in the church, but each time I had to go back to my promise and say, 'God I promised I'd do anything you asked me. I can't do this by myself and you'll have to give me the grace and power to do it. ...' That promise I made at that kitchen chair has been on me all my life. I have to be available to God. .... I stand amazed at what God has done. ... I'm only a 'farm boy', but God has poured blessings into my life beyond anything I could have imagined. He's given me responsible positions in the church world and in the business world. He's taken me around the world several times where I've been privileged to share my testimony. He's given me financial success so that I've been able to help the mission programs of the church. ... I can only say with the writer to the Ephesians as we find it in chapter three, verse twenty, 'He is able to do exceeding abundantly above all we ask or think.' "

What a testimony to God's grace, goodness and power! How frequently God has blessed Lavina and me, personally, through this humble servant. For Frank it all began with a promise made as a young man at a kitchen chair. For me it began with a promise I'd made as a young boy in a hospital bed. Whenever Frank talked about that kitchen chair, I thought about that hospital bed. Frank made his promise on his knees at a wooden chair, I made my promise in that hospital bed. Frank had said to God, "...I'll do anything you ask me to do for the rest of my life." I had said, "...I'll try to be a preacher of the Gospel."

Frank and Gladys and Lavina and I, with our children, were in Ethiopia because of those commitments made so many years earlier. Each of us had surrendered our lives to God trusting Him for whatever He had for us to do in His tomorrow. How marvelous to be available to Him! How wonderful are His ways! Ephesians 3:20.

We frequently spoke together of the marvelous ways of God in our lives. When the heat of the day had subsided and the cool, damp evening air moved in around us, there was time to share. On more than one occasion I'd read one of our favorite chapters from the Bible. Psalm 103 was high on the list.

In the nearby forest, the monkeys would call back and forth. A forest owl would plaintively hoot and call. Occasionally, a rat ran slowly across the rafters. Eventually the little midges and mosquitos became intolerable and we each went for the protection of our mosquito nets. We knew that God had blessed us through another day. We'd be safe in the night because we knew that He "neither slumbers nor sleeps." God be praised for His manifold mercies!

Worship in a Mesengo clearing

Mesengos brought in knotted strings
indicating new believers

CHAPTER SEVENTEEN

"KNOTTED STRINGS"

It happened by the light of a flickering candle. Lavina and I were sitting there in our stick shack trying to read a little by the inadequate light of the candle. We couldn't sit there very long because the mosquitoes were working on us. We had no doors or windows, just openings. During the day Mesengos crowded the doorway and leaned in at the window openings, curious to know what was going on. Only gradually, we taught them with sign language that whenever we ate, we wanted them to back off. They got the message and would move back twenty or thirty feet, still straining to see what they could as they shared their observations with animated speech and gestures explaining to each other what they thought was going on. But as soon as we were off our trek boxes indicating the meal was over, they came storming back. Once even one of the mules came in to investigate. And, inescapably, the chickens checked the place out on a daily basis. No brooms needed!

BY THE LIGHT OF A FLICKERING CANDLE

But now it was evening time and quiet. I was reading from a small book written by Joy Ridderhof, founder of Gospel Recordings, telling how God had led her through illness to establish that ministry. As I read her story of how God was blessing the use of disk records to reach people in remote areas, I turned to Lavina and said, "Honey, if we're going to reach this tribe, we're going to have to use those records." It was a simple statement, but was to have profound significance in shaping our ministry and the rest of our lives.

RECORDING OUR FIRST MESSAGES

When Kathy Hofmeyer, the GR recordist, arrived by MAF plane to spend a week with us at Godare, we had with us on the station a Mesengo who was completely bilingual in his own language and Anuak. In fact, we were never really sure whether he should be called an Anuak or a Mesengo. He was an ideal informant for me because I spoke Anuak and understood it well from my Sudan experience.

One of the interesting aspects of this effort was that Orac, this informant, was not a believer. The question was, "Could we use a non-believer to communicate the message of God's salvation effectively using the voice of one who did not know Jesus Christ personally?" My reasoning was that we would use his tongue like we use a typewriter key. We would look to God to be in control. We believed it would be honoring to Him. In any event, we had no alternative. I couldn't speak the language, that's for sure. There were no Mesengo believers at that stage. Theoretically and perhaps theologically it shouldn't be possible. But in practice it worked and for that we praise God and feel certain Orach was His provision when we needed such a person most.

We prepared and recorded a dozen 3 1/2 minute messages to fit the length the records could accommodate. We began working from prepared GR scripts, but I felt a need to try to communicate more effectively from within the world view of the Mesengo. I wanted, from his perspective, to be able to express in different ways why Jesus Christ was good news for him. It was a great challenge — our one opportunity during those seven days to do it right. We discarded GR's prepared script and wrote our own messages in the light of what we knew about Mesengo beliefs. We prayed earnestly for the Holy Spirit to direct our thoughts as we worked out the new messages. It was a great week. When Kathy left she said, " I can't remember a time when I've ever experienced such leading of the Holy Spirit in the attitude and availability of an informant like I have this week in the way Orach helped us express these messages."

Orach soon disappeared into the forest to return to his distant village along the Anuak border. I don't believe I ever saw him again. I've often wondered if he ever came to faith in the Christ about whom he spoke so clearly and eloquently on those records.

Kathy returned to the states and the tapes were mastered and became phonographic disks in Glendale, California where GR is based. More than a year passed before the first records and our heavy army surplus record players arrived at Godare. We began using them, but by then it was already 1967 and furlough time. Larry and Betty Zudweg and their two girls would build our permanent house while we were away and hold down the station in our absence. Part of the time the Kiefts would be back helping them. Lavina and I would be visiting churches in many parts of America telling the story of how God had led us to the Mesengo and how we needed their prayers and support for the challenge that lay ahead.

A NEW POSSIBILITY WITH CARTRIDGE PLAYERS

During that furlough, we were living with our family in Holland, Michigan in an RCA Mission house. It was a busy life and we had only a nodding acquaintance with our neighbors. One of these neighbors would have a tremendous impact on our future ministry.

Early during our furlough I was preaching on a Sunday morning in the Fourth Reformed Church just down the street from where we lived. In my message I told how we were going to be using records because it was a way we could multiply ourselves and the occasions when the message of Christ could be proclaimed. I explained how our stations among the unreached tribes in Ethiopia were one-family stations. The Mesengo were a widely scattered tribe, living in isolated clearings separated by an hour or two's walk. They were spread out over an area of nearly five thousand square miles of hills, valleys and rivers. It would be a difficult tribe for one family to reach for Christ. Gospel records could be carried by Mesengo believers to places beyond the missionary's reach.

The only problem was that the needles quickly dug down into the record grooves and the voice became distorted sounding like Donald Duck! But I went on to explain, "It's the only means we have to extend our reach and proclaim the good news of Jesus Christ in the language of the people."

Unknown to me, God was at work in that congregation that morning. After the service while finishing our noon meal, the phone rang. It was my neighbor, Dr. Ron Beery, who taught physics at Hope College and directed the choir at Fourth Church. He said, "Say, I caught a vision while you were speaking there this morning. I wonder if I could come over and talk to you sometime."

Later that afternoon he shared how when I was speaking about those records and their limitations, he was recalling his meeting earlier in the week with Dr. Ted Ward, a communications specialist at the university in Lansing. Dr. Ward had been sharing with Ron about a new child's toy just appearing on the market. It was a two-track cartridge player powered by flash-light batteries. They had been talking about its possible potential for educational programs.

Ron said that as I shared in the church, he began to think of the possibility of these children's cartridge players being adapted to do what the records were intended to do. The existence of such a cartridge player was news to me. I was intrigued and could see the great value of the message being put on a cartridge like that where it would retain its fidelity. And, it appeared that the beauty of these players was that they were light-weight, inexpensive and could be powered with flash-light batteries. Ron's question was "Do you think this kind of device would be of use in your kind of ministry?"

As I recall it, my response was, "Ron, you may have the answer we are looking for." I encouraged him to pursue his vision and urged that he share with me all he learned. Praise be to God! I recall saying to Ron at one stage, "Ron, you may soon find yourself so busy you'll not have time to teach full time at Hope College." That moment came earlier than either of us could have anticipated at that time.

Before we returned to Ethiopia, Ron had formed Portable Recording Ministries. As I recall it, he had three gifts of $500.00 each to put toward the purchase of the first thirty cartridge players. We contributed an additional $500.00 from a special gift for which we received the donor's permission to designate it for this purpose. We returned to Ethiopia six months later with the first 15 cartridge players. The other 15 went to our friends, the Swarts, working among the Galub people at the Omo. We were making history! We had the first "on-line" cartridge ministry anywhere in the world to proclaim the Gospel.

CASSETTES REPLACE CARTRIDGES

Within less than eighteen months, Phillips Corporation in the Netherlands perfected the cassette and were producing a small battery operated unit powered by four c-cells. For our purposes it was a gigantic improvement over the cartridge players. Very soon, these earlier units became obsolete and we were in a growing cassette ministry which later became known as "Teppi Tapes" and was based in the town by that name to which we had moved in efforts to reach additional language groups in that area.

MESENGOS RESPOND TO "THE BOX THAT TALKS"

During those early years the Mesengos came from all directions to see what was happening in their forest. They had never seen so large an open field as was the airstrip. They had never seen a saw which was able to take logs and turn them into planks. They had never seen bricks or concrete. They had never seen white people close up, and most of them had never heard of people who looked strange like we did. They came to see for themselves. Some, of course, came because they were ill and knew they would find help.

For whatever reasons, we felt God was bringing curious Mesengos to us so that we could minister to their needs and share the good news of Jesus Christ with them.

On many occasions, once their curiosity had been satisfied, we'd sit with a group of Mesengos on the hillside in our yard or almost anywhere at all, put down a cassette player and let them hear this fantastic good news about Jesus Christ in their own language by one who spoke as they did. I wish you could have been there to see their reaction. Frequently someone would hold his or her face tightly, turning the head from one side to the other to hear more clearly. Some spoke back to the voice coming from the "box that talks". They were exclaiming, "Tia" (I hear you) "Moko nyun" (It's no lie) or "Yang jet" (It's sweet). It was marvelous to behold. They were hearing the saving message of God's salvation. Mind you, there were no believers yet, but one day there would be because we knew from the Bible that "Faith comes by hearing" and "hearing by the preaching of Christ." It was happening before our very eyes and God keeps His promises that His Word will not return to him empty.

Sometimes in that kind of setting someone would ask to take the player home. They'd point across the river toward the mountains and say, "We live back there behind that mountain. We want them to hear this good news that we have heard. We'll return this 'box that talks' to you after they've heard."

What more could one ask? We'd show them how to put in a cassette and how to turn it over when it stopped talking. We told them that when the voice no longer spoke (the batteries would be dead) they should bring the "radioni" back.* In that distant village where this missionary's feet could not reach, the Gospel would be clearly heard. It could happen because of technology God had led people to develop in our time which we were harnessing in this unfinished task. What an exciting day to be alive and involved in Christ's mission to the ends of the earth. Our hearts were glad and we praised God often.

At that time there were still no believers. Players were being carried hither and yon by non-believers who were intrigued by a "box that talks" and by what it was saying. Eventually, there were a few who had accepted the message and believed the good news. One of these was a young girl named Argeem, about sixteen years of age. She and our daughter Carol and the Zudweg girls, Terry and Sherry, had often played and visited together. Argeem had picked up a lot of English. When the girls were away at school, Argeem and Lavina became close friends and they often helped each other. Lavina taught Argeem numerous skills in sewing and baking. As they shared together, Argeem's love for Jesus grew and she was eager to share the Gospel by means of cassettes.

"TIE A KNOT ON YOUR STRING FOR ME"

We discovered that the Mesengo had a neat way of keeping track of the days. Unable to read or write they had their way of checking off the days in relation to a specific event to indicate how many days had elapsed or how many days were left.

If a man was going on a buffalo hunt, he'd tell his family how many days he expected to be away. His wife would take a certain kind of grass, make it into a string, and tie one knot on it each day. On the day she tied her eighteenth knot her husband was expected back home from the hunt. Hopefully, he and his companions would be weighted down with a heavy load of meat for the anticipated feast.

The man away from home, in the same way, would be tying knots on his grass string. He knew he was expected back when he had tied eighteen knots. We thought they were exceedingly ingenious.

I shall always remember the day Argeem returned carrying an Ethiopian Air Line's flight bag we had given her. Inside was a cassette player, several cassettes, and dead flash-light batteries. Argeem had unzipped the bag and brought each of these items out. Then she reached in one more time and pulled out a grass string on which were tied thirteen knots. I had never seen this before. She quickly explained.

"I've been in my mother's village. Every time I put down the player, my mother and other women would gather around to listen. Sometimes when the machine would stop they asked if it would say it again. Sometimes when the machine stopped speaking I would tell them, 'I can't talk like this radioni, but I know that what it is saying is true because I am a person of this Jesus.' She went on, 'Before I left my mother's village, there were thirteen women who came to me and each one said, 'Argeem, I want to become a person of your Jesus. Take some grass and make a string and then tie a knot on your string for me.'" Unable to read or write, this was their way of signing on to register their commitment to Jesus Christ.

This was a day of boundless joy. I could see the tremendous potential of the cassette for evangelism. It was the key to our reaching the Mesengo people in the remotest places with the Gospel. It could happen because ordinary Mesengos like Argeem could communicate effectively using cassettes. All that was needed was a ministry like ours to help produce the messages on cassette and provide these cassettes, players and batteries in the languages required.

Later we saw numerous knotted strings like Argeem's. The longest string I ever saw was brought in by a middle-aged man named Elong. He'd been out on his own for six weeks across the Bako river some two days hike from our station. There this man was in an area where Mesengos and Daniir people overlapped.

Elong fingered the knots on his string coming to a larger knot near the middle. He explained, "These knots on this side are all Mesengos, but on the other side of the knot — these are all Daniir people."

Here was an illiterate barefoot Mesengo, a relatively new

believer in Christ, able with the help of a cassette player and messages in his own language, finding a bi-lingual Daniir to cross the linguistic barrier to communicate the Gospel in such a way that some fifty Daniir people, members of an unreached group, said to him, "Tie a knot on your string for me. I want to become a person of your Jesus."

The wonderful thing about the cassette is that it not only enables ordinary, even new believers, to be effective witnesses for Christ, but it also is a marvelous teaching tool. While sharing the Gospel in this way, the person carrying the player is growing in his or her understanding of the essential truths of the Gospel. Initially, the cassette emboldens and enables an untrained Christian to share the Gospel among those who would otherwise not hear. In the doing of that, the believer is learning the essential truths over and over again so that at an early date this believer is able to share freely and accurately even when the player is not in hand. It is truly a tool God has given us to harness for this purpose.

SEARCHING FOR ALTERNATIVES TO BATTERIES

Batteries, of course, put limitations on how often the message can be heard. But God also led us into a solution for that problem. Hand-crank cassette players and small solar panels to power players directly from the sun were part of His tomorrow for His mission.

We missionaries shared with each other how we were using cassettes. We frequently shared our observations about the limitations battery consumption placed on the use of players. We could not have dreamed then that in a few short years tiny solar panels would become available to power cassette players and to charge batteries which could be used repeatedly.

Balti, the most important ritual expert
and chief of the Mesengo.

The first Mesengo children to attend school.

CHAPTER EIGHTEEN

"THIS IS BIG TALK"

In the wilds of Ethiopia, a Mesengo chief puts down his gun and listens to the story of God's love.

"Peeni cin Obiing. This is big talk," mused the stocky and obviously intelligent Mesengo chief. His name is Gabrekidan, the chief from Batagur, a village some three hours' walking distance on the other side of the Godare River. He and I had been sitting for more than an hour in the early evening darkness. We were sitting on the step of the "Godare Hilton", the name given to the stick-and-grass guest house where our guests slept when we had an overflow of visitors.

"This is a big talk," he repeated almost under his breath as he listened intently to a taped message in the Mesengo language on one of our small play-back machines. "This is bigger talk than the other 'radioni' spoke when I heard it across the river," he continued. He was learning more about the wonderful things about Jesus.

Our first contact with Gabrekidan had come on one of those unforgettable days. We met under the most inauspicious circumstances more than two years ago. On that particular morning we looked up from the breakfast table and saw many Mesengos crossing our back yard. Most of them were carrying two spears rather than the usual one. Two spears spell fighting and bloodshed.

About mid-morning, I went to Chief Balti's village, which is less than a fourth of a mile from the mission compound. I found a large gathering of sullen tribesmen planning their revenge for a fight that had started the previous day over a wife dispute. The fight had been broken up by Bakle, the chief's oldest son, who was something of a hothead himself. He had waded into the group beating anyone unfortunate enough to be caught by the lash of a hippo tail he was flailing about. During those wild moments someone had also struck Balti, the chief — which is quite unthinkable. The tension was compounded the following morning when Balti awakened suffering from a severe attack of malaria. His body shook convulsively as he tried to tell me the source of the trouble.

As I spoke to them, I reminded myself that I came with no authority but that as a man of God, I wanted to tell them what God's Word said about fighting and killing. And I told them of God's great love and Jesus Christ, and how we are to love one another.

Before I left that morning, they all assured me that they would not leave the village to go out to kill. If they were not attacked, they would remain in their homes. But sometime that afternoon a messenger came to the door. He had come from Balti who feared the people were getting out of hand. The new factor was the arrival of the chief from Batagur with twenty of his men. Seeing Balti's weakened condition because of his malaria, they jumped to the conclusion that it was because he had been jostled the day before and they were sure he would die. They must take their revenge without waiting to see what the outcome might be.

While we were discussing the matter with the messengers, drums began to beat and the trumpet screamed its call for others to gather in the chief's village. We were frightened, to say the least. Since it was late in the afternoon, many would have been drinking and I didn't consider it safe to go to try once again to bring peace.

About this time, our little boy, Paul, came running into the house. The mother of one of his playmates had come quickly, snatched up her child, and had run off into the forest to hide. On such occasions it's a life for a life, and no one is safe, however young or innocent. Women and children were gripped with fear.

We stood in the doorway watching the messenger disappear down the trail. The shouting and confusion from the village could be heard plainly. It seemed that anything could happen. Straining to interpret the shouting, we saw a large group of Mesengos coming down the path toward the house. Paul dashed into the bedroom and crawled under the bed to hide. Lavina followed him into the bedroom and sat on the bed, quietly trying to reassure him. By then the men were at our back door, headed by the chief from Batagur. This was my first meeting with Gabrekidan.

They appeared to be friendly enough and we invited them into our living veranda. They all had guns and spears. For nearly an hour we reasoned with them and tried to persuade them not to kill. We urged them at least to wait until the next day. We were confident that by then conditions, now inflamed, would have had time to cool. It was not at all certain that Balti would die, we argued. Why should they take revenge without waiting? With God's help, sense prevailed. Somewhat reluctantly, they agreed to wait. And when their spirits had quieted, I had a wonderful opportunity to tell them about Jesus Christ. Gabrekidan was hearing the Gospel for the first time. God, through strange experiences such as this, often opened a door of opportunity for us to bear witness to Him.

Two days later was Sunday. Peace had returned to our community, and everyone was grateful and relieved. We met for worship on top of the hill near the center of this beautiful clearing in the forest. The sheer beauty of the day made it difficult to realize that two days earlier we were all gripped with fear and faced violence and death.

There were seventy-four present. Sitting in the center of the group was my new friend, Gabrekidan, the chief from Batagur about ten miles from here and across the river. With his heavy old Italian rifle stretched across his crossed legs, he listened intently as I preached from the First Epistle of John, chapter four. They heard of God's great love and learned that we cannot love God and hate our brother at the same time. God seemed especially near that Sunday, and the message appeared to fall on listening ears. Some days later I crossed the river and walked through the deep forest to Gabrekidan's village. We sat together in his barn and talked about Jesus. He asked penetrating questions about why they had never heard of Jesus before. I was ashamed and could not bring myself to tell him we'd been too busy with other things. As we visited together, I discovered that here was one of the most intelligent and ambitious Mesengos that I had met. Even his newly planted fields of corn seemed to reflect his desire for things that were worthwhile.

When I left his village, he spoke earnestly, saying, "Odola, you are going to your country soon. Don't stay away for a long, long time. If you do, we'll forget these good words you have told us. Come back when the corn is ripe." And just as I was about to disappear in the forest to head for home, he called, "If you'll come back, I'll have my men cut the trail so that you can come riding on your horse."

Now as we sat together on the steps of the "Godare Hilton," evening had become night and it was already too dark to see each other's faces. But the language from the heart sometimes expresses itself best without the aid of a lamp. And Gabrekidan was baring his heart to me. The sweet word of the Gospel made sense to him, and it was apparent that he deeply desired to know it better. It would only be a matter of God's own choosing when he would know Jesus.

"This is a big talk," he said, unconsciously, thinking aloud. "Before you came, we had never heard this. We Mesengos were told that the Melineer*¹ had come from a rock and were the offspring of God. We thought that the Melineer were our gods. We never knew from where the world came and how people began. The way of God has been lost to us."

That night before we parted with prayer, he said, "Odola, I want all my people to hear this talk. If you will come and spend a week with us, I will call all my people and they will come to listen to this word about Jesus." He went on, "Tomorrow I go to Teppi (seventy miles on the trail). I would like to carry with me a 'radioni', so that I can remember how to tell this talk to my friends with whom we'll be sleeping along the way."

Early the next day, he picked up a play-back. Three weeks later it was returned. Scores had again heard the "big talk" from the "radioni" that speaks Mesengo and tells about Jesus. Gabrekidan seems not far from the kingdom. But we remember the word of Jesus who said, "Except a man be born again, he cannot see the kingdom of God."

In Gabrekidan's village, as in others, stands a crude shrine. It seems simple enough — an emoy plant, a few stones piled up, the horns of a buffalo or two, and a few beads and bracelets scattered about. The stones are stained from the offerings of beer that have been poured out and from the blood of the sacrificed chickens which has been sprinkled about. It all seems crude and unkempt. But it is the tribe's link with the spirits of the ancestors. This is the seat of power and blessing and lies at the center of the life of the community. The ritual expert who receives the offerings and can announce blessing or curse is the Melineer chief. Ignorance and superstition link hands together at the shrine. Only Jesus Christ can set them free! He is the light of the world!

---

1. Melineer was the clan of the ritual experts.

"... I have been found by those who did not seek me; I have shown myself to those who did not ask for me."

Romans 11:20

CHAPTER NINETEEN

A "ONE-FAMILY" STATION?

The Godare River Post was a "one-family" station. But that doesn't mean we didn't have many additional people involved in opening up the work during our years in Ethiopia. Godare was one of the mission stations identified in the Illubabur-Kaffa (I-K) project. Others being opened during those years included the work at Chebera by Bill and Betsy Muldrow, the station on the Omo River being opened by Bob and Morrie Swart, and the work among the Surma people being opened by Don and Ginny McClure. There were to be a total of seven stations among seven different tribes, or language groups. Each was to have one family and be part of a network of stations in which Ethiopian staff would work with the missionary in the school and clinics. Missionary staff from larger stations in the Presbyterian mission would fly into these one-family stations periodically to supervise the Ethiopian staff. The idea was to set the resident missionary family as free as possible for evangelism and ministry in general. All of this was made possible because of the services of Mission Aviation Fellowship based in Jimma.

Our stations were linked together by a morning and evening schedule on the two-way radio system. These radios linked us to each other and to MAF. With these transceivers we ordered our supplies from Jimma, which in turn were flown in by MAF. In cases of emergencies or illness, a doctor from one of the other stations would come on the radio, diagnose the illness and prescribe the medicine to be taken.

More than once we were on the air asking advice not only for ourselves but about some patients who needed medical skills beyond our own. Sometimes we'd have MAF fly in to transport seriously ill patients or those who required surgery to the mission hospital in Mettu or Dembidollo. These hospitals were north of us about 30 minutes by air from where we lived.

Educational missionaries and medical missionaries appointed to supervise the medical and educational work at Godare, normally flew in on a bi-monthly schedule. They'd spend one or two days with us and we found this to be an excellent plan. Missionaries with the special skills required gave direction to this aspect of our ministry and set us free for other areas of ministry, especially in the area of evangelism and working with the growing Christian community.

From a letter to the states, dated October 23, 1966 we're given a progress report on how the work at Godare was progressing:

"The heavy rains are over and the sun is shining here at Godare this beautiful Sunday in the rain forest. Lavina, Paul and I have just walked home from our regular Sunday worship service. Birds were singing melodiously and from deep in the jungle came the regular call of the chime bird. Today at the service were 53 Mesengo people, dressed in leaves with a small patch of cloth or grass for covering. Slowly, almost imperceptibly, changes are taking place in the life of this people, and deep in their hearts God is at work. The seed is being sown and there is promise of an abundant harvest. On this day we again praise God for calling us to be His messengers to the Mesengo people. ...

"This has been a year of exhausting physical work, coupled with language study, witnessing and preaching. Of necessity a great deal of time and energy has gone into establishing our base. The long airstrip to accomodate a DC3 aircraft is completed. Hundreds upon hundreds of trees entangled by twisted vines and covered with hordes of biting ants have been felled, stumps dug

out, *holes filled in and dragged smooth. Paths through the jungle have been cut allowing the Landrover to be used to haul water, sand, rocks and timber for buildings. Thousands of bricks have been pressed. The houses for the clinic dresser and teacher have been completed. The school and clinic buildings are nearly finished and our own permanent house has the foundation in. ...*

"How sharply this year contrasts with our previous work and way of living in the Sudan! There, for 15 years the bulk of my time and energy was spent in sitting translating or in visiting in the villages absorbing language and culture and witnessing and preaching. Here there has been little time to sit, but each day has been too short as we have been involved in exhausting physical work, taxing one's energies to the extreme, and living under conditions that leave much to be desired. We, ourselves, are amazed that God, who gave us such joy in our work in the past, continues to fill our lives with joy and satisfaction in this entirely different kind of ministry. Truly it is of God's goodness.

"During recent weeks we've been doing considerably more visiting in the villages, making friends, witnessing and preaching. It is our goal to reach all within walking distance before we leave for furlough next July.

"The Mesengo live in family units with several simple houses situated within a distance of a hundred yards, joined by ill kept paths with brush, stumps and logs obstructing the way. But the quietness of these homes, hidden in the forest, offers a marvelous opportunity for personal witnessing to the things of God. This is quite in contrast to the Anuak village of the Sudan with its many people congregated in one place and the inevitable distractions which follow.

"The Mesengo will not be easy to reach with the Gospel. The physical barriers are many. The paths are incredibly difficult. The rivers are many, the mountain ranges are formidable and the people are scattered in isolated villages for distances up to 100 miles. And then the old customs do not change easily. The witchdoctor has a tremendous hold upon this people. The power of superstition, ignorance and custom hold the people in a vise-like grip. But Christ is greater than all these things. And it is He that we proclaim. With keenest anticipation we look forward,

anticipating the wonderful changes that will come in the lives of this tribe because of Him. What a rare privilege is ours!"

THEY CAME TO HELP US

We were greatly helped by the large number of volunteers and short term assignment personnel that came and worked with us for periods ranging from a few weeks to as long as two years. They came to work with us and often to do the tasks that enabled us to devote our energies to the real reasons for our being there. I could not have visited the villages, spent time with people, written those messages for the tapes or produced the cassettes which later played such a vital role in our effective witness to Christ if these people had not come to relieve us of the tremendous work load involved in opening work in the rain forest.

I think of Ed Pollock, Jr.. He was that young college graduate who gave several valuable weeks of his time in the very beginning. He walked in with us and helped get the work going on the airstrip and in helping clear back the initial camp site. He was able to rough it, sleeping in a hammock in the trees. He was nearby so that Lavina and Paul weren't left alone during those first weeks when I was frequently on the trail between Godare and Teppi.

Frank and Gladys Kieft made their first trip to the Godare within a few months of our arrival.

Within a few days of our first MAF landing, Frank and Gladys flew in and stayed with us for several months. They came with their boots and work clothes, some pots and pans and lived in a small tent on the hillside just below our grass house. During their entire stay we never heard one murmur or complaint from them .

Frank and Gladys were great fun to have with us, a great help and always an inspiration and example to us. The only complaint is that he worked us hard from sunrise until after sunset! They came out four different occasions for periods of five to six months each. Once when they left, as the little plane was disappearing from view, I turned to Lavina and said, "Honey, let's take a day off!" More seriously, we can never adequately express our gratitude to God for the Kieft's contribution to our lives and work. They came to work. When they saw a need they tried to meet it. Once, Frank even flew out a heavy cement mixer and paid the transportation charges from America. He said, "What good is it to you if that thing comes by sea and arrives six months after you need it. I'll see to it that you get it before it's too late." That cement mixer was like pure gold to us. What a relief after mixing cement in a half barrel with a hoe and a shovel! God be praised for lay people like the Kiefts.

YOUTHFUL VOLUNTEERS LIGHTEN OUR LOAD

There were others, similarly eager to help, who came out to make an essential difference. The first of these were Don Sill and Jim Cetan. Don was a graduate from Hope College and Jim was a pre-med student. Jim helped in that first clinic shack on which one of the volunteers put a sign reading, "Godare Medical Arts Building." Jim also supervised the digging of ditches on each side of the road that ran through the compound connecting our airstrip with the living area where our house was to be built. We dubbed this little stretch of road "Cetan Ave." We so appreciated Don and Jim who put up with less than adequate food and lived under very primitive conditions.

Our first MAF plane had landed on March 16th. During those ensuing weeks, the plane was in and out, often, several times a day and sometimes several times a week. What a joy to receive supplies that hadn't been damaged by being dropped from the air. The only thing we missed was the excitement of seeing those double sacked supplies hitting the ground and then flying and bounding along the ground of what was becoming the airstrip. Some of those bags scooted along some fifty to sixty feet. I'll always remember soap bars flying in all directions when a carton of 200 bars without protective sacking was dropped.

Lavina remembers vividly her experience with air drops too. I had trekked into Teppi to help with the loading and to help in making the drops. In lieu of roses, I had wrapped a glass jar of pickles in several rolls of toilet tissue and dropped it with a nice little "love note". It's good I did, too, because on that same drop one of the sacks with a carton of beans landed in a stump hole and had no way to scoot along the ground to lessen the shock. Lavina reported that 23 of the 24 tins of baked beans had ruptured. She had no can opener but used a pliers and screw driver to pry the tins open. She said she ate beans (not her favorite food) three times a day for three days before they soured and had to be thrown away.

But now with the strip open that was all past history. However, a great deal of work on the strip still remained. We had determined that it would pay in the long run for us to extend the strip so that a Dakota aircraft could land. This would make the building program so much easier and we wanted the larger strip because of some pressure for this from the Royal family.

TIES WITH THE ROYAL FAMILY

Her Highness, the Crown Princess, with her two daughters, personal secretary and body-guard came into the Godare on a special chartered flight one day to visit us. Lavina scrambled to figure out what to put on for lunch at noon. This was fasting time for the Orthodox Christians and Her Highness wouldn't be eating meat, eggs or any animal products. I thought Lavina was extremely creative with her menu. Most everything came out of our garden which had an abundance of vegetables and fruit. Our missionaries at Pokwo on the Baro River helped immensely by sending up tasty, frozen filets of Nile perch. We were greatly honored to have members of the Royal family as our guests. Dr. Don McClure had set that up and accompanied them on their visit to the Godare. We lived in the afterglow of this special day for quite some time!

We also had the privilege of being entertained by the Royal family at the palace in Addis Ababa. Once we were invited out to their summer palace at Lake Bishoftu for a royal dinner with the Crown Prince and his entire family along with special guests from among their ambassadorial representatives. After our humble circumstances at the Godare, it was rather daunting to sip and dine with the finest cutlery and glassware!

We always had a lot of good humor with our fellow missionaries on days such as that. I suspect they were just a little envious of us so we'd tease them that to shake our hand after returning would call for an extra dollar. After all, this was a hand that had only recently shaken the hand of the Crown Prince or of Her Highness the Crown Princess, no less! I've often marvelled at the tremendous variety of experiences one has as a missionary. They range from the humblest to the most sublime!

The work was made more pleasant by four young fellows from the states who came out in 1966 and spent the summer with us.

They were Harry Miersma, Duane Laman, Ted Wyngarden and Bill Van Eenenaam. They were all college age, full of fun and eager to work. They came with boundless energy, curiosity and a readiness to work and live under less than ideal conditions. It was a tremendous help and inspiration to have them with us. We had great times at work and great times sharing, especially after the work and heat of the day was over and on Sundays, pondering together the meaning of life and what God had in mind for each of them. It continues to bring joy to our hearts when we realize that Harry married and became a full time missionary and that Duane felt God calling him to be a pastor and went ahead with his theological training. Both men, with their families, are in the Lord's service today. We like to believe that their summer experiences living among the Mesengos and seeing their need for Christ and how missionaries were attempting to make a difference, perhaps in some small way, influenced them in making those large decisions that shaped their lives to be available to Him.

The memory of the companionship and vitality of those young men are precious to us even now, some thirty years after the event. With the joy comes a tinge of sadness when we think how Bill, a few years later, was tragically killed in a plane crash, leaving behind his wife and two children and family. He was always special to us.

THE VOLUNTEERS FROM KALAMAZOO

Larry and Betty Zudweg and their girls were with us for two years. Larry was skilled in building and had finished part of what was to become our permanent house when Haven Reformed Church in Parchment, Michigan sent us five men to help finish it and to work on many other projects then underway. These men all left their families behind to give us five wonderful weeks of their best efforts. We had great times of fun and fellowship along with hard work. They slept in our "Godare Hilton," a mud floor, stick and grass-walled building situated about twenty feet from where the new house was going up. Lavina and Betty scrambled to keep food on the table. Cooking with damp wood in the iron range didn't make it all that simple! I can still see them blowing on the stubborn flame to encourage it along.

We shall always be grateful to the families of my cousin, Dr. George Hoekstra, Frank Spitters, Brad Stonerock, Bill Smith and Ron Houtman for their willing spirits, encouraging their husbands and the fathers of their children to come.

These men were all skilled in their various professions back home. At the Godare they proved to be equally skilled as builders and mechanics. I can still see them laying out on the ground lumber we had sawed on our own mill, as they constructed those large wooden trusses for the roof of the house. Without lifting equipment they figured out how to move them and position them in a standing position on the walls.

It was these men that speeded the time when we moved up the hill from our grass house. This old house had served us well for three years but it was past time to move out. The roof leaked and the rat population hadn't diminished. In the new house it seemed pure luxury for us to have a clean, cement floor underfoot and to sleep with regular beds and mattresses again with no need for mosquito nets.

Even so, it was with some nostalgia that we tore the old grass house down. Our children lightheartedly complained, "Dad, you're spoiling the place, making it too modern." Perhaps they were thinking of the fun times we'd had as a family when the children took turns with the pellet gun shooting rats off the rafters.

A MISSIONARY'S CHILDRENS STORY

This brings back a fond memory. We always had marvelous evening times sharing in a Bible reading and prayer before calling it a day. It was during those quiet moments when I was reading the Bible that a rat or two would frequently appear on the sill or on the rafters. Sometimes one of the children couldn't resist the temptation and interjected into the reading, "Dad, there's a rat." I'd keep on reading, but sometimes the pressure increased. "Dad, there's a rat!" At that point, I'd give in and say, "Okay, get the pellet gun and be sure you don't miss."

That was fine except it could sometimes lead to a bit of confrontation between contenders for the gun. A minor war zone would erupt with one missionary child contending with the other as to whose turn it was. "Dad, it's my turn, he shot last night" Great fun! Missionaries and their children — no different from normal people! There was no telephone to disrupt, but some demonic angel seemed to instigate those rats to appear just when they could inflict the maximum disruption in our quiet time together. That may not be good theology, but there were times when I almost thought it might be so!

FOND MEMORIES FROM THE OLD HOUSE

That old house has many memories. But first, one experience from the very first shacks in which we lived. We never bothered putting grass around the outside so the sticks laced together gave plenty of room for insects and bugs to enter. And with no doors or windows at all, just openings, almost anything could get inside at will.

Not having a way to bake bread, Lavina frequently made pancakes and we ate these with honey we could get from the Mesengos. Bees loved that honey and we'd often have eight or ten bees sipping at the edges of our tin plates while we were carefully trying to eat without irritating them unnecessarily. With bees like that partaking from the same plate, one learns to handle the fork quite expertly!

The second generation grass house was much more spacious and after Frank Kieft came it had screen doors and screens over the window openings. This helped a great deal but mosquitoes and tiny midges often drove us to our cots early. These midges would itch between the fingers so intensely that one had to give up the battle and retire early.

Frequently, Lavina would put out on the kitchen work table a plastic pitcher of milk to sour overnight for pancakes she'd prepare in the morning. The pitcher was always carefully covered with a cloth to keep out any droppings from wall lizards or the rats. There was one morning, however, when we would have no pancakes. During the night rats had pulled the protective cloth off and had gotten into the pitcher — all three of them. Two had drowned and the third one was still frantically treading milk with his nose just above "water" trying to survive. I don't remember what we had for breakfast, but I know it wasn't pancakes.

UNPLEASANT IRRITATIONS

Army ants also had a way of invading our houses. Even the new house wasn't a match for army ants. They'd come in, marching two abreast, and fan out everywhere. Their sting was so hot that one couldn't really tolerate it. The only answer was to try to contain them in one section of the house by sprinkling either ashes or gamexine powder as a barrier to a room that they might not have reached yet.

Another contender to make life difficult for us, was the little jiggers we called "bojulies". During the dry season, they multiplied in any dry, powdery soil. Walking with bare feet was an invitation to them to latch on, burrow in and hatch. When this happened, the "nest" would grow from a tiny pimple to something as large as a small pea. They itched furiously and frequently became infected. Having several in one's foot at the same time wasn't at all uncommon. They had to be tackled with a pin or needle to dig them out. Afterward we'd soak the infected foot in a pan of warm, antiseptic water, put a bandage over the place, and try to remember not to walk with bare feet again!

Among the most unpleasant irritations we had to learn to live with was what the mango flies did to us. The Mesengos taught us which trees attracted these flies and warned us not to linger under them. Before we knew this, we were hanging our laundry directly under one of those trees with disastrous consequences.

These flies would lay eggs, especially on anything damp like laundry when hanging out to dry. Before we discovered that every piece of laundry had to be ironed, for which we used our charcoal burning irons, we found ourselves getting maggots under our skin. We made our discovery when I had what appeared to be three large boils on the shin of my leg. They were extremely painful and we got on the radio with the mission doctor who suggested I keep the leg elevated and apply hot packs to it. I followed the doctor's orders and later applied a bandage with drawing salve. Imagine my astonishment and horror the next morning when I removed the bandage and tried to get the core of the boil to pop out. What actually popped out was a large, full grown living maggot. Two others followed in rapid succession.

We learned that if we carefully ironed every piece of laundry, no exceptions — even wash cloths, towels and socks, we reduced the chances of this happening. Even so, we contended with them frequently, especially during the first few years. Once Carol, who was about twelve then, came running up the hill to me saying, "Daddy, look what's coming out of my eye." Coming right out of the eye lash area a maggot had emerged. We had thought she had a sty in her eye and never dreamed it might be one of those miserable maggots.

During the early years especially, whenever a pimple appeared anywhere on our bodies, we were on the alert for these maggots to develop.

We learned that we could use a lighted candle and let a drop or two of the melted, hot wax drop on the pimple where the maggot was maturing. The trick was to get the hot wax close enough, but not too close or it'd be very uncomfortable. Another trick was to hit the right spot. Once these two hurdles were surmounted, it got to be rather interesting to see this hidden enemy try to get through the wax for air at which point we would squeeze it like one would a pimple and it would come popping out. That whole procedure was quite distasteful and uncomfortable.

LIVING IN THE FOREST A NEW EXPERIENCE

These were all interesting challenges and provocations. Sometimes, we had additional excitement, and it was a lot more fun, when wild pigs invaded our compound. We tried shooting them by the light of a flashlight when they got into the sweet-potatoes. Once, I even shot through the screen when these wild pigs awakened us by their chomping on fallen, ripe, guava fruit right near our bedroom window.

The forest was alive with strange, frequently haunting sounds during the night. The Colabus monkeys chattered like machine gun staccato as they called back and forth to each other from trees on opposite sides of our clearing. Baboons could scream bloody murder when they engaged in their savage brawls. And there was a forest bird we never saw that would, only rarely, pierce the normal forest environment with a blood curdling, piercing cry like someone terrified and calling for help. But early each morning long before daylight the innumerable variety of jungle birds would begin to sing. The choir of the most beautiful songs one can imagine was our daily delight. Several times I arose early to go down the hill into the wooded area between us and the river. The variety of songs the birds were singing was out of this world. How privileged we were to be there in that unique place.

SNAKES A DEADLY THREAT

We were always on our guard for snakes. The small, deadly poisonous green mambas were in the trees and bushes. On the ground were the cobras and the pythons. The largest python we ever killed measured sixteen feet four inches and was about four to five inches in diameter.

The red cobras were dangerous, even deadly.

SMALLPOX AT GODARE

One summer our daughter-in-law, Sheryll, came out. It was such fun to have her. All the strange sounds at night were real threatening to her good sleep. It was interesting that when she first arrived and found we had evening devotions and Bible reading each night as a family, she thought we had "church" every night. At first, teasing playfully, she'd inquire, "Are we having catechism again tonight?" Before the summer ended, if there was the slightest hint that we might be cutting that devotional time because of some intruding factor, it was Sheryll who spoke up saying, "Dad, aren't we having devotions together tonight?"

Sheryll loved helping in the clinic and gave many small pox vaccinations that summer. We were experiencing the last outbreak of smallpox in Ethiopia before it was totally eradicated. I had never seen patients with smallpox before and it wasn't a pretty sight. Oozing pus-filled sores covered large sections of the body and there were high fevers. It was a dreaded disease among the Mesengo.

When the disease first struck our area, Chief Balti, who was also the chief ritual expert (witchdoctor), discouraged people from coming to the clinic to be vaccinated. Instead, he put up a small stick trestle about three feet wide and seven feet tall over the trail between his village and the clinic. He lived about a fourth of a mile from our mission compound. Balti assured his people that if they walked under the chicken he had sacrificed and spread with wings outstretched at the top of the trestle, they'd not become ill.

Well, it didn't work and Mesengos gradually came to realize that the only people safe and secure from the disease were those that Sheryll and our clinic dresser had pricked with the needle. Eventually, Balti himself, was pricked in the arm and began to tell others to follow his example. During our years at Godare, Balti was a frequent visitor to our clinic and encouraged others to come. Balti had a severe, incurable case of shin ulcers, made worse by his elephantiasis. We put hundreds of bandages on his legs and each time he heard the message of Jesus' love.

JOHN BOEREMA HELPS INSTALL THE TURBINE

We owe a lot to John and Harriet Boerema too. They came out in 1968 and spent some nine months with us. John and I had talked by phone from the airport in New York just before we left for Ethiopia. We'd spoken together briefly when we had visited Iowa. During our conversation John had said he'd be open to helping us. I thought a call before we left might be just the encouragement he needed. It proved to be so and in a few months they had made arrangements for their feed business and the farm and were winging their way toward Ethiopia.

We enjoyed them both tremendously. Harriet and Lavina did many things together and had great fellowship. For Christmas they baked mounds of cookies and threw a lawn party on the hillside in front of the house for the Mesengos. We had great fun over that after the party was over. Didn't take long! There must have been twenty or thirty who came. They had no idea about taking one or two cookies and a drink of juice. Each one loaded his or her paper plate with all it would hold before moving away from the table. In no time flat the table was empty! We laughed and laughed over our first Christmas party with Mesengo guests. I don't believe it was ever attempted along those lines again!

John and Harriet were there during those months I was installing the electric turbine and hydraulic ram. When those four young college-age volunteers had been out, Harry Miersma and Duane Laman had written a letter to their folks in California suggesting a turbine would be useful and had presented an idea on how the loop in the river could be cut with a channel to give a head of water sufficient to power it. I still remember how excited those fellows were when they shared a letter with us from their folks saying their church, First Reformed in Artesia, was excited about their proposal and wanted to make it a project for which they'd provide the funds.

We'd since checked the various kinds of turbines that would operate efficiently on a low head of around five to six feet of water. The unit we purchased would use up to 680 liters of water per second. The amount of water needed determined the width of the channel we'd have to dig. The order had been placed in Germany and the unit was now in the station waiting to be installed when John arrived. He was exactly the man we needed. John was patient, careful, creative, and methodical. When the job was completed, the turbine operated flawlessly without vibration.

Once the turbine and the water system were completed, our Ethiopian staff and we shared equally in its benefits. The water system provided the entire compound with a constant supply of water as near as the faucet itself. An overflow pipe enabled nearby Mesengos readily to fill their pots from the overflow instead of having to walk the seven or eight hundred yards to the river and carry the heavy pots filled with water back up the hill.

Having electric power twenty-four hours a day made it possible to have lights in each of the staff houses, clinic and school. Eventually, we brought in an electric freezer where we could store meat for staff and ourselves to share alike. A tiny Reformed Church in Colton, South Dakota gave this useful gift to Godare station.

In order to have fresh meat available, we purchased young bulls and steers in Teppi on market day. Once or twice a year Mesengos would walk in ten or twelve animals. These grazed on the airstrip where grass was in abundance. They helped keep the grass down and provided meat for the freezer as they were butchered one by one.

Keeping animals was a problem in the forest. The entire area was infested with tsetse flies and animal sleeping sickness was indemic. Every animal brought into the Godare had to be injected periodically to protect against sleeping sickness. Cattle responded well, but horses, mules, donkeys and dogs were never completely immune. Across the years we eventually lost every horse and dog we ever brought to the Godare. This always saddened us because we needed these horses to get around, but knew that their fate was sealed. During the final stages of the illness, the animals began to stagger about aimlessly, eventually went blind and either died or had to be destroyed.

TEACHING MESENGOS HOW TO GROW COFFEE

Mesengos were learning many new things. We introduced them to bananas, pineapple, mangos, peanuts and sweet potatoes, teaching them how to grow these things. We undertook an ambitious program of helping Mesengos learn to grow coffee as a cash crop. I'd learned what I could from coffee plantation people near Teppi about planting the spacing of seedlings, how to prune the growing trees and how to go about harvesting the ripened coffee beans. They told me how much of the forest should remain uncut to provide shade for the coffee trees. I passed this information along to the Mesengos as we worked with them. The MAF plane brought in thousands of seedlings which Mesengos planted in their villages. On the compound itself we had a demonstration plot with about 100 coffee trees for teaching purposes.

AL SCHREUDER, THE MIERSMAS AND LAMANS

Al Schreuder came out to help us one summer and later came back with his lovely wife Susan to spend an internship in Ethiopia as part of his theological program from Western Theological Seminary in Holland, Michigan. Al was strong and pleasant and was willing to live the most simple lifestyle. He had the markings of an excellent career missionary in the making. We could see that Al and Sue would be "top of the line" missionaries that God would mightily use.

That same fall Henry and Susan Miersma and their pastor, Dave Laman and his wife Lois came out to help for about three weeks.

We'd just returned from furlough ourselves and Larry and Betty Zudweg with their girls had been holding the fort in our absence. Larry was a good builder and had finished our permanent house while we were gone. We were amazed to see the beautiful, quartz stone fireplace he'd put in the living room. Larry had run across a stretch of rock in a clearing just off the compound. I suspect ours may have been one of the few quartz fireplaces in the world! Larry's specialty in the states was fireplaces and he couldn't resist the temptation. We were the benefactors of this labor of love and appreciated it immensely. Whenever we had guests our unique fireplace was a sure conversation piece!

LACK OF FOOD POSES A PROBLEM

We'd arrived home from furlough just a few days before the guests from America were to arrive. Food supplies were low. The Zudwegs were using up the supplies and hadn't replenished the larder anticipating we'd bring in what was needed when we returned from furlough. Somehow we hadn't realized how low their stock was. The problem was further complicated when we removed the lid from the barrel in the outside storeroom in which we had left a good fourth of a barrel of sugar. Imagine our horror and revulsion when we discovered that the cover had somehow slipped off at some time or other and a rat had fallen in. We discovered his shrivelled up carcass of bones and hair. Our imagination told us of what had occurred between the time we found him in this condition and when he had fallen in. It couldn't have been pleasant! You may be sure that we used sugar on cereal very sparingly those days until fresh sugar could be flown in!

The Miersmas and the Lamans were to bring in numerous supplies including our new dog, Zadick. They'd be coming on a DC-3 with a full load of whatever was needed including food and staples. Unfortunately, the pilot became lost and about the time they should have arrived, he was asking our travelling guests if they had any idea where the Godare was. Eventually, the pilot gave up, turned back to Jimma and landed with minimal reserves. This could have ended in tragedy!

So instead of coming with numerous supplies, our guests came in the next day with MAF and minimal supplies. Having four additional people to prepare food for when there is none poses a real problem when the closest food store is a hundred and twenty five miles away. We shared our plight by radio with the other missionaries. It was Maji station that came to the rescue and sent what they could when the MAF pilot diverted to drop them off on his way back to Jimma. They must have heard Larry on the radio one morning saying, half in jest, "Either fly in food or prepare to fly out the bodies!" It was serious enough that our guests huddled one morning and seriously discussed leaving on the first MAF plane available because of fearing they were a burden to us because of the food crisis. Lavina and I talked them out of it and food supplies did reach us and everyone lived happily ever after!

We had a great time with the Miersmas and Lamans. The women enjoyed each other and pitched in planning and cooking for all us hungry men. We still talk about the morning when, as we men came through the door into the kitchen, we found Susan scooping up a freshly baked mulberry pie off the floor. It had slipped out of her hands as she pulled it from the oven. She had a mind to throw it away, but we restrained her and said, "Not on your life, lady. The floor was just mopped this morning. We don't get mulberry pie every day in this house. You don't go throwing that away." I can't remember a homemade pie tasting better!

Henry and Dave erected the fence around the fruit orchard and house area. We had brought in metal posts and adequate barbed wire. They did a first class job like people used to do on the farm.

The other important task accomplished was putting in the headgate in the channel to the turbine at the river. We'd been using the turbine, but the headgate itself still had to be put in. Like good soldiers Henry and Dave stuck with Al Schreuder and me at the river until ten o'clock one night. We had to complete that task in one pouring of cement. They were dog-tired guests accompanying a very weary missionary as we trudged up the hill the seven hundred yards with a two hundred and fifty foot climb to the house. I can still see young Al Schreuder jumping into the rain barrel half full of rain water standing under the eave at the corner of the shop. He had a good bath, but, as I recall, the rest of us did it with a little less noise and less water.

PAUL HAS RHEUMATIC FEVER

Sleeping was somewhat difficult for lack of covering and space. The forest was always damp and sleeping on the floor could be quite chilly for a little guy like Paul. Weeks later, I recall my returning from Ghimeera following a couple of days of meetings. Lavina had been alone with Paul and was very concerned. She described how Paul had a fever and that his joints seemed to be hurting him. She said that he couldn't stand the weight of a bedsheet on his toes. Without knowing more, I suspected rheumatic fever. When we finally got him to the doctor, it proved to be just that. Lavina had a very sick little boy in bed for three months. Part of that time was spent in Addis Ababa where medical care was available. The Lord mercifully spared him from perceptible heart damage. Much concern and many prayers were said for his full recovery.

THE KIEFTS, BROUWERS, STAUBLE AND OTHERS

The Kiefts were back at the Godare for a five month stint when Carlton and Warren Brouwer from North Holland and Harold Stauble from Kalamazoo came to help. Carly and Warren were both professional builders. Carly, Warren, Frank and Harold put up a beautiful little mud and cement brick house for short term staff we anticipated in the years ahead. During this same period, Harold took our old Landrover and completely overhauled its engine. Hours and more hours on the saw mill and the rugged use to which it had been put on the airstrip and hauling sand, rocks and dirt for the bricks had taken their toll. It had only a few miles on the speedometer, but long hours on the engine. When Harold finished his work, the vehicle looked as old as ever, but it ran like new!

Roger Koppenol from Michigan and Tony Heinen from Wisconsin came out to help us build the itinerant airfield at Keto. Right after my first landing there, the men from Keto invited me to one of their homes. It was a simple mud-walled, grass-roofed house but it had a spectacular view out across the valley. We were about ten or twelve of us and I was sharing the Gospel as one would share good news he'd recently heard. I was telling them that because of what Jesus had done in giving His life on the cross, God would freely forgive the sins of anyone who was sorry, turned away from them and asked God's forgiveness.

While I was sitting among them sharing, one of the men suddenly spoke up. He said, "I'm so glad that we didn't quit working on our airstrip. We almost gave up because the work was so difficult. If Mr. Roger and Mr. Tony hadn't come to help us, we'd never have completed it."

And then another spoke as he asked a question. He wanted to know if God would forgive him. He said, "I've quarreled badly with my neighbor. Every year we'd quarrel over the boundary separating our land. One year the rocks would be moved over by my neighbor and the following year it'd be my turn to reset the stones making the division between our fields. We cheated each other and we hated each other. If we confess our wrong to each other and to God, will God forgive us?"

Yes, I'm glad, also, that they never gave up. Without that airstrip they'd never have heard this good news of God's readiness to forgive all who repent and believe the good news centering in Jesus Christ.

DAVE BAST AND DAVE PETERSEN

A couple of choice young fellows who came out for a summer, were Dave Bast and Dave Peterson. They were there when the astronauts made their first landing on the moon. Dave Bast later said that at that time where he was deep in the jungle rain forest in Southwest Ethiopia, the men on the moon could reach home before he could. ... We had a great and wonderful summer with these two Daves. They were of sterling character and fun to be around. I knew Dave Bast's father, Henry, well and often said to Lavina, "He's sure a chip off the old block. His mannerisms are just like his dad's." I consider that observation to be a first-class compliment to both Dave and his father. His dad had been one of our dearest friends. It often seemed that just when we needed a special word of encouragement, a letter from Dr. Bast would show up. The Lord knew!

David Petersen was a young man whose behavior and disposition reminded me always of the passage from the Gospels where Jesus said of Nathaniel, "Behold, an Israelite indeed, in whom is no guile."[1] He was sincere, considerate and tender of heart ... always thoughtful of Lavina and her work load in trying to keep hungry mouths filled under less than ideal circumstances. Twenty years later the two Dave's still speak fondly of the wiener roasts on the hillside, late Sunday afternoons when we opened tins of anemic wieners to put on home-made buns that Lavina had baked in her wood oven!

Dave Bast returned to the states to prepare for the ministry. After serving several churches, he was chosen to succeed Dr. William Brownson as Words of Hope's radio minister. Dave Petersen went on to become an outstanding surgeon who specializes on the hand. We count it a privilege to have had them with us during their formative years. They gave us more than they will ever fully understand.

AL AND BETH SMITH FROM MINNESOTA

Another great couple who came out to help us for two full years was Al and Beth Smith. They came out as Christian Service Corps missionaries. There coming overlapped one of our furloughs and they held down the fort at the Godare while we were gone. They deserve special praise for sticking it out alone at the Godare when the radio went bad and they had no contact with the outside world. Only a few could have tolerated the isolation and potential danger facing them under those conditions. They were good soldiers and met a real need to man the station, working with Ethiopian staff and nurturing the growing Mesengo church. Al had grown up on a farm less than a mile from where I'd lived as a boy in Minnesota. Beth also had close ties as her mother and I went to the same little church and Sunday school when we were children. Al and Beth did a great job and are included among our dearest friends.

HARRY AND PAT MIERSMA

Finally, last, but by no means least, are Harry and Pat Miersma. Harry had once come as a volunteer, but was now back with his lovely wife, Pat, who was also a trained nurse. They took over from us at the Godare when we moved to Teppi to establish a new base from which to reach several other unreached tribes using the MAF plane and cassettes. Harry and Pat came out as RCA missionaries and were God's provision to carry the work among the Mesengo forward so that we might be released for the new Teppi Tapes cassette ministry which was based in Teppi.

Other volunteers also helped us get that station opened but we'll wait to speak of their contribution when we come to that part of our story. Then and now, we praised God for His faithfulness and help in providing us with the means for the task and for the people who came out to help us. We praised God then and still do for the churches that assisted volunteers and short term missionaries by providing finances that enabled them to come. Godare a "one-family station?" I'd say, with overflowing thanks, that it was much more akin to the celebrated "extended family" so common to Africa.

1John 1:47

"Therefore, my dear brothers, stand firm. Let nothing move you. Always give yourselves fully to the work of the Lord, because you know that your labor in the Lord is not in vain."

1 Cor. 15:58

CHAPTER TWENTY

HOPES AND FEARS

Bakle, chief Balti's oldest son and heir apparent, wasn't living in the Godare area when we first moved in to open our station. This had important implications affecting our relationships with him once he returned to the Godare some eighteen months after we first arrived. When he appeared on the scene, he came with a hostile attitude. We had the feeling he wished we weren't there!

Our dealings were with Balti. It was he who had assured us of his cooperation and that he welcomed our coming to the Godare. From the beginning, it was apparent to us that Balti had enormous power and influence over his people. At times it appeared that he had the power of life and death in his hands.

When we first arrived, nothing happened without Balti's involvement and approval. If he told people to help us, they helped. When we paid helpers their wages, they counted them out to Balti and he took a few for himself. During the early months, no one worked more than a day at a time. Usually, it was far less than a day and no one ever worked by the week. At the end of each day's work, however long or short the day, we had to pay each one his or her wages. Payment was always in 5 cent coins.

As we came to know Balti and the Mesengo people better, we began to understand their *world-view*. Mesengos believed that the Creator God was far away. They recognized His existence and acknowledged him as the giver of sunshine and rain. However, they didn't worship Him and on a daily basis their concerns were about keeping unfriendly spirits satisfied and at bay.

The Mesengo had many superstitions. Some were quite humorous. Our son, Mark, as a young boy loved to hike, fish, hunt and explore with Mesengo boys his age. After returning from one of those hikes visiting villages across the river, Mark shared with us a strange experience. He said that when they came to a certain place where the path suddenly veered off in another direction, his Mesengo friends all stopped. They picked up small switches and began to switch their buttocks, threw these switches on a pile in a certain fashion, and then moved on. He said they'd told him that a leopard had crossed the path there and they did this to protect themselves from him.

In the early days when we were exploring the river for possible sites where we could put our hydraulic ram to push water up the hill into the station, I had asked Balti to provide a man who could help me research this. Balti kept dragging his feet, so one day, growing impatient, I was able to get one of the men to take me to a nearby falls so I could check it out. That evening when we returned, Balti was so furious with this man that he threatened to kill him. I learned that Balti claimed a mysterious power over these falls and that they had some superstitious views about spirits who resided in that place who also gave him special powers.

THE COFFEE TREE INCIDENT

Another strange thing occurred when workmen from Teppi located a coffee tree just off the compound. I had told the workmen that I was very interested in learning where wild coffee might be growing. I hoped that eventually we might be of some help to the Mesengos in helping them grow coffee as a cash crop.

On this occasion, Lavina and I had just returned from our first trip out to Addis Ababa with the MAF plane. Upon our return, the workmen from Teppi were excited to show us a coffee tree they had located nearby. In fact, they had already planted several volunteer seedlings they had found growing near this tree. When they showed me the tree, I was surprised at how scrawny it looked and decided I should prune it so that it would become more productive.

I thought nothing more about this as the tree was actually growing in the midst of vines and brush just off the compound. It wasn't long, however, when we discovered that Balti wasn't at all happy with what we had done. I had no idea that this tree was anything other than a wild tree growing in the forest. I learned differently when Balti and his man, Alemayu, and I pushed our way through the undergrowth to visit this scrub tree which was only about ten feet tall. I was astonished to see these two men kneel down and begin talking to unseen spirits. I learned that it was a sacred tree which had connections with someone who had died long ago. I never fully understood, but it was apparent that it was more than just a wild tree growing by itself. They thought I had been disrespectful when I cut its branches. I don't know whether I was fully successful or not in trying to indicate that I had pruned it so that it would produce coffee beans. They had no interest in harvesting coffee from it and I'm not sure they believed what I tried to explain to them. My usage of Mesengo language at that stage didn't make for the most efficient or certain communication. I did know one thing, however, and that was that Mesengos saw things far differently than I did and that I'd better learn all I could about them if we were to communicate the Gospel to them effectively.

BALTI
CHIEF AND RITUAL EXPERT

The Melineer clan to which Balti and other less important chiefs or ritual experts belonged, were considered to be gods and to have power over the spirits. On our survey trek when I made my first contact with the Mesengos, I asked an Anuak speaking Mesengo in the Korme area what the Mesengos believed about God. We were walking along the trail fifteen or twenty feet behind the leader, the Mesengo chief in that area. Pointing to the chief, he said, "Pa Jwoka eni?" (Is he not the god?)

In Balti's village there was a typical shrine with the emoy plant. It had some stones, a broken pot and another that seemed to still be intact. There were a few scattered beads and that was about all there was to it. When they made beer, a little of the new beer was always first spilled on these rocks. I was told that this was to honor and keep the ancestors happy.

Balti performed numerous sacrifices of chickens. People would come in carrying a chicken. At the appropriate moment, Balti, who had bad-looking legs with shin ulcers that never completely healed, would come out of his hut or arise from his stool. He'd point to his spear leaning up against the grass fence. Someone would fetch it. All was very informal. Someone held a gourd with a little water in it. Another held the chicken and stretched out its neck. Balti would slowly run his spear across the chicken's neck, severing it so that the blood flowed down into the gourd. The chicken never seemed to make a fuss like when I was on the farm and we'd chop a chicken's head off for Sunday's dinner.

The people who brought the chicken were squatting on their knees waiting for Balti to sprinkle them lightly with the blood and water. If someone showed up late, he'd rush in and join the others already gathered there. Before the blood was sprinkled, the spear was put back to lean along the grass fence and the chicken was put on the ground. The chicken was eventually plucked of feathers and cooked but it had no relationship to the ceremony so far as I could determine. It was just another chicken for the pot.

Sometimes if a person in the village was too ill to come to Balti to have him sacrifice the chicken, he'd put some of the blood in a hollow tubular stalk. They would seal up the end with mud and sprinkle the blood on the sick person in the village.

Almost no Mesengos kept sheep or goats. When you saw such an animal in a Mesengo village you knew it was there for some superstitious reason. I recall one Sunday seeing someone come up the hill leading a goat on the way to Balti's village. They were bringing it from home to have Balti cut off the tip of its ear to make an amulet. This tip of the ear was taken back home along with the goat. The amulet with the tip of the goat's ear was put on a string made from the fiber of the bush with the nettles and worn around the neck by the woman in the village who had been experiencing poor health. The goat itself was staked in a shady place next to some emoy plants. Every day they gave the goat preferential treatment. They spoke kindly to it and gave it beer or fermented honey water. The idea was to keep the goat happy so that the bad spirit causing the illness would leave the woman and be attracted to live in this goat.

People were constantly coming to Balti to be blessed by him. They would hand him something like a cooked Godare root or possibly a short string of beads. Usually, they knelt in front of Balti when they did this. Balti would take the object to be blessed, pass it under one of his armpits, spit on it, remove it to his other hand and repeat the procedure under the other armpit. It often appeared that he was talking causally about something unrelated to what he was doing — just having a normal, friendly conversation about almost anything. Before it was over, Balti would hand the item back to the person who brought it and this individual would wrap it in a leaf of some sort and carry it back home to the village. It appears that the idea was to convey Balti's blessing and power to a particular felt need in that person's home or village.

Frequently, we'd see young people come up to Balti and he'd spit ever so lightly on their chest or stomachs to bless them. When I got to know him better, I'd occasionally, in good humor, lift up my T-shirt and kid Balti that I could use a blessing too, always being careful to call it all off by backing away before he might think I was serious about it. Balti had a great sense of humor and loved to tease, especially the children. People loved him but also feared him greatly. He was a complex person. He was shrewd, calculating and shared in one way or another in the lives of the Mesengo people. His power and reputation extended to the far reaches of the tribe.

When we'd be working down at the river, we'd frequently see six or eight Mesengo men and women passing by on the trail leading up the hill in the direction of Balti's place.. They'd be carrying heavy pots of honey they had collected from their beehives which were positioned high in the trees throughout the forest. When I'd ask them where they were going, they'd call back, without stopping, "Weenga. weenga" (life or spirit) They were bringing these as gifts to Balti. He received many such pots of honey. Some of the honey was turned into fermented honey water into which they had shaved the bark of a certain tree to give it a drug-like effect. Others were carried by Balti's people into Metti and turned into cash. With the cash they were able to purchase heavy, old Italian army rifles. With these they could marry, kill each other and celebrate on occasions like marriages and especially in connection with deaths.

A MESENGO BURIAL

We always knew when someone had died and the burial was taking place because of the heavy rifles being fired in that place. It appeared that the more important the individual the more shots were fired. When a new mourner arrived, he'd eventually aim his gun in the direction of "nowhere" and fire.

One morning we became aware of a death just over the hill beyond the upper end of the airstrip. Throughout the morning individuals or groups of two or three came up the hill from across the river. They passed through the compound and continued on the vine-covered trail leading to that village. We'd heard a few shots during the morning and finally decided we'd go and have a look.

This is what we saw. This older man who had died had already been buried. The grave site was almost in the center of this small clearing. Women had put a small temporary grass enclosure around the mound of the grave. There were only a few shacks in this small clearing and the forest pressed in closely. As was their custom, an area of at least thirty by forty yards had been cleared of any vines or small sharp stumps. Several women were still working at that. Most people were just scattered around, sitting there, saying very little to one another. It was all extremely unorganized and informal.

Lavina and I, quietly, sat down among them on a small log. It wasn't long before one of the women ran in from behind us, put her grass skirt between her knees and took a nose dive into the air, falling flat out on the ground with a crashing thud. She was stretched out full length with her hands extended beyond her head. This was the way Mesengo women expressed their grief. Almost immediately, a couple of women rushed forward, grabbed hold of her and restrained her, forcibly, as she struggled against them, bringing her back to where she had been sitting. At this same time, other women were throwing themselves on the ground in this same way. It all seemed confusing and terribly tragic. The hopelessness and despair was overwhelming.

After this had continued for some little while, on our left and across from us, we saw a man come running across the cleared area with his spear in hand high over his head in a position from which he could throw it. He ran past the grave site to the opposite side of the clearing near the edge of the forest. Suddenly, he stopped abruptly and made menacing movements with his spear arm in several directions as if he were going to throw it each time. He then turned the spear around with the shaft pointing away from him, with the two-edged blade facing his own body. He took this spear and began violently and vigorously, with strong force, repeatedly coming down on the top of his head with the sharp blade, cutting his scalp deeply each time.

The entire gathering seemed to be getting emotionally worked up with a gun or two also being fired. At that point, we decided it would be in our best interests to quietly slip away and return home.

In the Sudan we had witnessed this same, utter despair and hopelessness when people died and were buried. The early morning wailing of the women was haunting and so extremely pathetic. Now among the Mesengo we were seeing this same hopelessness in the face of death. We had long before this noted the numerous cuts and deep scars on the foreheads or on the top of the heads of Mesengo men. It was their way to express sorrow and it was a proper way to ritually participate in such events. Both men and women also shaved their heads bare when a member of the family died.

It was significant to us that when we asked Mesengo believers how they would characterize or identify distinctive marks of a Christian, setting a person of Jesus Christ apart from people who had not yet accepted him, they always remarked that believers no longer cut their heads with spears. They had heard and embraced the fantastic good news that Jesus had conquered the power of death, set His people free from fear and had given them the assurance of life beyond the grave, a life which would never end or diminish. Interestingly, another distinguishing mark they always mentioned was that a person of Jesus Christ gave thanks to God for his food before he ate. And they always added that Christians no longer sacrificed the chicken. For Mesengos, both of these distinctives were obviously visible and important!

In trying to communicate the Gospel, we had to know these customs and learn to express the good news of what God intended for the Mesengo through Jesus Christ within the context of their world-view.

ORAL, TRACT-LIKE MESSAGES ON CASSETTES

When we began producing the oral, tract like cassettes, nearly every message, in one way or another, began with the words, "This is good news for us to listen to. It is good news because it is in our language and we can understand it. It is good news for old men and women. It is good news for young men and for the young women carrying the babies on their backs. It's good news for our children. It's good news because it is from God, the one who created the world, the God we thought had gone away and left us.

"The good news is that this Creator God never left us. And, if we will stop and think we will realize that this is true. It was the Creator God who has been giving us sunshine and rain. It was He who gave us the children in our homes and supplies us with the food that we eat. But we never worshipped Him or gave Him thanks. For this He should be angry with us and we deserve to be punished.

"But the good news is that this God loved us so much that He said, I will send my own dear Son from heaven to earth to show them what is in my heart. The name of God's only Son is Jesus Christ. We never knew what God had done, but He has sent people to live among us to tell us this good news. ... "

These messages, from different perspectives, told this good news from God. Each message led up to the central affirmation that Jesus Christ had given His life as the perfect sacrifice and therefore no more chickens need ever be sacrificed again. "Jesus came out of the grave having defeated the power of the evil one who destroys and kills. Jesus has great power and we need not ever be afraid again. He is powerfully present through His spirit which he sent to live with us and in our hearts. If we will put our trust in Him, He will protect us from every evil thing. And when we die, He will take our spirits to be with Him in heaven forever. This is the good news from God.

"And this Jesus told His followers to go everywhere in the world with this good news. Today, this good news from

God has come here too. We have heard it in our own language. We must turn away from the things we know God will not like, and give our lives to this Jesus who loved us that much. ... "

When Mesengo's heard this good news, some would respond with comments like, "Yaang jet." (This is very sweet) or with "Moko nyun." (It is not a lie).

But it took time before some among them took the plunge of faith and committed their lives to Jesus Christ. For some, it was when they realized Jesus' power to heal and experience His loving care through the clinic. For others it may have been when they saw Jesus behind the help they received when hungry and about to starve. For all, it was the divine power of the Holy Spirit who, in His time, opened blind eyes and gave the gift of faith, doing it in His own mysterious way as when the wind blows and we cannot explain where it comes from or where it is going.

DIFFERING RESPONSES TO THE MESSAGE

For some, it was a leap of faith they found impossible to make. I recall the Sunday when many were being baptized. Among the people waiting for baptism was Gadi, a smaller witchdoctor. She had had double cataract surgery in the mission hospital at Metu where Arlene Schuiteman was a nurse. Gadi had been greatly blessed by this. She wanted to commit her life to Jesus and had come to that service to be baptized along with the others. We'd sung many of the new Mesengo songs of praise. The sermon had already been preached and everyone to be baptized had come forward. Gadi, remained sitting on the ground with her paraphenilia. Slowly, she arose, turned away and made her way down the hill to her stick shack below the compound. In her hands were the paraphernalia she relied on to keep peace with and have power over the evil spirit world. It was her living and her livelihood. Village women visiting the service had whispered words of fear in her ears. She was persuaded that to be baptized was to risk her life. Sadly, she turned away and to our knowledge never committed her life to Jesus.

On the other hand, there were instances of great courage when new believers were unashamed of their allegiance to Jesus. Argeem is a case in point.

Tom Nichol, from Mettu hospital, one of the medical doctors who visited Godare clinic periodically, did a double cataract surgery. He did it in our clinic on a bare wooden table. I was his assistant and amazed at what I saw! After the surgery, this lady had both her eyes bandaged and we carried her over to one of the vacant staff houses. Argeem offered to stay by her night and day to tend to her needs. Later she told us how non-believing Mesengo women would pass by, coming in from the villages, and taunt her. They would tell her she was foolish to be sitting with a woman who wasn't even a relative of hers. They said many other unkind, sarcastic things, but Argeen said, "I'm doing this because I belong to Jesus who wants me to help others." Argeem was meeting a real need and modeling the life of Jesus so very beautifully.

This woman's case was most interesting to us. After the bandages had been removed and she could move about, she still insisted that the small girl who had helped her before the surgery continue leading her with this stick which she clung to as she was being led from place to place. This continued longer than it should and we were concerned as to the success of the operations. Then, one day in our back yard, Lavina came out to greet her and chat. This woman began to recognize that Lavina was wearing a bright red skirt. Then she looked higher and saw what long hair Lavina had. At that point, she suddenly took her walking stick and with exuberant joy threw it ten or fifteen feet into the air and began shouting that she could see. It was a joyous moment of truth I shall never forget. She realized she could see again! For it we praised God with happy hearts.

CHASED BY A DRUNKEN MESENGO
WITH A SPEAR

During our years among the Mesengo, especially those first few years, there were times when we really were alarmed and afraid. I can scarcely adequately describe our fear and the danger facing us on that day when angry, drunken Mesengos came on the compound late in the afternoon. We had a serious misunderstanding with Balti over an incident in which a young man had attempted to drive the Landrover. (How he managed to move it, I'll never understand) Later that afternoon, when Mesengos were on a high from their fermented honey water drink, laced with the bark of the tree that gave a drugged like effect, they came on the compound with evil intent.

Larry Zudweg and I were sitting, casually, in front of the office across from the clinic when I saw a group of men coming across the compound in front of the school. They seemed excited and suddenly, Bakle stopped, crouched down behind a tree about fifty yards from where we were sitting. He raised his rifle, pointing it in our direction as he took aim. I jumped to my feet and said to Larry, "The man is going to shoot. Run."

Larry responded by saying, "You've got to be kidding."

Quick as a flash, I said, "I am not, man! Run!" We both took off running down the mission road toward our houses. As we began to run, a big, strong Mesengo, under the influence, picked up his spear and began chasing us. He ran after me twirling the spear over his head ready to be thrown. I could see that we weren't going to get away. I turned around, stopped momentarily, raised my hand and in English said, "No, man, no," wheeled around and ran.

Two women jumped out of the bushes and tripped this drunken Mesengo whom I later came to know was named Ocoor. He stumbled and fell and we were able to get away. Larry peeled off into the forest below on the side. By this time, our wives had heard the commotion and were making their way up the hill to find out what was going on. I nearly collapsed into their arms with the words, "They're going to kill us all." It was the most indescribable moment of terror I had ever experienced. The women steadied me on my feet and we made our way as quickly as we could make it to the nearest building, the outside storeroom, rushed in and closed the door. We were worried as to what had become of Larry. All I could think of was Auca Indians. What a relief when Larry, after ten or fifteen minutes, showed up unscathed.

We were now all in the storeroom along with our little boy, Paul. We learned later that several of the Mesengos with their heavy rifles were lying in the coffee grove waiting for us to come out. Obala, our clinic dresser, came over and advised us to stay out of sight until their anger was cooled and they were less drunk. He helped with comforting words and by bringing over something to eat as we were going to stay hidden until morning.

Larry, Betty, Lavina, our little boy, Paul, and I were in the first room of the shop where the tools were. We immediately decided we should crawl over the six-foot-six inch metal roofing sheets which served as a wall separating this room from the next which was the middle room having its own outside door. We're still amazed that these women managed to crawl over it and get between the low roof and that wall. Once we were all over the wall, we were locked in there for the duration.

There were barrels of supplies in there and we moved them around a little to give us added insulation should the Mesengos decide to shoot through the wall. We were huddled pretty closely together and sleep didn't come quickly or sustain itself. In the early part of the night we heard the Mesengos shouting and milling about under the influence of that fermented honey water. But it gradually diminished and before mid-night all was quiet.

We had to deal with the lack of toilet facilities in those cramped quarters so that our dignity was retained. We all managed somehow, but were exceedingly happy when morning came and Paul Obala told us he'd been talking with Balti and Bakle and the other people in the village and he was sure it was safe for us to emerge. Conversations early that morning with Balti helped resolve the misunderstanding and they apologized for what they had done when drunken. They assured us that we should sleep in our regular house again and that they didn't want us to be afraid of them.

We were still skittish and uneasy about how the morning might develop when it was time to tend to our morning radio broadcast at which time all the stations checked in with Jimma. I tried to alert them to our situation without unduly alarming them. At the same time, we all felt they should know the possibilities for evil in those events. We signed off with a request that if we didn't come back on the air by noon, they should assume the worst and arrange to investigate things at the Godare. I'm sure every radio was tuned in much of the morning and that when we came on the air saying there seemed no further need for worry, many prayers of thanks to God went heavenward. At Godare, we too, gave unceasing thanks to God. He had mercifully rescued and saved us from a dangerous set of circumstances which, in part, were of my own making. We had learned important lessons. I, personally became a wiser, more careful and sensitive person because of what we had gone through. In practical terms, I learned that late afternoon among Mesengos was a wrong time to try to deal with complicated, sensitive issues requiring compromise and understanding.

THE MAN WITH THE SPEAR IS BAPTIZED

But the story doesn't end there. The marvelous, unspeakably good news is that within a year, Ocoor, the man who chased me with the spear gave his heart to Christ. It was my great joy to baptize him in the precious and powerful saving name of Jesus Christ. Ocoor became a dear friend. I once tried to purchase the infamous spear he carried that day, but he was unwilling to part with it.

Within a few months of his becoming a believer he moved with his family to an area closer to Metti about 30 miles away. He took with him a cassette player, cassettes and batteries.

Later he began purchasing his own batteries in the town of Metti so that he could keep his player operating. Ocoor won a number of people to faith in Christ. Perhaps the most important among them was Elong, the son of their local chief. Elong is the man who went across the Bako river and returned after two months with that knotted string having on it over one hundred knots.

THE INCIDENT INVOLVING BAKLE'S WIFE

The harrowing experience we had had, served us well in reminding us how to respond to various tense situations that arose from time to time during our remaining years working with the Mesengo. One incident I remember well, was the morning I came from our morning chapel with the staff and workmen. As we were having breakfast, Lavina said that while I was in chapel she'd heard a lot of loud noise in the village just beside our compound. This was where Bakle lived.

After breakfast, I thought it might be well for me to wander over there and see what the problem might be. In doing so, I stumbled into a situation that shocked and frightened me.

This is what I found. As I came around the corner and out of the brush into the village, I found Bakle sitting on a log with a hippo tail in his hand. Several women were huddled together near him, one of whom had her arms tied with grass rope so that her elbows nearly touched behind her back. She was one of Bakle's five wives. It appeared that she was about six or seven months pregnant. Across her bare abdomen was a nasty wound from the beating Bakle had given her and which was the noise Lavina had earlier heard before our breakfast. Two women were sitting near her with a gourd of water and they were occasionally using a smaller gourd to pour small amounts of water over her head which ran down over her bare breasts over her injured belly. It was a pitiful sight.

I sat down beside Bakle on the log. I wished I hadn't come. I was too frightened to speak and didn't really know what to say anyway. Bakle was nervous too. He was wearing knee high rubber boots, had his legs crossed and was swinging his foot back and forth nervously. His wife turned her head toward me without speaking. Her expression was so pathetic and I could see she was wanting me to do something to rescue her.

I had learned, previously, that Bakle was accusing his wife of being pregnant by another man. He'd been away for months and when he returned, he found his wife to be expecting a child. He was now in the process of beating her until she would reveal the guilty person.

I finally spoke softly and carefully. I recall telling him that I sympathized with his problem. I said that even the Bible teaches that adultery is wrong. But, I went on, the Bible also tells us that we are not to kill. I knew that he was trying to kill the baby she was carrying so that she would abort.

After I had spoken, Bakle responded icily as he pointed to the sky, "When the sun is over there, he said, she will talk."

I left for home and the work of the day. Around ten in the morning, I saw his wife walk ever so slowly and painfully past our back door toward the overflow pipe from the water tank. She washed her wounds and slowly returned to her village.

A few days after this incident, Bakle and a group of at least twenty grown men were at our back door. It was early in the morning. Bakle was wearing his revolver and also carrying a heavy rifle. To my knowledge he was the only Mesengo with a handgun. Bakle had stopped by to tell me that he and his men were heading across the river to deal with the man who had impregnated his wife. When I urged them not to kill, he assured me that "no guns will cry". He had stopped to report to me because of a somewhat strange relationship in which he respected my moral authority but feared I might report him to the government for his behavior.

By mid-afternoon, we began to learn what had happened. When Bakle emerged out of the forest into the clearing in which the guilty party lived, someone fired a shot and killed one of Bakle's men. Bakle, enraged, sought out the man he wanted and shot him, cold-blooded, through the head. Chaos followed. People - men, women and children - were fleeing for their lives. We began seeing people coming up the hill from the river and passing through the compound. These were pitiful, bedraggled women and children trying to hide somewhere to be safe.

The following morning, Bakle and his men came up the hill and walked past the compound without saying a word to us. It was apparent that they had large guilt feelings and were fearful that I would report them to the government. Eventually, without my involvement, the government in Metti learned about this incident. Bakle was picked up and spent about a month in jail. He was then released, after which he returned to the Godare and again lived beside us. It was some weeks before he acted normally toward us because he mistakenly assumed that I had reported him to the local governor in Metti.

BAKLE BECOMES A FRIEND

Eventually, tensions eased and we were again on quite a friendly basis. When we began teaching Mesengos how to grow coffee and brought in coffee seedlings for them to plant, Bakle took the lead in encouraging his people to take advantage of this opportunity. Bakle himself had the finest little coffee plantation and we became quite good friends. The day even came when he and his wives were baptized. On the day we left, I saw him cry because he was so sad to see us leave. God's ways are indeed mysterious and His mercy is beyond measurement.

"Fear not for I have redeemed you; I have called you by name, you are mine. When you pass through the waters I will be with you; and through the rivers, they shall not overwhelm you; when you walk through the fire you shall not be burned, and the flame shall not consume you."

Isaiah 43:1-2

CHAPTER TWENTY-ONE

OUR VISION GROWS

These first few years in the forest we'd learned a lot about Mesengo customs and habits. They were what anthropologists describe as a "slash and burn" people. With their small axes and knives they hacked down huge trees to clear small areas where they could build the simplest kinds of stick houses. Many of their houses were little more than stick shelters with open sides except the house in which people slept. These could also be securely closed. Their houses were scattered around the clearings with no apparent rhyme or reason.

Sometimes an individual man cleared back a forest area by himself where he'd build a shack or two and locate his family. Others would work communally helping each other clear back the forest for new plantings. Women had huge, baked, earthen crocks in which they fermented the corn mash. This was the magnet that attracted Mesengo neighbors to come and help someone clear his area. This beer was not that potent and, in many respects, was the stimulant to their diet needed that day for abnormally heavy work. These "working bees" were usually, happy social gatherings with only an occasional time when some beer may have gotten a little too potent and an individual or two went too far.

The Mesengos had a most interesting way to show the depth of relationships on occasions like that by their peculiar manner of drinking from a gourd. Two persons, normally men with men, but occasionally a man and woman, would drink simultaneously from the same gourd. Two persons would be sitting side by side and having a gourd of beer or honey water in front of them. While they were quietly visiting together, one of them would pick up this gourd and lift it to their lips. Their heads were side by side, facing the same direction, and with their mouths close to each other, as they took a small drink from the gourd. They did this in a leisurely fashion until the gourd was eventually empty. To me it always appeared that it would be very difficult to drink with another person at the same time from the same container, but the Mesengos handled it with no problem. And they did this without spilling a drop!

Felling the trees for a new clearing was a big, social event, made more pleasant by the abundance of food in the drinking involved.

Once the trees were felled, some weeks would pass before the brush had dried sufficiently to be burned. Even when fired up the logs and larger branches and stumps all remained as before. The Mesengo never cultivated their soil in any fashion whatsoever. Dura (sorghum) seed was simply scattered among these stumps and branches. Maize was planted using a long stick to make the hole in the soil into which the kernels were dropped and stepped on. The only hoeing a Mesengo did was to cut back, and that very haphazardly, those new growths that seemed to be getting out of hand. The men did the chopping and burning, but the women and girls did most of the planting. Boys and girls guarded the fields from monkeys and baboons when the corn was beginning to ripen. Sometimes a musically inclined person would select certain kinds of sticks, split them and tie them together with vines in racks of five or six, separated by eight or ten inches. These were strung up to hang freely suspended between poles looking like our wooden fence posts on each side. Beating these crude musical instruments, they created quite beautiful combinations of melodious sounds. Apparently, it was music the baboons and monkeys preferred not to come near.

Mesengos, however, didn't rely only on their small, unproductive plantings for food. Men also hunted for wild pig and they set fish traps in the rivers. The women worked extremely hard in searching for and digging out edible roots over a wide area in the surrounding forest.

Mesengos were noted for their honey-collecting skills. One man might have as many as forty to sixty hollowed-out, log beehives in forest trees scattered over a wide area. By lacing smaller 3-inch poles up a tree trunk, Mesengos had learned how to reach the first limbs of the taller trees having trunks too large to climb. Agile men climbed up on these three-inch poles securely laced to the larger trunk. Having reached the lower limbs, they would hoist up their beehives on vines tied together like a long rope. The honey collected was their cash crop, but it was also their daily diet during long periods during the dry season. When mixed with water and allowed to ferment only a little, it was a pleasant, nourishing drink for them and popular as a soft drink throughout southwest Ethiopia. But Mesengos also often scraped into the honey water the bark of a certain tree. This combination had a drug like effect on those who drank it. Sometimes if there was too much bark or if the drink was allowed to ferment too long, it caused those who imbibed too long to become irritable and argumentative. It seemed that Mesengos didn't stagger from this as one would expect to see when one is drunken. Instead, they seemed to become unpredictably hostile and contentious.

Mesengos stayed in their clearings for three or four years, at the most, and then moved on, clearing another small plot as before. Useable sticks and grass from their abandoned houses were tied up with vines and used again for the new structures on the new location. The old village site was left to grow over with vines and brush. Large sections of the forest had been cut back like this, making room for the Mesengo. It was a never ending cycle of slash and burn, staying in one place a few years, abandoning it to grow over again, and moving into a newly cleared site.

When travelling through the forest and visiting Mesengo villages, we'd normally spend an hour or more in thick, uncut, original growth before emerging into a Mesengo clearing of scattered shacks and unkempt fields. To move ahead, one followed a crooked path through this clearing to the opposite side, reentered the forest and continued on to the next clearing. During our early days, these trails were uncut with many areas having low, uncut vines making walking difficult. Mesengos feared raids from hostile neighboring tribes.

Lavina and I were itching to trek out over these trails to Mesengos scattered about in these forest clearings. We had good news to share with them and were eager for the opportunity to preach it to them in their language.

While John and Harriet Boerema were with us, Lavina and I could get away to do this. Once we were out for eighteen days. We had with us ten young Mesengo Christians who helped carry supplies and whom we wanted to train in evangelism. They could witness first-hand how we went about it and our hope was that it would stimulate them and encourage their hearts.

AN EIGHTEEN DAY TREK

Lavina and I each had a horse that we could ride or when we were tired of the saddle we would be leading our animal behind us. The horses were sometimes a big help in carrying us up the steep hills. The area between us and Teppi, the direction in which we were moving, was characterized by rivers and streams flowing toward the Bako river. Every stream and river meant a steep hill, mountainous like, that one was either climbing or descending. Long stretches of level terrain were outnumbered by the hills and peaks. This made for tough going.

We'd been on the way less than four hours when Lavina's horse balked. She was coming up out of a steep gully, when the animal stopped, backed down into it, with Lavina falling off. In those tight quarters with brush on both sides, her horse kicked her in the hip. It was really painful and I thought we should consider calling the trek off and returning home. Lavina wouldn't hear of it and after awhile said, "I'll be alright. Let's get moving." I admired her for her spunk, and made a secret resolution that this would be the last time this horse would kick my wife. When we reached Teppi, I'd take him to the Saturday market, sell him and come back with a different animal. And, that's exactly what happened!

KONKON

Our first big stop was the village of Konkon. We stayed there two and a half days. I preached and we mingled with the Mesengo people throughout the day. Lavina prepared food at appropriate times from the supplies we were carrying in our trek boxes. At night we slept in jungle hammocks we'd strung up in the forest just on the edge of the clearing. During the night we heard many frightening and ominous sounds. Dogs barked incessantly, monkeys chattered and called back and forth to each other. We even heard a leopard coughing somewhere in the distance, and we thought we heard leaves rustling indicating a snake or python might be moving about nearby.

But the most exciting moment was on the morning of the third day when we were preparing to leave. An older man, a woman with a baby in its carrying pouch on her back and a little child beside her came to us and said that they wanted to become people of the Jesus we'd been telling them about. Our joy was tempered by the fact that we were leaving and there were no other believers in that entire area and we had no one to leave behind to teach them. What could we say? I remember well the words that the Lord gave me. This is how I concluded our conversation. I said, "It is true that we are leaving, but remember that Jesus is not leaving. You have seen how we talked to him when we prayed. You, too, must talk to him every day just as you heard us doing. He is strong and powerful and able to protect you from every evil thing. Trust him completely. Some day somebody else will be coming to this village with these same words about Jesus. Listen to him. He will teach you more. Until then, we too will pray for you many times."

We put our arms around each other and commended them to our Lord Jesus, and then we left. Because of illness, I never, personally visited Konkon again. But the story doesn't end there and we'll return to it at the appropriate place.

TEPPI

When Lavina and I finally reached Teppi, we camped on a hillside beside one of the major trails leading out of town. It was right near where the road turned. This was a Saturday and the town was overflowing with people, including Mesengos from that region, who had come into the market. Such market days brought hundreds of people from several different language groups. They came with donkeys, horses, and on foot. They brought sheep and goats, other livestock, grains and items of every description to bargain, sell or purchase. It was the important day of the week when everyone dressed up and came to town. Relatives and friends met in the market and shared news. More than should have made their way to the "Tej Bets" (shops where people sat and drank beer and moonshine.) More than a few found it more difficult to return home than to come.

Lavina and I had already begun a ministry in Teppi. We'd opened a small book room where Bibles, tapes and a small amount of Christian literature were sold. We'd also rented a room where we could keep our cots, simple cooking utensils, and a few supplies. We'd come in with MAF and spend a week visiting the various "Bunna Bets" (coffee houses). We'd play our tapes in whatever language was needed. Most of these houses were congregated by people who spoke the same language. Each group had its own houses they frequented most. On the market day, we'd play our tapes in the market for people who would otherwise never hear. It was a great opportunity and our hearts longed to find a way to take full advantage of it by having a permanent base in that town.

But now on that Saturday afternoon, we were camped on the edge of town on the far side. Our ministry at this stage was focused almost exclusively among the Mesengos. As we pitched our tent and spread ourselves out, we brought out the cassette player and began a tape with Mesengo music. We knew that Mesengos loved to hear their small Mesengo piano boxes being played on tape. It would soon attract a crowd here too.

CURIOUS MESENGOS IN TEPPI

Mesengos leaving town turned in to see what was going on. They were attracted by the music and curious about these strange white people. Before long, we had quite a crowd, invited them to sit with us and listen to the "box that talks." I wish you could have seen the expressions on their faces and heard their barely audible comments. I shall never forget one old woman sitting there - legs extended and feet crossed, listening intently. I saw her turn to a woman behind her and say, "Why haven't we heard this before? I wish (and she mentioned someone's name) were with me to hear what we are hearing."

I never ceased to marvel at the Mesengo's positive response to the good news about Jesus when they heard it in their language on cassettes. I was then and remain now convinced that the cassette was no accident of history, but that the cassette is part of God's provision to be utilized to proclaim in every language the good news of His beloved Son.

Eighteen days from the time we started out, Lavina and I arrived home at the Godare. We were tired, hungry and exhausted, but our hearts were glad. The young men who had helped us were excited to share from their experiences. It was good for the people we had visited and it was a catalyst to the little church developing at the Godare. That night we praised God together with John and Harriet. He had spared them during their time of danger and he had brought us back safely. And when we prayed for the new believers we'd left behind in Konkon, we knew there was rejoicing among the angels in heaven. I had every intention to return to Konkon at an early date.

Our vision was growing. From the time we'd first assembled our gear in Teppi for the trek into the Godare, we felt a special burden for this town. It was only a matter of time before the urge to base ourselves in Teppi became irresistible. But before that would happen, a number of important pieces had to fall into place. Could a replacement be found to take over from us at Godare? On what basis could we receive government permission to open a mission work based in Teppi? These and other important details were pondered, prayed over and awaited implementing in God's tomorrow.

CHECKING ON NEW AIRSTRIP POSSIBILITIES

We'd often flown with MAF between their base in Jimma and Godare. Sometimes it was a straight line and other times we'd fly by way of Teppi. Flights I seem to remember best were those I made with our son, Denny, as pilot or with Vern Sikkema. The reason I recall my flights with Vern is that I often heard him comment as he looked down below. He'd say something to the effect that "I think we could get an airstrip in there." And when we flew over the old Italian strip at Gecha about fifteen minutes northeast of Godare, he'd say, "We should try to drive in there with a Landrover someday and see how much work would be involved in reactivating it."

You guessed it! The time came when Vern and I flew the old big-wheeled Porter aircraft to Gore and borrowed Kert Hultgren's Landrover to try to reach Gecha overland. One of the tires on the Landrover had a patch on it the size of a maple leaf. It looked unreliable, but with speeds never exceeding a few miles per hour, it wasn't a real problem. We had only one flat that last evening going up a long, stony hill approaching Gore from where we had started out.

Vehicles hadn't been over that road or trail from Gore to Teppi in years. The Italians had built the road during their occupation of Ethiopia, but once they left, like the airstrip, it had been abandoned.

It took us more than a day to do the fifty or so odd miles from Gore to Gecha. The local governor was excited when he heard us driving in. He put on a big feast, killing a sheep and serving us their very best injira with wat that evening long after dark. In the morning, the governor, a few officials, forty or fifty local men, Vern and I walked out to the former airstrip site. There were no trees or stumps on it but it was a mess with grass humps everywhere. Cattle grazed on it and it really was a huge cow pasture without fences except for the one that crossed the strip near the lower end. I remember that one because when we eventually landed and had our first take-off that fence seemed dangerously close to our wheels as we cleared it and were in the air.

The governor promised to have his men hoe off the humps and smooth the strip so that we could make a landing if we'd fly in as soon as we returned to Gore.

On our way out, we gave a ride to a young man dressed in a business suit. This was unusual dress for those parts. He turned out to be a young member of the parliament in Addis Ababa. When he learned that we were planning to open the airstrip in Gecha and begin an itinerant ministry with a medical team, he said, "You have to do this in my country too." He explained that he was from the area beyond the mountainous ridge to the west. His father was one of the most important landlords in that whole region. He said, "If you'll do this for my people there, my father will build you an airstrip so that you can fly in."

The landing at Gecha was successful. About three months later, Arlene Schuiteman, an RCA nurse working at Mettu hospital, came on the radio with startling news. She normally didn't call Godare but that morning she called in, "Three five, three five this is three nine. Do you read me?"

We said, "We read you loud and clear; go ahead."

This was her message. Peace Corps people had been in that area some fifteen or twenty minutes north of Godare. They were there in connection with the drive to stamp out smallpox. They were now back in Mettu and told her that two airstrips were being built in the area north of us. They were, in fact, airstrips being built under the direction of the big landlord, the father of our passenger returning to Gore, that member of parliament. Again, we marveled at how the Lord puts things together. A, seemingly, chance hitchhiker catching a ride and catching a vision resulting in the opening of an entirely new area to the Gospel. ... We thanked Arlene, signed off and pondered where it would all lead to.

DARABATA

Less than two weeks later, Harold Kurtz, the mission's general Secretary and also a skilled pilot who flew his personal 185 Cessna called on the radio. He said he was going to check out these airstrips and see if he could locate them. He wanted to know if I'd be interested in riding along. He'd come into the Godare first and pick me up. I jumped at the chance and by mid-day we were flying back and forth over that ridge which sloped off toward the east into a huge valley. We eventually found what appeared to be the strip that was closest to being completed.

We began circling the field, flying closer and closer to the ground. A tall tree just off the upper end was a menace and later had to be removed. People could be seen running from their villages in our direction. There was tremendous excitement among them to be sure. Their hard work had paid off. The plane was actually there and they were wanting to see it on the ground.

Finally, after we touched the wheels once or twice flying in the direction he eventually would have to take off in, Harold pulled up and said, "Fasten your seat belt and shoulder straps securely. I think we can make it."

He flew out over the valley and turned back for his approach. We came in over where the field dropped off sharply some eight hundred to a thousand feet to the valley below. Our wheels hit the ground and the plane shuddered from the vibration. It was a rough field. The speed, to me a lay person, seemed incredibly fast. My adrenaline was flowing freely. But it soon became apparent that Harold had it mastered and we were rolling to a stop. When we opened the plane's doors and stepped onto the soil, the people were ecstatic. They were pushing in from all sides with people shouting and talking together with uncontainable excitement and exuberance. In that setting, my first words to Harold were, "Harold, let's give thanks to God."

Harold climbed up on the wing of the plane, sat there with his legs dangling down, and prayed in Amharic. Some understood, but most only realized he was praying to God. The language in that area was Oromo. Almost before Harold finished his prayer the people began to clap spontaneously. I have often thought, they had every reason to clap for joy. Their lives would never be the same. The good news from God had also come to them. With that good news they would also receive medical care and learn how to live a better life. Our hearts were glad.

This airstrip was known as Darabata. The other strip the Peace Corps people had reported to Arlene still needed a lot of work on it. Eventually both strips were opened and we began a regular itinerant ministry from Godare. Key elements in the ministry were the visits by our medical dresser with modern medicines and the use of players and cassettes with tapes in the language spoken by those people.

The Darabata strip, like nearly every strip we opened, had undulations and low spots that had to be corrected. Usually, after the first landing, we'd fly in our little garden tractor with its plow attachment and go to work.

SOLOMON GIZAW

The work on the Darabata strip was especially interesting because of the young fifteen or sixteen-year-old lad, a nephew, the landowner had entrusted with the work in his absence. While we plowed with the little tractor, this young lad, who was named Solomon, was supervising several teams of oxen pulling their plows. We liked this young man from the first time we saw him in action. We discovered that he was enamored with our tractor. He appeared just to love to feel it vibrate and would jump at the chance if we'd only allow him to operate it.

That young boy went off to the government school in Gore but stayed in Kert and Lillie Hultgren's hostel. Later that fall when revival broke out in the hostel among the students, this young lad, Solomon, gave his heart to Christ. When the Hultgrens eventually moved to Jimma, he accompanied them. Kert taught Solomon how to drive the Landrover and he proved to be especially adept at learning mechanical skills like changing the oil or adjusting the brakes. If it was mechanical, Solomon loved it.

Included in Kert's responsibilities in Jimma was his purchasing of supplies for missionaries living in the outposts. These had to be sought out and purchased in the local stores or marketplace. Solomon was Kert's right hand man. Eventually, he did most of the purchasing and packing himself and delivered them to the hanger where MAF had their planes. This gave Solomon a feel for what MAF was all about and he endeared himself to the MAF pilots and mechanics. They recognized that Solomon had the potential of becoming an MAF pilot if only he could get the education and training needed.

We had to leave Ethiopia before Solomon had completed his high school education. We kept in touch. Things became difficult in Ethiopia because of the revolution in which the communists took over and eventually destroyed the country.

After completing his high school work, this young man tried various means to secure a passport so that he could leave Ethiopia legally. Many his age were fleeing the country to become refugees in the Sudan, Kenya and other places. But Solomon was determined to leave Ethiopia legally. After more than two years of abortive effort, he said he simply gave up trying and surrendered his futile efforts to the Lord.

If God wanted him to leave Ethiopia, God could open the way. Solomon tells of the great peace he experienced and how almost immediately things began to fall into place.

Unknown to him, we were working on his behalf in America. Hope College sent him the important papers the Ethiopian government required before they'd give him a passport and an exit visa. Glenn Bruggers, the Africa Regional Secretary for the Reformed Church in America provided funds for his ticket to the states. Mr. Kieft offered to help with funds to supplement his scholarship from Hope. It all came together at the exact moment the Lord had planned.

This young man worked hard to help cover expenses while at Hope. He struggled academically as he tried to pay most of his own way and keep up his studies at the same time. Even before graduation from Hope, he began his aeronautical training in Grand Rapids, Michigan. All was successfully completed and today Solomon and his wife, Genet, and children are flying for MAF in Uganda. In Kampala they have an additional fruitful ministry among Ethiopia refugees and have succeeded in planting a church among them. They dream someday of flying for MAF in Ethiopia, their original homeland.

GOD'S PROVIDENTIAL LEADING

It's difficult to realize that it all started with bits and pieces coming together in Ethiopia. How marvelous are the ways of God. An MAF pilot years earlier observes, "We should be able to open a strip over there." A hitchhiker is given a lift. He talks to his father who builds an airstrip on which MAF could land. A young lad helps make the strip useable, goes off to school, gets converted in a revival among students, becomes the mission's purchasing agent's helper which introduces him to MAF. He dreams of the possibility of his becoming a pilot for MAF. In God's timing it all comes together. So many played a part. But it was God who made it happen. Today this young lad, now married with a lovely wife and family, is flying for the Lord in Africa. How thrilling to be part of God's great master plan to take the Gospel to the ends of the earth. We see it happening just as Jesus predicted. "This Gospel of the kingdom will be proclaimed throughout the whole world as a testimony to the nations and then the end shall come."

CHAPTER TWENTY-TWO

CONTENDING WITH ILLNESS

The Godare River area was not a healthy place to live. The Mesengos themselves suffered many illnesses. All of the tropical diseases were evident — dysentery, malaria, smallpox before it was eradicated during our years there, tuberculosis, sleeping sickness, colds, flu and others plus their being afflicted with infections and tropical ulcers. We saw middle-aged people become permanently old following a struggle to survive a severe illness. And then there was endemic elephantiasis plainly seen in the water-logged, swollen feet and lower limbs of men like Balti, Gimti and many others we knew. Certain areas were identified as having an unusually high number of women with huge goiters, larger in size than I could ever have imagined. These women could barely talk because of the huge, four- to- five inch growth of swelling around their necks and under their chins. Right from the beginning we tried helping with treatments and modern medicines. Within a year we had a good clinic building and a trained Ethiopian dresser [1] on staff. Paul Obala, an Anuak medical dresser, came up from the Gila river station and served with us most of our years at Godare. The good news about the clinic spread and people came from ever more distant villages. Severe injuries or extremely ill patients were carried in on crude, home-made stretchers.

MESENGO STRETCHERS

These stretchers were interesting and represented a lot of creativity. Usually they were five-or six-foot light poles tied together with vines to give a two foot base on which the patient could lie. To prevent the patient from rolling off, they fashioned a protective canopy of light sticks like a half-circle over the patient, spacing them so that three or four of these prevented the patient from falling off when they went down steep banks, crossed rivers or encountered rocks or logs on their journey.

When these pitiful stretcher cases came in, their were always fifteen or twenty people who took turns carrying. It was truly a major, desperate, last ditch effort they made to find help. All these kinds of cases sickened our hearts because of the human tragedy and pain they were suffering. Sometimes it was too late to help, but other times we saw dramatic recoveries. There were times when we'd send these stretcher cases and other kinds of patients out with the MAF plane to one of the mission hospitals. Each time these crudely fashioned stretcher cases came in, we had the opportunity to share the love of Jesus with people who knew little if anything about who He was. Tape players were listened to in the outpatient houses and there were always numerous people beside the patient who were hearing this good news from God.

CONTENDING WITH PERSONAL ILLNESS

No, the rain forest where we lived wasn't a healthy place to live. Lavina did much better than I did. This was strange, too, because when we started out for the mission field, way back in 1948, Lavina was considered to be the frail one. People in Bignell Chapel, where we'd served as their student pastor for three years, were concerned that Lavina might not be healthy enough for the rigors of the tropics. They'd seen her getting pneumonia and struggling with a virus for many months. During our first months in the Sudan, I gave her regular injections to build up her red blood count. But she fooled everyone and proved to be much less prone to sickness than was I.

MALARIA

Getting dysentery was taken for granted. Malaria was something we protected ourselves against by taking a couple of little pills once or twice a week. In the Sudan, these pills had been quite effective, The malarial strain in the rain forest was much more resistant. I remember once when Paul had it. He was less than five years old then. At breakfast time, I'd made a comment about what a beautiful day it was. Around ten that morning, Paul went into his tent and his fever began to increase rapidly. At one point, not feeling at all well, he called out with a tearful voice, "I thought you said it was a beautiful day." Paul was feeling miserable. His malaria was the kind that flared up every forty eight hours. During the off day he felt quite normal, but on the following day it was a different story. With medication, it normally took a week or ten days to knock out the fever. Tiredness and listlessness lingered much longer.

I had severe malaria on several occasions. It left one really feeling unwell, discouraged and lacking in ambition. After one of those sieges, Lavina and I joined the rest of our mission in Addis Ababa for our annual mission meeting. This was six weeks after I'd finished my treatment. When Dr. Mary Smith met Lavina, before Dr. Mary and I had run across each other, she said to Lavina, "Where's Harvey? I hear he looks just awful." Malaria was no fun!

FILARIASIS

I also became infected with that nasty elephantiasis, or filariasis. Before I realized what it was, I was itching a small three or four inch patch on my shin for weeks. During our furlough a skin specialist said he thought it was some kind of a fungus. Later, back in Ethiopia, while I was in Addis, we decided to check it out with a tropical disease doctor in one of the hospitals there. He took a little snitch of skin from that area and put it under the microscope. What he saw excited him. Under the microscope was a wiggling parasite he identified as the one causing elephantiasis. He called in his students and each had a turn at observing this thing doing its antics. Although this disease is common in Ethiopia at lower altitudes, I got the impression that they didn't see these kinds of parasites under the microscope very frequently in hospitals in Addis where the elevation was well over 8,000 feet.

Treating this disease is a long-term proposition. The disease is caused by the numerous little black, elephant-back flies down along the rivers. When they deposit their eggs on a person's skin, one or more become host "worms" in the human body. These, in turn, spew out countless microfilaria into the blood stream and these, again, damage the lymph glands causing fluid to collect in the lower extremities of the body.

I was diagnosed as having them and treatment began promptly. The medicine used at that time was extremely toxic and required one to spend at least twenty four hours in the hospital in the event the reaction was too severe and required an antidote. The first treatment began with one half of a half of a small pill. This dosage was gradually increased until at the end of three weeks I was taking a total of nine of these little pills a day. Antihistamine helped control the reaction, but even so the itching was pretty awful the first couple of days each time one took the course. I was still taking treatments for this regularly when we left Ethiopia in 1976 and continue to experience the after effects of the damage done. It's a nasty disease.

HEPATITIS

The most serious illness we encountered was a case of severe hepatitis which put me in bed for nearly three months. At the onset, I'd been feeling unusually tired for more than a week. In fact, I was so exhausted that I'd have to return to the house to lie down several times during the day. I had an important meeting with the governor in Teppi that I had to keep. Vern Sikkema, one of the MAF pilots, had night-stopped at Godare and said he could drop me off in Teppi in the morning on his return to Jimma. This was Sunday morning and he planned to leave early so as to be home in time to attend church with his family.

I took an aspirin before leaving with him for Teppi. I felt extremely unwell but never suspected hepatitis. In Teppi I put up my tent, crawled in and lay there feeling terribly ill. Later in the morning, when I went out I saw that my urine was the color of mahogany, I knew that something serious was afoot. I ate absolutely nothing that entire day and lay in the tent waiting for my appointment on Monday morning. One of the merchants came by around nine in the evening and offered to help. He urged a sip of tea on me which he had kindly brought over.

I kept my appointment with the governor in the morning. At mid-day MAF, by previous arrangement, landed in Teppi and flew me back to the Godare. The next morning, I spoke by radio with Dr. Dan Reynolds, one of the mission doctors who was in the Pokwo station. After I described my situation, he said, "You have hepatitis, man. Go straight to bed and stay there. Try to drink lots of fluids and fruit juices. There's no medication for hepatitis. You need rest and more rest. It'll take weeks before you're recovered." That was bad news, indeed.

As soon as we finished talking, before going to bed, I hiked down to the river one last time to check on the turbine. John Ojulu, who took care of the turbine, went with me. I wanted to be sure it was operating well and properly lubricated. I went over everything with John, and slowly trudged back up the long hill. I fell into bed completely exhausted and stayed there until the plane came in to fly me to the hospital in Addis.

Lavina gave me the tenderest, loving care anyone could ever wish for. I know it was a great strain on her to have this responsibility. She found her strength and courage in the Lord and never faltered! Those were difficult days for both of us, but the Lord was present and very precious to us while we were learning new lessons in patience and in what it means to trust Him completely.

Dr. Dan Reynolds was on the radio with Lavina every day inquiring as to my progress and making suggestions. The MAF plane flew out blood samples on a weekly basis. The reports were never encouraging. My liver was badly swollen. One of the doctors put it this way when he said to me, "Your liver was badly stepped on." For weeks my skin was as yellow as an old, plucked chicken hanging in a butcher shop. I lost twenty-nine pounds during those three months. I was a very sick man.

Even so, there were also times of levity and we could chuckle and laugh together. I remember once receiving a note from Mary Alice Jordan, who with Chuck was in the Adura River station near the Sudan border. She sent up a humorous little note with MAF, saying, "I hope you're not lying there thinking the Lord is pacing back and forth in His office every day wondering how He can get along without you!" We enjoyed it thoroughly. In it was an important reminder that the Lord was at work in ways beyond us.

One of the great truths I learned during those days was that the Lord's work didn't stop among the Mesengo because I wasn't personally involved. He was continuing to bless the witness of Mesengo Christians and we kept on hearing of new people coming to faith in Christ. I had nothing to do with it. God was marvelously at work showing mercy and kindness to these people who had been in great darkness. There was no direct correlation between my involvement and the final result. The Lord was getting along without me just fine! It was God's mission, not mine! An important lesson that continues to encourage our hearts even now.

OCOOR COMES TO PRAY FOR ME

Dr. Reynalds had urged Lavina that outside visitors should be kept to a minimum. He said, "Harvey needs all the rest he can get." But there were exceptions to the rule. Let me share a marvelous experience. One afternoon there was a clap outside our kitchen door in the back. Lavina went out and discovered that Ocoor and several of his friends were standing there. They had been on the trail for three days. They indicated that they wanted to see me. Lavina told them that the Dr. had advised against my having anyone come in. Ocoor protested that they had come because they had heard that Odola was ill and they wanted to pray for him. With that, Lavina couldn't resist and invited Ocoor and three of his friends to come in.

They came into the bedroom. They sat on chairs and someone sat on the floor. Then Ocoor said, "Now we are going to pray for you." He identified the men who were to pray. One of the two men selected got stuck in the middle of his prayer. At that point, Ocoor put words in his mouth and the man prayed line by line the words Ocoor was giving him. It was a moving, beautiful, unforgettable experience and we praised God. You will recall that Ocoor was the Mesengo who had tried to spear me on that dreadful afternoon several years before. How wonderful is the grace and power of our Lord Jesus Christ.

After a month in bed at home, Lavina was concerned that I get to a hospital for whatever help they could give. Denny was flying in an area just north of us that particular day. He and his mother were on the radio as he flew. Den suggested that he fly in Dr. John Cremer from Dembidollo to have a look at me and decide what should be done. He flew in that same afternoon and decided this missionary needed to get into a hospital in Addis without delay. The next day, MAF flew in and I was carried on a cot by four Mesengo men to the plane and we were on our way to Addis Ababa.

An excellent tropical disease doctor from England began caring for me in the Haile Sellasi hospital. Lavina stayed in the mission guest house and made it out to the hospital twice every day. Our dear friends, Bill and Marilyn Vineyard who were with the American Embassy in Addis, were able to get all the tin fruit juices I needed from the government canteen. They probably don't realize how important their special contribution was to my recovery.

The Lord mercifully restored me to the point where, thirty days later, I could get out of bed and go the mission guest house in Addis. At first, even with Lavina to lean on and using a sturdy cane, I could barely walk. Recovery was slow and I spent most of the next thirty days in bed.

But God has marvelous blessings for us through adversity. How marvelous and, yes, strange are His ways sometimes.

THE VISIT BY DR. CLARK AND MR. OGILVIE

By this time we were back from Bishoftu, a beautiful, relaxing vacation and conference center operated by the Sudan Interior Mission (SIM) located on a beautiful crater lake about forty miles outside of Addis Ababa. Now I was spending the best part of every day in bed in the mission guest house, trying to gradually recover my strength. Dr. Roy Clark was in from his hospital at Mettu during this same period. He was concerned with my slow progress.

One morning he came to the room where I was lying in bed and Lavina was sitting on a chair beside me. With him, Dr. Clark had brought a man I had never met before, but of whom I had heard. His companion was an older, former SIM missionary by the name of Ogilvie. This man was known for his eccentric ways and was also recognized by some to have an unusual spiritual gift of healing. There were many stories circulating about this man and how he wandered about from place to place casting out evil spirits and healing the sick. He was an unusual person, to say the least.

These two men said they'd like to anoint me with oil and to pray for me. I had no objection and was greatly pleased. They took the little vial of oil and anointed me. Placing their hands over my liver area they began to pray for me. I recall how warm their hands were — much warmer than an ordinary hand normally would feel. They prayed for me in English and they prayed for me in tongues. Then Mr. Ogilvie began to prophecy, speaking in beautiful poetic English. He was saying that the Lord is healing you of this disease. He is leading you into a larger ministry etc. etc. Then he turned to Lavina and speaking in poetic form again said to her that the Lord was healing me, leading us into a larger ministry and that she shouldn't be concerned about anything because God was leading and would supply our every need.

When the men left the room, Lavina and I looked at each other and both of us knew that God was in it. God had sent them to minister to us. What these men didn't know is that during my illness, I had frequently shared with Lavina my burning desire to open a new work at Teppi from which we could reach out to four or five unreached peoples groups using cassettes. Each time I talked to her, Lavina had seemed less than enthusiastic about it. She kept urging me to not worry about those possibilities yet. First I had to get well and then we could talk about possibly opening a new station.

These were the kinds of differing viewpoints we frequently shared with each other. But when these two men left our room that morning, both Lavina and I were at peace over this matter. We both recognized that God was calling us to open that new station and that in His perfect timing it would happen. What a marvelous experience for us. The Lord had ministered to us in this unusual, somewhat unconventional way. I wasn't healed instantaneously, but felt then and now that a healing process began that day which was directly related to the men who anointed me with oil and prayed over me in English and in tongues. Six months later, when I again met Dr. Clark he shared this with me. He said, "When we came in to anoint you with oil and pray for you that morning, I felt sure that you had cancer of the liver."

Only God knows! But this we do know that whereas once I was weak and ill, I'm today strong and well. It was Jesus Christ the great physician who mercifully restored me to health. My deepest longing was and continues to be that I be available to Him for whatever tasks He has for Lavina and me to do for Him!

The bout with hepatitis had an enormous impact on our lives and ministry. It was apparent that my complete recovery of strength and vigor was going to take years rather than months. We were going to need to rethink how we were to minister to those who became believers in villages where this missionary would not yet be strong enough to reach. Hiking over rough terrain, climbing steep hills and crossing river and streams was beyond me. But by this time we knew that some of God's most fragrant flowers are often found among the thorns of life.

PERGATIIN GOES TO KONKON

Let me share one of the important events of that period. You will recall that in the village of Konkon, Lavina and I had preached and shared the Gospel on our eighteen-day trek. You will remember how we'd committed those two new believers to the Lord and promised them that one day somebody would come to their village and teach them more.

It was a young man by the name of Pergatiin from the village of Dampay, about four miles out, that God raised up to visit that village. One day Pergatiin came to me and said he'd like to go with a cassette player and teach the people of Konkon. Pergatiin, himself, was totally uneducated. He was a young man of about twenty years of age, but he'd never been to school and had never learned to read. We sent him off with a cassette player, a double set of batteries so that he'd have a second set when the first ones went dead, and we gave him a number of different cassettes with the essential Christian message. Occasionally, Pergatiin came in to pick up fresh batteries.

Then came that wonderful day when Pergatiin came in with a knotted grass string having 37 knots on it. He reported that there were 37 people who had believed in Jesus and they were wanting to be baptized. This was exciting, good news but it posed a problem. How were they to be baptized when this missionary was too weak to make it those eight hours to that village? It didn't seem right that they should be denied baptism because this missionary couldn't reach them.

It seemed that we had two options. We could tell those people they had to wait a year or two until this missionary was sufficiently recovered so he could come and baptize them, or we could consider ordaining a Mesengo whom the growing church at Godare could identify and commission for that responsibility.

ROKET IS ORDAINED

I discussed these matters with Harold Kurtz, our General Secretary. He'd taken some courses at Fuller's School of World Mission and was eager to have our mission take bold initiatives to help the developing churches become truly indigenous in their application of the Gospel. He was most open to the possibility of doing something very unorthodox. Harold and I were both firm believers in indigenous leadership guided by a contextualized theology.

With Harold's blessing and encouragement, I began meeting with Mesengo Christians worshipping at Godare to share with them the need I saw for someone to be chosen whom we could train and entrust with administering the sacraments. I explained to them why I felt it was important for the Konkon believers to be baptized and share in celebrating the Lord's Supper. They understood that I was unable to walk that far and that without selecting and commissioning someone for that task, these believers would have to wait far too long.

It was beautiful to hear them discuss these matters and finally select the person they felt we should train and entrust with this responsibility. Do you remember my telling you about Roket? He was the young lad whose finger I had sewed back on during our early days at Godare. He was the young man who preached in the villages with his stiff finger, holding it high overhead and saying, "Gopan omo mo!" (There just one way)

Their unanimous choice was this young man, Roket. By now he was a married man with small children. He'd learned to read Amharic in the school and was beginning to understand more and more when he read from his Amharic Bible.

On an appointed Sunday, Harold Kurtz was with us for the special ordination service. What joy to share with Harold in laying hands on this choice young Mesengo. That same service, Roket baptized his first new believers. He did some things a little differently than I would have, but I was determined to allow him to make his little mistakes and to find his way in his new responsibilities. He also led his first communion service in which we used tomato juice and native, pancake-like bread.

When Roket returned from Konkon, in his little record book he had written the names of all the new believers. I never baptized another person from among the Mesengo. They were now able to perform the essential tasks to enable a church to grow and mature. In retrospect, the decision we had made was probably one of the wisest decisions we could have made. I have no doubt that the Lord had led us in making this unorthodox decision to ordain a man who had never been to a theological seminary or a formal Bible school. When all missionaries left Godare and Teppi, the young church was able to function in every respect. We had set in motion a totally indigenous pattern with indigenous leadership which the Holy Spirit could prosper and use. God blessed the Mesengo in unusual ways after we all left and today it is reported that more than 90 percent of this tribe have come to believe and are within the Christian fellowship. To God be all the honor, glory and praise!

1. equivalent to a male nurse.

CHAPTER TWENTY-THREE

EXPANDING THE MINISTRY FROM TEPPI

Teppi was always on our hearts and minds. From the very first time we stopped in Teppi, it seems the Lord had created within us a sensitivity to the challenge, needs and opportunities there. By this time in our ministry from Godare, we realized that Teppi would be an ideal location to base a cassette ministry. In Teppi we would have access to five or six additional language groups. For one thing, this would facilitate our production of master cassettes in these needed languages. Teppi would also be an excellent place from which to fly out with MAF to airstrips we could open in strategic places among these language groups. Teppi already had an excellent airfield on which Ethiopian Airlines came in at least twice a week. During the coffee harvest they flew in five or six times a day hauling out those precious beans.

A REPLACEMENT FOR GODARE

But before we could get serious about a move to locate ourselves in Teppi, we must have a replacement to continue the work among the Mesengo. God wonderfully raised up Harry and Pat Miersma to fill this need. Harry had been there before when he came out for that summer with those other three young college students. Pat would be a tremendous asset with her nursing skills. Harry's church,

The First Reformed Church in Artesia, California was behind them. This church had already made a tremendous contribution to the work at the Godare. They had provided the hydroelectric plant and Harry's folks had been out there along with their pastor, Dave and Lois Laman. The Reformed Church General Program Council approved, and with supporting churches, Harry and Pat soon were ready to come and set us free to open the new work in Teppi. We could see God's leading and were constantly praising Him.

GOVERNMENT APPROVAL FOR TEPPI

The other hurdle that needed to be dealt with was the basis on which we might receive government approval for a station in Teppi. Normally the government required a commitment from the mission to operate a school and a clinic before receiving approval to open work. In Teppi, however, there already was a fully staffed, upgraded health center as well as a large school with grades from one through eight. The challenge was to offer something to the government they would recognize as important to warrant their giving permission for us to open a work in Teppi. We were constantly talking about and praying over it.

The thought finally came to me that we could offer the government a unique language learning program using cassettes. Most of the other language groups outside of Teppi town knew little or no Amharic, the official language of Ethiopia. We would offer a program in which we prepared oral, language learning tapes enabling people to learn Amharic, moving from the vernacular to the national language. We could offer this valuable service so that people coming into the market would understand Amharic and when government officials spoke and gave out orders the people could understand what was said in Amharic.

The moment came when I was in the proper official's office in Addis Ababa. I was sitting across the desk from an important official in the ministry of education. I carefully shared what I have just described. This man was greatly interested and even became excited as we discussed these possibilities. I told him that the ideal place from which to launch this kind of program was Teppi because of the government airstrip there and the ready access to the vernacular languages needed as part of the language lessons from the vernacular to Amharic.

As our conversation concluded, this official stood up behind his desk. He extended his outstretched arms toward me and with considerable emotion said, "Mr. Hoekstra, this is a program that all of Ethiopia needs. ... can you suggest a ten-year plan for the whole country. ... we will give you blanket permission for your district." He promised and did write the necessary letters of introduction to the local governors in whose districts we'd be carrying on this ministry.

This official, like most government personnel, was an Orthodox Christian. Before parting, with some hesitation, I shared with him my observation that while many of the people in those rural areas where we'd be working were nominal Christians, many had little or no real understanding about the Christian faith. I asked if there would be any objection to our putting the essential Christian truths on cassette in the vernaculars as part of this program. I said, "We don't want to wait until they learn the Amharic language to tell them this good news from God which both you and I believe." He raised no objection and I took that to mean we could go ahead but not to raise the matter officially.

I left his office on cloud nine. I was ecstatic with praise and thanks to God. The door to opening our cassette ministry from Teppi was open. God had not only provided the personnel needed to ensure the ministry at Godare was in good hands, but He had opened the door for us to move to Teppi.

MIERSMAS, HETRICKS AND TERPSTRAS
BUILD THE NEW STATION IN TEPPI

The next question was where to locate our base in Teppi itself. I knew that we wanted to be as close to the airport as possible. Our larger plan was to continue opening new airstrips into which we could fly with MAF from Teppi just as we had begun at Godare. If at all possible, we should be right beside the Teppi airstrip itself.

Again, the Lord was going before us. We were able to purchase a small plot, sufficient in size to accommodate two houses, an office and recording room and a storage, workshop building. To avoid a great deal of time consuming effort, we and the Mission agreed that we should erect prefabricated buildings available from a German firm in Addis Ababa. But before making the move to Teppi we must first take our furlough in 1971. After that, Lavina and I would return and make the move to Teppi. When the moment finally arrived, Harry and Pat Miersma were already on the field. They would help us open the new station. Harry was an excellent builder as well as a great young missionary. From the states, two volunteer couples came from the First Reformed Church in DeMotte, Indiana, Steve and Laverne Terpstra and Larry and Linda Hetrick. They came out and, with the help of Harry and Pat, during their month in Teppi literally built the new base, including erecting a protective fence around it.

LAVINA WAITS AT THE GODARE

Lavina remained at Godare during those first weeks to relieve the housing problem. She'd have given anything to be with the gang in Teppi but common sense dictated otherwise. She says it helped her a lot on those days when Denny, our son, was flying in the area. He'd come on the radio and say, "Mom, I'm flying overhead this morning. How about my dropping down a few minutes and see how you're doing. And, I'll be ready for a cup of coffee with you by that time." Lavina would scurry around the kitchen and by "coffee time" she'd turned out a delicious, home-made cake or a batch of cookies. Denny knew he could count on that.

Later when we were all settled in our new place in Teppi, Jim and Betty, Denny and Carol and the little ones all flew in once for a week-end. It was really something special to have two of our sons and their families working beside us in Ethiopia as missionaries. When they came with the MAF plane to Teppi, we'd open the wide double gate and Denny would taxi in. He'd tie down right in front of the house with the plane secure behind the closed gate.

But I'm ahead of myself. We're still back there getting started living in tents with volunteers doing the work. A lot would happen before Lavina and I were home together in our new station and work.

Before the big trucks arrived from Addis with the prefabricated buildings, the men had laid the cement floors of the two houses. There were two because the program also called for a medical person to be based with us in Teppi. Each airstrip opened would have regular visits by trained, Ethiopian, medical dressers equipped with modern medicine. A nurse would occupy the second house to supervise that aspect of the ministry. The competent nurse who came to do that was Leatta Weidenbach. She came to us from the Dembidollo station but had previously served for a number of years in the Presbyterian mission in Yaoundi in the French Cameroon. Important health lessons were also put on cassette and were an intregal part of the medical program.

A SERIOUS LEG INJURY

On the Saturday afternoon of the day the trucks arrived from Addis bringing in the pre-cut houses, I suffered a serious accident with my trail bike in Teppi town. I had gone from the site into town to purchase some small item needed. The town itself had one main street running through it on each side of which were mud-walled, metal roof shops where

331

cloth, soap, salt, sugar, tea, coffee, cooking oil and other basic supplies were sold. Interspersed among them were "Tej Bets" and "Bunna Bets" where people gathered to drink and visit.

The market area itself was nearly deserted by this time in the afternoon and the trails leading out of Teppi were crowded with men, women, children and animals making their way home. Some of them would be travelling for several hours and would arrive home well after dark.

But, many were still crowding that street in Teppi as well. Some had stayed a bit longer than they should have in the drinking houses. As I threaded my way, ever so slowly, through this crowd on my trail bike, one man suddenly grabbed my handlebars rather than making room for me to continue moving along. I put my foot out to keep my balance and stop. Somehow, in doing this I twisted my leg in such a way that the femur crashed into the head of the tibia and I fell. The pain was excruciating and unbearable. I was going less than five miles an hour and it hardly seemed possible one could receive a serious injury under those conditions. I lay there moaning and groaning. People tried to assist me but I begged them just to leave me and I'd be alright. After lying like that for a minute or two, I thought I'd better try to get back on the bike and head back to our site across the airfield. On one leg I managed to get my injured leg over the seat and started the bike with its electric starter. I hadn't gone more than a couple of feet when I again fell. Apparently the pain was too severe and I simply couldn't manage by myself. Again, I lay there with unbelievable pain.

About this time, Harry and Pat drove up with the Landrover. Someone had run from the town to the base and reported what had happened. In due course, I was placed on a cot just under the eaves of the workshop which had been the first building completed.

You'll recall now that the trucks from Addis had just arrived before I left for the store. A storm was building up rapidly and the men and their workmen were working furiously to get the supplies under cover before it struck. Within moments a colossal, late afternoon, tropical rain storm descended on us. The wind was blowing so furiously that the tents were threatening to blow down. Everyone, both the men and the women, were struggling frantically against the elements. The rain was now coming down in sheets. I was under the protection of the overhanging metal roof, but the water was running off on me and I was helpless to move. It was too ridiculous to describe. When the folks discovered my plight they came to the rescue, but later we had many good laughs over that chaotic scene.

At that time, I didn't know, of course, how serious my injury had been. We only knew that the pain was almost unbearable and we had only aspirin to relieve it. I shall always remember, with unspeakable gratitude, the way Harry and Pat, nurse that she was, kept coming to me during the night to inquire how I was doing and to give me more aspirin. Whenever they came, I was awake! It was a very long, dark night!

In the morning MAF came in on an emergency flight and flew me to the hospital in Mettu. Poor xray film failed to indicate the extent of my injury. The doctor put a cast on it and the next day I was flown home to be with Lavina at the Godare. The swelling and pain became unbearable and we had to cut off the cast to bear it. Finally, a week later, we decided I should get into Addis Ababa and have it looked at in the hospital there. I was sent to the Leprosarium where a skilled Indian-born British orthopedic surgeon re-xrayed the knee and said I had smashed the head of the tibia. Surgery would be required.

After the surgery Dr. Fritchie said the injury gave the appearance of a parachute accident. He was extremely pessimistic. He said he couldn't bring the tibia back to where he wanted it because it was already nine days since the accident had occurred. He told how cartilage and large amounts of blood poured out of this hugely swollen knee when he operated. He said, finally, "I've tried to give you a leg on which you can get upstairs, but your mule riding days are all over." He was so dismal in his prognostication, that his Indian wife, who was also a doctor, rebuked him and said that with God all things are possible.

ART AND FRIEDA VANDERPLOEG

Teppi station would be opened without my help. My leg was in a cast for seven weeks and when it came out it was as stiff as a plank of wood. Physical therapy followed and bit by bit improvements followed. This was the period when Art and Frieda Vanderploeg were volunteer host and hostess operating the mission guest house. Art was God's gift to me during those weeks we had to be in Addis. Lavina and I stayed in the guest house during which time I waited for the cast to be removed and continued with physical therapy.

I recall how I would lie on my stomach on the floor in the mission house with perspiration rolling off my forehead as Art put his knee on the back of my leg where it was supposed to bend. He would pull up on the foot, release it and pull again until it moved a little. I could barely stand the pain. Eventually, it bent far enough so that I could sit on a chair and pull the foot back by myself. Every day for one solid month Art drove me to the physical therapist, a competent Swedish lady to whom I owe so much. When I finally began trying to walk with the help of the bars, it was obvious that there was too much wobble at the tibia for me to get along without a helping brace. For six months, I walked with a cane and every day dressed myself with a heavy metal brace which was anchored in the heel of my shoe, hinged at the knee and strapped around my leg with a six-inch belt just above the knee. It seemed likely that I'd need this sort of brace the rest of my life.

LEARNING TO WALK AGAIN

Eventually, we were back at Teppi. Our volunteers had done their job well and had long since left for America. Harry and Pat went back to Godare among the Mesengo. Lavina and I were back at Teppi settling into our new home and ministry. I was walking with a brace and the help of a cane. Every day I tried to force the knee to go a little farther until finally I had almost achieved the full range of what it originally could do.

One day, I decided not to put on the brace, hung it up in the outside shop and never donned it again. I still walked with a cane, but my pain was minimal and I knew that God was gradually giving me back my leg.

I may never fully know why this kind of accident happened when it did. I believe, however, that even in the tragedies of life, God overrules them for good. In ways we cannot chart or predict God receives honor and glory through it. Sometimes we cannot understand but accept by faith what God says in His word, "All things work together for good to them that love God and who are called according to His purpose." For myself, I can only praise God for lessons sickness and injury have brought into my life. Some of His best secrets and insights were shared during my most difficult experiences. And, we are absolutely certain that nothing in life or in death can ever separate us from the love of God which is ours in Christ Jesus our Lord.*1.

"YOU'RE THE MAN WITH THE MIRACLE LEG"

This accident happened in February of 1972. Seven years later Lavina and I were in South India visiting in the home of Sunjeeve Savarirayan and his wife Esther. Sitting beside him was another guest who was a personal friend of the surgeon from India who was in Addis during the time of my accident and had operated on my knee. As we were sharing together, this other guest suddenly leaned forward and said excitedly, "Then, you're the man with the miracle leg!" Dr. Fritchie had told him how when we had been in India the preceding year we had visited his leprosarium and he had been amazed to find that I was walking without pain and without a limp. He recognized it as a miracle of God. I totally agree!

When I think of my marvelous recovery, however,I sometimes think of the story I heard about the man who was being complimented on his lovely garden saying something about it that only God alone could make such a beautiful garden. The man, whose garden it was, responded by saying, "When God was doing the garden by Himself, it didn't look nearly as nice as now when God and I work at it together!" I did what I could to help, but, seriously, I know that without God's powerful, healing hand, I'd still be a cripple today. To Him belong all the honor, glory and praise!

The work in and from Teppi prospered. New airstrips were opened in the surrounding area. Eventually we had seven airstrips into which MAF flew our medical dresser and an evangelist with cassettes and players. The vernacular messages about Jesus Christ were always more popular than the language-learning lesson tapes. But both were an integral part of our ministry and without either it could not have been happening.

We had some great experiences at those airstrips. Normally, just our Ethiopian staff did these itineration flights. They'd go out on a Monday and return on a Friday. They had a regular circuit to complete before returning and starting all over again. Occasionally I was privileged to accompany them. It was always an inspiration to see how God was blessing their outreach and how people were being helped in the name of Jesus.

TED POLLOCK'S PREFABRICATED STRUCTURES

I recall the week we were improving the Gecha airstrip. We'd already put a small prefabricated building on the edge of that strip. Ted Pollock, the mission builder at Ghimeera, had designed these so they would fit into an MAF plane and could be transported to the site. Ted had helped us put this one together. Two or three of us with a couple of local people helping would have one of these prefabs ready to sleep in by nightfall.

Ted was a creative genius as a builder. He figured out building structures that would fit into the MAF plane so they could be transported from his workshop in Ghimeera to whatever new post needed them. All our first buildings at

Godare had come in that way. Once Ted and three of his children had come in to spend a week with us putting up the staff houses, clinic building and the school buildings. We supplied the home-made bricks, sand and cement needed, and Ted was there with the roof structure, roofing, doors and windows. Every mission station benefitted from Ted and his wife Dolly's skill and dedication. And when their children came out, it was an entire family making an inestimable contribution to the Lord's work.

I really appreciated those prefabricated, one room structures beside the airstrips. Before we had them, I'd sleep wherever the local people found an empty room. Often, it'd be in some abandoned trader's storeroom or in some unused shack no longer needed by the local folks. Their hospitality was enviable, but the only problem was the rats. I learned that if I'd bring with me a rat trap and start trapping just about dusk time, I could catch as many as three to five in an evening in my room where I'd soon be sleeping. This seemed to discourage the rest of them and I could get quite a good night's sleep. ... Army ants were another problem. More than once I had to abandon where I was sleeping and wait elsewhere for morning to dawn. With the small prefabricated buildings, we had a wooden-type floor and it could be locked securely during the day when I was out. Another big advantage was that our medical person and the evangelist and I could all be rooming and eating together and enjoy each other's company.

GECHA AIRSTRIP

But now we were there at Gecha with Harry and Pat Miersma, my teen-aged son Mark, and myself. Pat helped the medical dresser and served as our cook and dietician. We men kept the little tractor and plow running from morning until night. We plowed that entire airstrip, six inches at a time. Much of that week we experienced periods of shower and rain. At sixty-five hundred feet it was chilly cold when the rain was falling. Heavy fog settled in periodically. Frankly, we were all eager for Saturday when the MAF plane was scheduled to collect us and fly us home. But, alas, Saturday it rained most of the day and their flight was canceled. By the end of the week our mood was somewhat gloomy. The bounce was gone! We'd worked hard. Our food supply was greatly diminished and we were ready to take off. But God had other plans. We'd know better in the morning when the sun was shining.

Sunday morning came and early in the morning while we were still sitting around eating, we saw a single individual coming across the airstrip carrying a ram's horn. He walked out in front of our temporary clinic to the edge of the airstrip, put this thing to his mouth and we heard a piercing call that echoed and re-echoed in the surrounding hills and mountains. He did this several times. It wasn't long before people began coming in to where we were camped. Some were ill and wanted medical care. We'd been there all week. This was Sunday, a day of rest. But we knew we couldn't say, "There are six days in which to be healed!" Human need had to be met, sabbath or no sabbath. The medical dresser began seeing sick people.

When nearly a hundred people had gathered, I began to preach, speaking in Amharic with the help of an interpreter. My Amharic wasn't that extensive, but out in the country I dared to manage. Eventually, I asked Yisahak, the clinic dresser to prepare his heart to preach. When he joined us, he preached awhile and when he grew tired, I'd try it again. Near the end, I remember saying to them that this scene in front of me reminded me of the days of John the Baptist. I told how the crowds had come to hear him and how John had said it was time for the people to repent because this was God's time and this was the time God was coming to visit and heal His people. As I spoke of the need to repent from our sins to receive God's salvation, one of the men stood up and began to confess his sins. This led to several others sharing similarly until finally someone said, "This will take too long. We all have sinned against God. We should all confess our sins to God together."

I was amazed to hear many of them pouring out their hearts to God. Eventually, we all bowed our heads, closed our eyes and I led them in prayer. When I opened my eyes, I discovered that a huge tropical rainstorm would soon be upon us. The people scattered quickly and headed for their villages. It was a morning I shall never forget. Our disappointment on not getting away the day before was turned into joy. How wonderful, mysterious and decisive are the ways of our God. Indeed, His ways are past finding out. On Monday morning, we were all back home. Our hearts were full of joy! How good God is!

SALLI AIRSTRIP

Once on another airstrip, at Salli, the evangelist, medical dresser and I had come in on Monday. I'd spent many hours improving the strip with our small garden tractor and plow. But now it was time to leave. The plane had come in, the door had been taken off and the seats of the plane were on the ground. The men were busy loading the tractor and gear. At that moment a man came up saying he had a toothache and wanted to know if I could help him. I decided I could extract it and relieve him of his pain. In the early days I extracted teeth without novocaine just using a regular pliers. But my cousin, Dick Hoekstra, in Chicago had a neighbor who was a dentist. While visiting Dick and Clara, he brought his neighbor over and this kind man provided me with four dental forceps and showed me where to inject novocaine to deaden the pain.

So when my patient sat on that MAF plane seat beside the plane, I injected him with novocaine, waited the right amount of time, and then rather skillfully extracted his tooth. People standing nearby saw that it didn't appear to be that big an ordeal and before we left, I had extracted a total of five teeth in a half an hour. I used to say facetiously that I charged each one fifty cents and that all bills were still outstanding! Seriously though, having a toothache for those people was no laughing matter. Their methods of dealing with it were quite primitive. I was only a "quack" but to them I was a real professional! Which reminds me that the definition of an expert is "an ordinary person giving advice or services away from home!"

Lavina and I went together to some of these airstrips. Sometimes we lived in our little yellow tent and at other times we set up shop in a local school building during vacation times. During some seasons of the year, fog would come rolling in and you'd literally be "living in a cloud." I remember one morning after we'd finished our breakfast, Lavina and I were having our devotions together. When it was time to pray, we both bowed our heads, closed our eyes and talked to God. On this particular occasion, when we'd finished praying, we couldn't tell where we were. The fog had moved in during those few minutes we'd had our eyes closed and completely enveloped us. The fog was so dense that we couldn't see but a few feet from where we sat. We were amazed and completely surprised! We knew that very soon the sun would be fierce and chase the fog away as if it had never been there at all. So it was on our itineration airstrips!

DR. CREMER AND THE WOMAN WITH THE TUMOR

The strangest experience I ever had on one of those itineration airstrips occurred when Dr. John Cremer from the Dembidollo hospital and I went out together with Yisahak and Getachew, the evangelist. We were living in a tent on the Gecha airstrip. One afternoon around four o'clock a group of people showed up with a woman who had an enormous, abdominal tumor. It was huge and she was extremely uncomfortable. Dr. Cremer examined her and decided he could drain off a good bit of that fluid making her feel a lot better. He explained that this wouldn't solve the problem because it'd come back again, but, at least for now, it would help her immensely.

So we invited her into our tent and put her on the air-mattress on the floor. Dr. Cremer tapped her abdomen and began draining fluid off into our twelve quart bucket. He explained that he had to drain this fluid off over a period of two or three hours lest the patient go into shock. You'll never believe this but I carried out at least two buckets of fluid and dumped it out in the bush.

By this time, it had already become dark. There was no way we could send her away as she'd have to walk back to wherever they'd come from. It was much too cold for her to be put outside.

There was only one thing left to do. She would spend the night in the tent with us and their entourage could make their way to the village and collect her in the morning.

John and I laughed over our ridiculous situation the rest of the week. Here were two missionaries spending the night with a strange woman breathing garlic in their faces while we protected her from the cold and permitted her to gain strength so she could leave in the morning. When morning finally came, her relatives were back. She got up off the air mattress, went outside and they all slowly began to head out toward their village. We never saw her again and I've often wondered if she saw the humor in the situation like John and I did. We had truly become all things to all people in the hope that we might at least win some, even as was said by the Apostle Paul when he wrote to those Corinthian Christians so long ago.

THE MINISTRY IN TEPPI ITSELF

We had a small, compact, neatly laid out compound in Teppi. Located directly beside the airfield and up about a fourth of the way from the lower end was an excellent spot. Ethiopian Airline planes touched down amost directly in front of the house and were barely one hundred feet off the ground at that point on take off. The MAF plane could taxi and stop right in front of our large gate. When they night-stopped, we opened the gate and they taxied in, parking safely in our front yard. We loved it.

In the center of the compound between the two identical residences was my office, recording studio and supply room for the medicines. The medical trek boxes were inventoried and restocked in that room.

My office was a place where we kept our records and accounts. Here I could read, study and prepare lessons, conduct Bible studies or meet with callers. I had an excellent library with a complete set of Calvin's Institutes, Lenski, the International Commentary, Hastings' Dictionary of the Complete Bible, the Gospels and the Church. My Greek lexicon, word studies and the International Bible Encyclopedia were my frequent companions. In this same room, we did our high speed duplicating of cassettes.

Between these two rooms was our recording room. It was never insulated as well as I would have liked, but it served our purposes adequately and many beautiful cassettes in Kaffa, Mocha, Oromo, Shako and Amharic were produced in it.

Amara, a keen young Amhara speaking man with great sensitivity about the nuances in Amharic and the languages in which we were working was my recordist. I had trained him from scratch and he did well with the state of the art available to us during that time. One of the larger projects we undertook was to do an oral translation of several books of the New Testament from Amharic to Shako. Kani Naro, one of the evangelists who was almost completely bilingual narrated the text on tape in his language. It was recorded verse by verse by Amara — slow, methodical and tedious but they got the job done. This oral translation proved to be a great blessing to the Shako people, most of whom were illiterate.

The recording room wasn't as acoustically acceptable as we wanted, but the major problem came from a friendly rooster outside. Invariably it seemed that when this rooster knew we were in there, he would march right past the back window, stop and crow lustily several times. He eventually paid for his folly by appearing on our Sunday dinner table!

There was an Orthodox church on the north side of town. We didn't have a church building of our own in Teppi, so we rented an abandoned trader's shop down the dirt road leading out of Teppi to the south. Even before that, we met on Sunday mornings on the veranda of our house with Getachew doing the preaching. Getachew told me that he first met us in the little book store we had opened years earlier in Teppi. He said he had come in and wanted a Bible in Amharic so badly but had no money to buy one. He still remembered with great thanks to God that before he left, we'd given him a free copy. Getachew at that time was just a young man trying to earn a living by teaching the children of Amhara officials during vacation time so that they would have an advantage over the rest of the students when school resumed in the fall.

Getachew had gone to school in the SIM in Addis Ababa. He knew and loved the Lord. He was excited that we had moved to Teppi and was eager to help us in any way he could. He also had artistic ability and our volunteers from America were able to put him to painting the inside of the new houses.

TEPPI WORSHIP SERVICES

Getachew loved to lead those worship services on our veranda and to preach. He used an empty oil drum for his pulpit. Right from the beginning, by his own initiative, he organized prayer times and developed a choir. During one of the summers Solomon Gizaw, the lad who became an MAF pilot, was in that choir singing and playing his guitar. How marvelous and wonderful are the ways of the Lord!

When we began in that rented building, we put in crude, log benches, held off the ground by five inch forked legs. They were later replaced with solid benches made by skilled carpenters. That little church was often packed with as many as twenty or thirty walking sticks leaning against the outside wall just outside the door on muddy days. Sometimes a dog or two showed up with the worshippers and it wasn't unknown to have a goat or sheep tied to the building.

We saw wonderful things that God was doing in those services. We witnessed first hand the effect of demons on people there when sometimes one or even two or three would begin laughing like hyenas and were making disturbances. On such occasions the service continued normally, but other members would quietly usher these persons outside and lead them to the little grass prayer room situated about twenty feet away in the back. While Getachew was continuing his message, we could hear folks praying in that little room that Jesus would drive out the demon and heal these disturbed persons. I personally witnessed persons who had been making those disturbances become calm and quiet in that prayer room. But before this happened, the individual under the power of prayer would suddenly fall over from a sitting position and lie there as if death had come. After perhaps a minute or so, the person would open his or her eyes, sit up and be perfectly normal.

In the main service, we also saw people moved by the Holy Spirit to confess their involvement in devil worship. Some took off bracelets that had been put on their arms by some witchdoctor. Others had heavy brass bracelets opened and removed after the service. God was marvelously at work in this church. It was not at all uncommon for Getachew and a small group of deeply committed young people to spend entire nights in prayer. Healings of sick in answer to prayer were frequent testimonials.

PRAYING FOR THE SICK

I still remember the morning when a man came across the airfield, came through the gate and was at the office where Getachew, several others and I were having our morning Bible study and prayer time. This man wanted Getachew to come and pray over his brother. The sick man had been in bed for some days and was unable to walk.

Getachew and his companions invited me to accompany them. We soon found ourselves in the back of one of those small merchant shops. The sick man was lying on a cowhide strung bed on which there was a thin cotton mattress and a sheet. Chairs had been arranged for us to sit on. After exchanging pleasantries briefly with the brother who had fetched us and had gone on ahead, Getachew opened his Bible and read the passage from Luke where it tells us that the power of the Lord was on Jesus to heal.*2 He spoke briefly of Jesus' great power to save, his power over demons and sickness and exhorted us to have faith and to pray.

At that point, Getachew and his three companions got up and quietly surrounded the sick man's bed. They laid their hands on this person's body and began to pray. They all prayed at the same time. Sometimes they were praying in their own languages and sometimes they were praying in tongues. These men were literally agonizing in prayer to the point where they were perspiring profusely. After fifteen or twenty minutes, they stopped praying, urged the man to believe in Jesus' power to make him well and then we all left.

Two days later, the man who had originally come requesting Getachew to pray for his brother, came excitedly across the airstrip, through the gate and into the office where we were again having our Bible study. He was exuberant. His brother was walking. Our response was a time of praise and thanks to God! Good news like this travels and no doubt contributed to the growth of the church and the acceptance of the Gospel in that area.

With the participation of these keen young men, we also started other preaching centers. One of these small worshipping groups was loaned a cassette player. Every Sunday, a different woman would take the player home for that week. Each morning when the women met, as was their custom, to drink coffee together in one of their homes, the woman would bring her cassette player and they had a time of listening. This was a marvelous way for them to grow in their understanding of the Christian faith and the one who had the player during her week considered it a great honor to have been entrusted with it.

DISTURBANCES WHILE PREACHING

During the dry seasons, these young people and we would go out with the Landrover to a place on the northeast corner of Teppi. People from this small center of shops and homes would gather around as Getachew or I would preach. It was amazing to see the tricks that Satan used to bring confusion into those times of preaching. Dogs would get into a vicious fight, or an animal might threaten to wander off. One Sunday there was a young woman who was acting very strangely. They said she was crazy and that normally she was chained inside the building. On this occasion she was sitting on the dirt and pulling her dress up in unseemly ways. She also made strange noises we didn't understand. The woman seemed to be attractive, but was mentally unstable or possibly demon possessed. I shall never forget how Lavina quietly sat down beside her, took hold of her hand and placed her arm around her. Eventually, they were both standing and Lavina was lovingly embracing her until the service ended. Lavina's loving touch was used by God to quiet this pour troubled soul's heart, quieting it with His peace. It was remarkable to observe. We left that village heavy-hearted because we feared that after we left they'd treat her as before, chaining her and keeping her like a dog of whom everyone was afraid.

KANI NARO DOING THE WORK OF AN EVANGELIST

Kani was a Shako-speaking young man with about three years of formal education. He loved the Lord, knew Amharic and read his Bible avidly. In the late afternoons Kani would frequently visit different areas of the town and surrounding villages with his cassette player. On one such occasion he found himself in the village of a local witchdoctor. This ritual expert was willing to listen, but the young woman who prepared his food and participated in some of his ceremonies was very resistant and tried to make disturbances. This woman's name was "Workit." We had first been introduced to her years earlier by her father. On one of those treks that Lavina and I made into Teppi, spending several days in our rented quarters, Workit was brought to us by her father. She was a young girl then and severely crippled by polio. The father offered me a bull if I could send her to a hospital and have her legs straightened. This poor girl's one leg was frozen in the position it would have if one was sitting on one's buttocks with knees bent. The other leg was twisted out of shape in another contortion. She could only move about by putting one hand on the ground and waddle along with her skirt dragging in the dirt or mud.

WORKIT RESPONDS TO THE GOSPEL

This same Workit was the young woman that Kani Naro, ten years later, was contending with each time in the witchdoctor's village. Local people said she was demon possessed. Workit was the assistant to the withdoctor. She lived in her own house nearby. It was Workit who brewed the coffee, participated in the rituals and frequently poured the beer on the special stones honoring the ancestors.

One day when Kani was in her village he said, "Workit, come here once and sit beside me. I have something important I want to tell you." Although she had never showed interest, on that occasion she responded and sat quietly as Kani carefully told her the message of salvation in Jesus. Before Kani left that afternoon, he asked Workit if she would like to keep his cassette player overnight. She accepted his offer and he gave her his player with the Gospel of John on cassettes in her Shako language.

She listened intently to the cassettes, listening over and over again until the batteries were dead. Her heart was drawn to the message from this beautiful Gospel. In the morning when Kani returned, she begged him to leave his player with her so that she could learn more. Kani, however, said, "No, but if you will go to the missionary, she will give you a player that you can keep in your house and listen further."

The very next morning Workit and a small girl who always walked on the trail with her, came to Lavina. Kani explained to Lavina what had happened and how eager Workit was to learn more about Jesus. Lavina gave Workit a cassette player with several cassettes in her language, and demonstrated to her how to operate the machine. Workit took the machine home and began listening carefully. Eventually, she surrendered her heart to Christ and was baptized.

This terribly crippled young woman came to be a very gifted, influential, charismatic leader. She eventually had in her house a box with a cassette player and every cassette we produced in the Shako language. Her friends and neighbors were frequent guests in her home or yard listening to these cassettes. On Sunday mornings, before the church service began Workit had a listening time with her growing circle of new believers. Every Sunday you would see Workit leading this Bible listening group from her home the fourth mile distance down the dirt road to the church. This severely handicapped woman went out as far as four or five miles to reach people with the message of Christ on cassette. Always she had some young girl beside her carrying the player and the tapes for the day. Workit was truly a triumph of God's mercy, grace and saving power in Jesus Christ.

Kani Naro, the Shako evangelist, also made extensive use of cassettes as he reached out in the direction of the coffee plantations Southeast of Teppi. He'd begin in an area by visiting homes and playing his cassettes in the Shako language. Eventually, he'd identify some person who appeared more interested than others and who might be a natural leader. Even before this man became a committed believer, Kani would entrust him with a player and cassettes. This individual loved his recognized status and enjoyed inviting others to listen with him.

This freed Kani to move on to another area and repeat the process. Occasionally he'd return to the village in which he entrusted this village leader with that player. Using the cassette players and the personal confirmation of the messages like this was greatly blessed by the Lord. I know of at least three areas where Kani had gotten groups of people to accept the message and commit their lives to Christ. It was a pattern I believed evangelists could use to plant churches successfully almost anywhere in the world. Years later I discovered in Bangladesh that they were using this same approach very successfully with five evangelists using fifteen players.

MANY OPPORTUNITIES IN TEPPI

In Teppi we had many opportunities to share the Gospel using cassettes.

WITH STUDENTS

On the opposite side of the airfield across from where we lived was a large government school with hundreds of students. We let it be known that students could come in the afternoon and pick up a player to use in their homes in the evening. They would pick up cassette-players after school was dismissed and drop them off in the morning before their classes began. We had several players going out like this on a regular basis. In this way the Gospel was getting a wide hearing. We knew that the cassette was making an essential difference and that the Gospel was being heard where without the players it wouldn't be happening. The cassettes in the hearer's own language was the tool of choice to plant the seed when an overt Christian witness might not be welcomed.

WITH PEOPLE REQUESTING PLAYERS

Sometimes individuals we had never seen appeared at our door and asked if we'd loan them a player and cassettes in their language. Some professed to have come from a distant village and wanted their people back home to hear this good news. We frequently gave players out to folks who came like that, but I must confess that I was often a bit nervous and wondered if we might ever see that player again. At the Godare, we never doubted that our players would be returned, but Teppi, being a town with people of different cultures and backgrounds, raised some questions about the wisdom of our doing this.

IN THE MARKETPLACE

On Saturday the town was filled with visitors from villages in all directions — people who were in town because it was market day. These market days were extremely popular, almost like holidays when people got together for business and for social contacts. Our evangelists went into the market area every week with cassettes in whatever languages were represented there. They were careful not to play their cassettes up close to where the sales and trading was taking place lest they antagonize those who wouldn't appreciate any additional distractions. Normally, they found shady places under trees where people gathered who were waiting or just socializing. Countless numbers heard the Gospel who would otherwise never have heard. A seed was being planted. I could picture an evangelist or another Christian eventually visiting those distant villages from which some of them had come. When this visitor would begin speaking about Jesus, the seed would have been sown and the comment might well be, "That's the same message we heard in the market when we heard it from the machine."

Lavina's letter home, dated August 29, 1975, tells how the church was developing in Teppi and about her personal ministry with the women:

"Eveything here is okay and we just rejoice in what God is doing in the hearts of the people. On Sunday morning at our worship service, a man from the Shako tribe stood up and asked the evangelist to come and remove the three bracelets he had on his arms. They were put there by the witchdoctor to please the spirits.

But now that he was a Christian, he no longer needed them and he wanted to trust in Jesus only. It is encouraging to see the response of the people. ...

"Last Sunday they elected elders in the church and we are hoping that they will choose a man to be recognized as their pastor soon. The little mud house we rent for a church is getting too small, so they are wanting to build a church near our home. ...

"I have a sewing class for the women on Friday afternoons. There are 14 women and more are wanting to come. Fourteen women is about all I can handle at one time. We are making patchwork quilts and I don't have enough of the squares of material for more people. "On Friday afternoon we have a women's Bible Study. One of the Amhara speaking girls leads the meeting and does real well. It's a joy to see the girls taking a share in the worship services. I go out visiting the women in their homes, trying to make one or two calls a day. I take one of the school girls with me to translate as I don't know Amharic well enough to do it on my own. The women love to have me come and they are very hospitable, always serving tea, strong sweet black coffee, hot sweet milk, bread and honey or the national food of injira-ba-wat. It's great to have this contact with the women. ..."

In another letter, dated September 21, 1975, Lavina shares her joy in seeing what God is doing in Teppi:

"It is a joy to see God so mightily at work in the hearts of the people in this area. There is a significant response to the Gospel among the Shako people.

"Yesterday was a busy day. We had a very good service, some 150 people in the little house we use for the church and about 40 or so on the outside. Our services are about two hours long and it gets hard on my back to sit that long on the benches without a backrest, but the people don't seem to mind that much. They just love to sing and really have a great time. ...

"After lunch we were invited to a Shako family's home. The couple are new Christians so a group of us went to their home and had a little Bible study, prayer and song service. The tiny hut was simple and crude with a huge fire burning in the middle of the

351

floor where the wife was preparing coffee. It was a joy to see how radiant they were and the love and presence of Jesus was in our midst.

"She served us coffee, thick and black, with a pinch of salt and red pepper along with roasted ears of corn. When the chickens began coming in to roost on a board above our heads, we knew it was time to go home. As we walked through the forest in the semi-darkness and drizzling rain, our hearts were full of joy, overflowing for this family and their new life with Jesus."

1. Romans 8:38-39
2. Luke 5:17ff

CHAPTER TWENTY-FOUR

BACK WITH THE MESENGO

It was time for us to take a vacation. We had come to Addis to pick up our car from Jim's house and head north toward Gondar and Axum, site of the ancient rock churches of the Orthodox church.

Paul was a boarding student at the Good Shepherd School for missionary children located in Addis Ababa. Our son, Jim, and his wife Betty and little girl, Andrea, were at Good Shepherd, where Jim taught and was in charge of their physical education program. Down the road leading from the school to the city, another son, Denny, and his wife, Carol, and three boys lived. Dave was married and lived in Holland, Michigan. Carol Joy had graduated from Hope and was about to be married. Mark was pushing ahead with his aeronautical training in California.

THE REVOLUTION BEGINS

After enjoying a few days with our children and grand children in Addis, Lavina and I headed on the road going north. Revolution was in the air. Rumors of an impending coup were rife. At that moment, however, things appeared to be calm enough for us to take that long anticipated holiday.

The first night out we were alarmed to hear the news on our trusty, little, portable radio which went with us wherever we went. The government in Addis Ababa was under siege. Parliament had been disbanded and His majesty's palace was surrounded by rebel soldiers loyal to Mengistu. They told of roadblocks being erected, making travel hazardous and uncertain.

Instead of vacationing, the very next morning Lavina and I headed back toward Addis Ababa. We made it through just in time as roadblocks were being put in position before darkness fell to prevent any movement in or out of the city. These were ominous days. Ethiopia would never be the same.

While still in Addis, we had a small taste of what lay ahead. Here's from a letter to my folks, March 5, 1974:

"We are all well and safe! These have been days of uncertainty, but better than we had feared. Lavina and I were very nearly mobbed one day in the car. We were shaking like leaves. ...The teachers and students are all on strike. ... Good Shepherd School may have to close too.

"There have been some who were killed and shots have been heard at night. Most say it is not yet settled. Last week our Embassy had us all pack emergency bags with water, a blanket, food and passports. But for now all is relatively calm except for rumors and more rumors."

During those early days of the revolution there was a great release of energy and enthusiasm among the people, especially among the students. Many thought that democracy had come at last. During those first few weeks the newspaper was exciting to read. News never printed before was circulating freely. The radio and television seemed to have no restraints on what they showed or said.

But, alas, the new liberty was short-lived. Very soon censorship returned and freedoms were restricted. Eventually, the same students that had marched leading others to bring down the government, were again demonstrating against the abuses and lack of freedom under the new government. On the streets of Addis Ababa scores of people, even hundreds, were eventually mowed down and killed. We were told that bodies lay in piles on the streets with permission to identify them and remove them being denied for many hours. We were told of one mother who lost six sons during a massacre on the streets of Addis.

THE KABELE

The university had long since closed and the students were being dispersed throughout Ethiopia to educate the masses. These youthful revolutionaries helped organize local communities to have their own political action groups, police and administrative structures. Every city, town and rural area had these students among them promoting and giving direction to the revolution. Chairman Mao's "little red book" was as common in the hands of these students as is the Bible in the hands of believers on their way to a Bible-believing church. In every community Kabeles, local people's organizations, were formed where the people were reeducated and organized to act together. Students were sent out in groups of various sizes to provide communist leadership within these Kabeles throughout Ethiopia. Regular, weekly meetings were held where attendance by the local people was mandatory. Ominously, the Sunday meetings were routinely scheduled for the same hour as Sunday morning worship. Where the church was strong, people continued to worship as before and merely showed up late for the Kabele meeting. Where Christians were weak, attendance at worship services suffered. Later, when Ethiopians had learned to suffer under communism, Christians refused to compromise and endured the consequences with joy for the sake of Christ.

In the Kabele meetings people were encouraged to express their likes and dislikes. Everything now belonged to them and they had power to make decisions. Taking their cues from Chairman Mao's little red book, enemies of the revolution were to be "smoked out," identified and dealt with. People who possessed too much were despised and abused. Some paid dearly, even with their lives.

In our area, these kinds of meetings stopped after a few months. Like in other areas, the dissidents had by this time been identified as people expressed themselves in their new, democratic meetings. These "enemies of the revolution" were dealt with appropriately and it was not uncommon throughout the country for such people to be imprisoned for varying periods of time, and some were killed.

In Teppi, as in other places, the traditional functions of government manned by a local administration and police continued. Alongside, almost like a parallel government, the local Kabele organized and controlled the people. They built crude jails of sticks and poles to imprison those who broke their rules. Before they had guns with bullets, we'd see them practicing with hand-carved, wooden replicas of the real thing.

Local people were required to be at their appointed places of work in the fields or on the coffee plantations. No one was permitted to leave the area controlled by a local Kabele without permission. Anyone entering the area of another Kabele had to check in, report his reason for being there and prove that he had permission to be away from his own Kabele. Eyes and ears within a Kabele reported any suspicious movements or activities. All roads had countless check points where every passing vehicle was stopped, searched and people were questioned. The control over the people was unrelenting. Some, even in Teppi, were killed for perceived non-conformity and disobedience. Fear and suspicion tainted relationships and produced intolerable tensions.

NATIONALIZATION PRODUCES SHORTAGES

Property was seized and redistributed by the new people with power. Regulations and more regulations restricted what people could say or do. People suffered much and many were disillusioned. Very soon shops and stores began to run out of staple products because trading licenses were refused and the new cooperatives intended to replace them were not yet functioning. In Teppi even soap, salt, sugar and cooking oil were in short supply.

Food also became expensive and often there was little to buy in the local markets. Why should this be so? What happened in Dembidollo illustrates how this came about. Prior to the revolution that area was prosperous and thriving. Perhaps the mission's educational program taking students all the way through secondary school contributed to this relative prosperity in that area.

.   When the revolution began, there were some thirty- one tractors in and around Dembidollo in Western Ethiopia with an assortment of needed implements to go with them. The local Kabele leaders required the owners to turn these tractors and their implements into a designated place with the promise of compensation. One year later, a Presbyterian missionary builder based in Dembidollo, reported that only two or three of those tractors was still operable. Tires on some were ruined when assigned drivers refused to change flats and instead drove them without inflation back to the center where the "tire man" could deal with it. This missionary reported seeing open crankcases being rained on.

The inevitable result was that food became expensive and scarce in the local market at Dembidollo. An area in Ethiopia which was once supplying surplus grain to other parts of the country, was now hardly able to feed its own people. These kinds of policies contributed to the national disaster when rains failed causing widespread starvation in other parts of the country.

The revolution was undoubtedly provoked by obvious injustices of too few having too much property, prestige and power. Tragically, in the attempt to rectify long standing grievances, this same revolution unleashed horrendous displays of jealousy, envy and revenge. Thousands of innocent people were vilified, harassed and hounded. Countless thousands were falsely accused and imprisoned or killed. Ethiopia was far from being happy. Before it was finished, the country was destroyed and the revolution failed.

REVOLUTION FELT IN TEPPI

It wasn't long before we began to experience the effects of the revolution in Teppi. The Kabele meeting of local people was held at least once a week under the shade of a big tree on the corner just outside our compound beyond the fence. Often their meetings were characterized by anger and shouting. Sometimes Lavina and I would look at each other as we were eating about that same time and wonder if they began shooting how much protection the thin asbestos siding on our prefabricated house would offer.

We had planted several hundred eucalyptus trees along the front of our property outside the enclosure. By this time they'd grown to about three inches in diameter and some of them were thirty feet tall. One Sunday morning when we returned from church, we were astounded to find that every tree had been chopped down. The local Kabele had done this while we were away without asking permission or offering a word of explanation. Later they told us that everything now belonged to everybody, including our small grove of several hundred trees. This was communism playing itself out!

One Sunday afternoon our Christian young people were putting on a special Easter program. Extra chairs and benches had been arranged on the lawn in front of the office building where the group would be performing on the cement platform there. Many guests as well as our own church people were present. During the service, I noticed that several young men sitting near the front were turning around frequently and communicating with other young men sitting toward the back. At one stage, about ten or twelve of these young men, mostly out of town university students politicizing the Kabele, on signal, jumped to their feet and demanded that the service stop. They began wildly turning over chairs as people jumped to their feet in shock and dismay.

Our Christian young people tried to calm the situation. I saw that one of them was motioning to me not to say anything and leave it in their hands. The situation was chaotic and fraught with danger. I had determined to remain silent, when those causing the trouble demanded that I answer their questions.

I found myself standing on one of the benches near the front. Chairs were strewn about in disarray and these young men were dispersed among them. One of them, in a very loud, threatening voice, demanded to know what we were doing in Ethiopia. He ridiculed our ministry saying that we were spoiling the people and doing nothing for the country.

I chose my words with great care, but reason was thrown to the wind. I explained how the village people were now receiving medical assistance through our itineration airstrip ministry. I spoke of our language learning programs on cassettes helping people understand the national language. But it was apparent that they didn't want rational explanations. They simply wanted to show their power and intimidate the Christians and us. I was shocked by the way they unashamedly, blatantly blasphemed the name of Jesus.

Just as abruptly as it began, so it ended. One of them said, "That's enough for this time. Let's get out of here." They kicked over a few more chairs and left through the open gate. As they began crossing the airstrip, we saw them attack some of our people who were carrying their hymbooks and Bibles. They began ripping pages out of them and scattering them in the air. (Once we were told that this same crowd had put a Bible in an outside privy in town to be used as toilet paper)

After they had all gone, an amazing thing happened. Instead of our group being angry over the abuse they had suffered, they knelt down among the scattered chairs and praised God and prayed for the salvation of those who had just treated them so shabbily. We gave thanks that God had protected us in a situation that might well have gotten out of hand with serious consequences.

That evening, there was a knock on our door. Kani Naro had come from his village, Bible in hand. He had come to comfort us and to pray with us. It was such a beautiful experience to have this young man show his concern for us and to hold us up before the Lord. It had been a rather terrifying experience. Kani's coming was a token of God's goodness as He ministered to our need that night before we tried to sleep.

ASSIGNED BACK TO GODARE

During this same period, Harry and Pat Miersma left the Godare and returned to America. Harry and Pat felt called to a different kind of ministry and, having received the required additional education and training, they began their long-term missionary career with Wycliffe Bible Translators. We thanked God for the good years they had given to Ethiopia, for the way they had helped us in Teppi and especially for their years among the Mesengo people in the rain forest at Godare. The big question now was, what do we do about the Godare?

The mission felt that Harvey and Lavina should return to the Godare. John and Gwen Haspels and their children, new missionaries ready to be assigned, would soon be available. The mission said that we should remain in Teppi long enough to orient the Haspels to the ministry there. In their opinion, we were needed at the Godare more than in Teppi.

During those deliberations, our hearts were sometimes heavy. We loved the Mesengo people and the years we'd had at Godare. But we also loved the ministry in and from Teppi. God had led us into a fruitful, challenging ministry with a strong itineration outreach from seven new airstrips. We were happy and fulfilled. The mission was urging us to be open to the change and to seek God's leading with them. In the end, they came forward with an argument that was beyond dispute. "Look," they said, "you are the only missionaries in the entire world who speak the Mesengo language. You have the gifts, experience and language ability needed there now."

It was, indeed, a powerfully persuasive argument. In the end, the Lord convinced us that we had to surrender the work at Teppi to another, and return to the rain forest, Godare, and the Mesengo people.

While we were wrestling with our decision, I took my Suzuki 185 hsp. trail bike past Metti in the direction of Godare and turned south on the trail toward Korme. I'd gone about fifteen miles, when I was abruptly halted by a log across the path that I couldn't get over or go around. This was the end of my journey for that day.

Leaving the bike there, I walked some distance ahead until I ran across two young lads whom I'd known at Godare. Almost immediately, they shared with me that one of their friends was very ill with a fever and they'd like me to go with them so that I could see what was wrong. They assured me that the village to which they wanted me to go was near. As I had so often experienced in Africa, the word "near" has a very wide area of meaning. It was a long hike. But, eventually, we were in this very dark hut and I discovered a terribly sick young man burning with fever.

I began reminding the young men whom I'd known at the Godare of how we had taught them to pray and to believe that Jesus has power to heal. I asked them if they still remembered and believed that. Assuring me that they did, I asked them if they'd pray with me and they said they would. These two young men and I laid our hands on this body burning with fever and we prayed. The young lads and I were all praying at the same time, just talking to Jesus and asking Him to please make this young man well again. Before leaving, we arranged for someone to give him some hot tea and to be sure that he drank plenty of water.

I arrived in Teppi well after dark and shared my experience with Lavina. About a week later, one of those two fellows was clapping outside our gate. He brought the good news that the young Mesengo man we had prayed for was well. Less than two weeks later that very sick young man, now well, was clapping at the gate. He was praising God with us for his recovery.

IN NAIROBI

While we were living in Teppi, I took three weeks out to attend the Fifth Assembly of the World Council of Churches. I went as a reporter for the "Church Growth Bulletin" of the School of World Missions, Fuller Theological Seminary in Pasadena, California. During our previous furlough I'd begun a doctoral study program there relating to the World Council of Churches. Attending the WCC Assembly in Nairobi was part of my research activity. The magazine I represented entitled me to that coveted badge, indicating I was an accredited member of the press corps registered to cover the meeting. My press corps identification badge entitled me to go anywhere the representative from Time magazine or any of the larger publications went. It was a marvelous way to cover the meeting.

It was a great experience to sit beside Dr. John Stapert, editor of the Church Herald, every day for three weeks sharing reactions, observations and our evaluation as to what was happening. My account of those events is covered in my dissertation which was published in 1979 under the title, **The World Council of Churches and the Demise of Evangelism,** My book was well received by both the evangelical community and the ecumenical community. It received favorable reviews and was commended for fairness and good documentation. My only regret is the title itself. Had I been in America when the publishers chose the title, I would have insisted on a positive title like "The World Council of Churches and Its 'New Mission'."

FINAL MONTHS AT GODARE

In the summer of 1976, Lavina and I returned to the Godare and the Haspels took over the work in Teppi. Al and Sue Schreuder were in Teppi in connection with Al's internship program from Western Theological Seminary in Holland, Michigan. When the Haspels went for furlough, Al and Sue were there alone, standing in the gap!

We had six wonderful months among the Mesengo. In God's kind providence, they are among our happiest times in Ethiopia. It was marvelous meeting old friends like Ocoor, Elong and Argeem.

I hadn't seen Elong for two and one half years. When he one day appeared on the compound, I learned how, on his own, he'd been using cassettes all those months. He said he'd moved across the river and was living way out there beyond the highest mountain peak on a ridge sloping down toward Gambela and the Baro river. He told how he'd gathered a small group around him whom he had taught and who worshipped regularly. He'd buy new batteries in Gambela and had kept his player functioning that entire period.

Elong was with us only a couple of days, picked up new and additional cassettes in the Mesengo language, and then disappeared in the forest heading down toward the river and in the direction of Gambela. I never saw him again.

Only eternity will reveal what people like Elong and others are doing to share the Gospel among their people. But this I do know, it was the cassette that enabled them to get started and to learn the essential truths about Jesus Christ. I suspect that most of those machines have long since fallen silent. But the foundation has been laid and with their phenomenal memories, they are still drawing on that fountain of information and instruction from God's word, first made plain to them in their own language from cassettes.

A LETTER HOME CONFIRMS OUR HIGH HOPES

It was Elong who had gone across the Bako river and witnessed among the Daniir people. His grass string with 105 knots on it was his record of what had happened. One hundred and five people had said to him, "Elong, take some grass and make a string. Tie a knot on your string for me. I want to become a person of your Jesus."

Some period of time after Elong had been in that area, several people came to the clinic from that general direction way out beyond the Bako river. They'd come to bring in a sick person, found the help they needed and, during their stay at Godare, professed their commitment to Jesus Christ.

At that time, I was hesitant to do so, but felt this family should be baptised on the basis of their faith before they went back to their distant village beyond the Bako river.

Our letter home written three years later, dated April 1, 1976, seems to confirm that we had made the right decision and our hearts were greatly encouraged:

"Do you remember about 3 years ago when I wrote about this father and his three sons from the Daniir tribe that came and wanted medicine, but who believed while here and were baptized in my office before they left. They also took a cassette player back with them with two cassettes. Well, this week Ojatiin, the first person among the Mesengo to believe and be baptised, told me of a Mesengo friend of his who has visited them from time to time. They are three or four days across the Bako River from here. Ojatiin said their faith has been firm and that there are about 20 believers in this family's village now. We were thrilled and encouraged by this."

The first seed had been sown with the help of a cassette player by a middle aged, illiterate, barefoot Mesengo named Elong.

BALTI DIES AND IS BURIED

Chief Balti had become an old man since we'd last seen him. He'd moved closer to the mission and had a little shack just off the airstrip near where that huge tree had once stood. I visited him frequently, but he was already too ill really to comprehend clearly. It was heart breaking to see him slipping away without ever having committed his life to Jesus. During our years at Godare he would sometimes attend our worship services. He was often in the clinic. There were times when he'd come into our house. We'd sit together on the veranda. When he was alone, I could share with him about Jesus and he'd respond with understanding and appreciation. If others were with him, however, he never entered into a serious discussion with me. He'd usually respond with some joking comment that didn't always make sense.

In many respects, Balti was a very weird person. Other members of his family were all a bit peculiar too. It's strange, but I had noticed already in the Sudan that frequently persons who were odd or who had had a traumatic experience, like having been knocked unconscious or who had fainted and revived again, were the ones who frequently had become witch-doctors. There was something eccentric about many of them and most of them I met were extremely clever and captivating. Some of them were well off, judging by the standards of their own people.

Balti, also, could be extremely cruel and unforgiving. He once shot his twenty year old son in cold blood. Shot him right in front of the young man's mother when the son and he argued. He was under the influence at the time. When Balti was under the influence of that fermented honey water, he was cantankerous and unpredictable. I had been afraid of him more than once.

He died while we were there during these last few months. I was there beside him. He lay in his hut unaware of those around him. His breathing had become heavy as his chest heaved up and down. The Mesengos knew that the end was near. Earlier in the day they had come to borrow shovels and a pick-axe with which they were preparing his grave. When they had it prepared, it was typical — a circular hole about three to four feet in diameter going down less than five feet. Half way down along one side was a ledge of soil they had left projecting out. On this ledge they would position the bark strips to shield the body from the dirt when they filled in the grave.

Even before Balti breathed his last, a woman was busy stripping layers of thin bark off a small pole from a tree that was used for that purpose. She was rapidly accumulating many thin strips about a half inch in width. Only a few people were sitting there with us waiting for Balti to take his last breath. When he did, Alemayu and another man went inside to remove all the bracelets and charms from his body. There were many of them. While they were doing this they asked if I could send home and ask Lavina for a white sheet in which they might wrap the body.

Once the body had been stripped of everything, they tied his body tightly with these strips of green bark, tying him in a fetal position. When finished, he was a ball shaped figure less than two feet in diameter. Around these tied remains, they wrapped our white sheet and again tied it with the green strips of bark.

Men had come with a crude, homemade stretcher of poles between which there was a square platform of light sticks tightly laced together. The platform was about three feet square. Before Balti's tightly wrapped, ball shaped body was carried out and placed on this platform, someone blew long blasts on a bugle Balti had owned. It was blown only on very special occasions and this was one of them. Several people with guns also fired shots into the air.

Balti's body was placed on this simple stretcher and four men carried him slowly down the hill along the edge of the airstrip to the waiting grave. At the grave site the same clearing described in an earlier chapter was being done. Women were soon throwing themselves on the ground. One woman was singing a lengthy and mournful funeral dirge. At one stage, a young woman went completely berserk, threw all caution to the wind, and ran in among the stumps and vines, throwing herself on the ground repeatedly. People ran out to catch her lest she injure herself on one of the sharp, protruding, small stumps hidden everywhere among the vines and brush. Many shots were fired during this whole procedure.

After the burial, the people who had prepared the grave and carried the body took water and washed themselves carefully some distance from the onlookers. Again, the hopelessness of the whole situation with its pagan practices was overwhelming and depressing.

The next morning when I returned to visit the village in which the grave was located, I found several men sitting on a small log. They had been cutting their heads to show their grief. In front of one was a small hole in the ground. In it I saw at least a cup or more of fresh blood.

CHOPPING DOWN BALTI'S BEEHIVE TREES

Once during the weeks immediately following Balti's death, I was working in the outside office just in front of the clinic. It was nearly noon and time to go home for lunch when all of a sudden we heard a nearby tree come crashing down. A few minutes later two men were walking down the mission road in the direction of the airstrip, each carrying a small Mesengo ax over his shoulder.

When I went for lunch I noticed one of our trees on the compound just behind where the saw mill was located was missing. It had been chopped down. When I inquired who might have done such a thing without permission, I was told that when a chief like Balti dies, his people go throughout the forest and cut down any tree in which he may have once placed beehives. After fifteen years, I was still learning things about the Mesengos that I'd never known before. I would probably have been much more perturbed had it been the stately shade tree overshadowing our house!

WITHOUT MAF

During our last weeks at the Godare, MAF was grounded. Revolutionary forces had forbidden them to fly into several areas, including ours. Our radios were still functioning but we couldn't fly anymore. The Haspels had been assigned to live at the Godare during our upcoming furlough. Because they'd be delayed, we'd been asked to stay over an extra month so that we could overlap with their coming and turn the work over to them responsibly. We were quite happy to do that, the only problem being that we wouldn't have sufficient food for that additional month. With MAF grounded, we had a first class problem. Even if we somehow managed the food problem, we still wondered how we'd all get out of the Godare to catch a flight from Teppi to Addis and then on to America. We decided we should take one step at a time. It was essential that we bring in additional food supplies as there was nothing we could find in Meti or Teppi to tide us over.

USING THE TRAIL BIKE TO FETCH FOOD

Paul, who was fifteen then, and I decided we should go out with the trail bike as far as Teppi. I'd fly on to Addis, have discussions with the mission about possibilities after furlough, and bring back sufficient groceries to supply our need until the Haspels arrived. Mesengos encouraged us saying that the trail between Godare and Metti had been cleared and we should make it easily on the bike.

On that Sunday afternoon, Paul and I made an exploratory trip in the direction of Teppi. We went several miles and found the trail was indeed cut. We encountered a problem with logs lying across the trail which we'd have to cross over. We solved this problem by cutting two boards measuring about two and a half feet in length and six inches in width. We drilled two holes in one end of each through which we put a rope that would be draped over the log and could be lengthened and shortened to accommodate whatever size log we encountered. This, actually, worked great except on three or four foot diameter logs we sometimes encountered.

On Monday morning, Paul and I started for Teppi with a small bag of sandwiches and a couple of chunks of cheese. Lavina told Sue Schreuder in Teppi by radio that we hoped to be there by late afternoon. We had just over fifty miles to go and, with the path cleared like the Mesengos had said, it should be a lark! It turned out to be anything but!

About two hours out, we came to a river over which they had failed to put a little bridge. The water was about chest deep. Paul and I were there alone. Should we turn back or wait for things to develop. We decided to wait. In about an hour, at least a half dozen Mesengo men and a couple of boys had reached our point and were sitting around with us. We solved the problem by cutting two poles, lacing the handlebars and the seat to them and getting the bike across with the help of strong, willing Mesengo men who were sure footed even on the slippery stones in the water. They literally hoisted the bike above their shoulders so that only the tires were wet.

Once across the river, we discovered that the trail ahead was uncut. The path was slippery, overgrown and wet. We literally had to pull the bike up these steep hills with a rope and restrain it similarly when going down. Two boys about fourteen or fifteen years of age stuck with us the remainder of the day. Finally, it was totally dark and about eight o'clock at night. The chain of the bike came off and we gave up. The Mesengo boys said they could lead us to a place where we could sleep. We walked over an hour to a tiny Mesengo village.

In the open-sided shack were several men and boys with their sleeping mats and there was a narrow bed made with sticks laced together with vines. A bright fire was burning in the center of this hut. That would be our hotel for the night.

The people were extremely hospitable. They said Paul could sleep on the stick mat and they would let me have the bed. We had no padding to lay over the sticks on which we later tried to sleep. Our clothes were wet up to our hips from the wet vines and undergrowth. We found places in the roof over the fire to dry our tennis shoes and socks. We tried drying our trousers, but I'm not sure how successful we were. About one in the morning, Paul came around the fire over to where I was lying and said softly, "Dad, I haven't slept yet."

I said, "Paul, why don't you take my bed for awhile and I'll see if I can get our clothes dry."

Paul tried my bed but soon decided it was too hard and rough. He discovered a filthy bark cloth somewhere, rolled himself up in it and fell asleep under my bed beside the fire. Later when I lay down, I could feel it whenever he turned over and gave the bed a bump.

When morning came, the Mesengos shared a gourd of black coffee into which they always put hot peppers. Quite some brew! I've always said that it takes only a little to remove one's hair. I'm living proof for the truth of that statement! We had only one small piece of cheese left about the size of my thumb. I offered to share it with Paul but he refused. Years later he told me, "You know, dad, the reason I didn't take that cheese is that I thought you needed it for strength." Bless his young, caring heart!

Mesengos accompanied us back to the bike and when the mud and brush that had caused the chain to come off the previous evening had been remedied, we resumed our journey. Mesengo men helped greatly by cutting bad spots. Our pace was very slow. During the day we found roasting ears and survived on that until we reached Metti around five that afternoon. We were warmly welcomed and they fed us tasty injira and wat, the normal Ethiopian highland food. We still had ten miles to cover between Metti and Teppi. It was nearly nine o'clock when we showed up on the compound and were welcomed by Sue Schreuder. She said Al was out for a few days north of Teppi on trek.

Lavina was greatly relieved in the morning to learn we'd arrived safely It's an experience Paul and I will never forget and one we'd prefer not to repeat!

PAUL RETURNS TO GODARE ON FOOT

I took Paul the ten miles back down to Metti in the morning on the bike. There we arranged for companions to accompany Paul on his trek back to the Godare, some forty miles from Metti! Quite a hike for a young missionary kid, all alone in the forest except for his Mesengo companions. On the way he survived on roasted, shelled corn and sweet honey water. Paul said that home looked awfully good to him. It took him several days to recover from the rigors of the journey with inadequate food, no place to sleep properly and the long distance he had walked.

I returned that morning with the Suzuki to Teppi, caught the plane in the afternoon and flew to Addis Ababa. Before leaving I asked Sue if she could buy a horse for me in the market on Saturday. I had no intention of trying to ride that bike home and knew a horse would be much easier. I already had a saddle in Teppi so when I returned from Addis, the horse was waiting and my transportation was assured.

RETURNING TO GODARE ON HORSEBACK

I engaged three men to accompany me and carry the cartons of groceries. That night, I slept in a Mesengo village, using a new Mesengo beehive for my bed. This was a village where they were making these hives. They would cut ten to twelve inch logs four and a half to five feet in length. These logs were split in half and hollowed out. When they put them up in the trees they would band the two halves together again with vines to constitute a whole log. In it were small openings for the bees to enter. The ends were stuffed with grass and brush. When they collected the honey, they would go up into the tree, carrying a smoking torch to the hive to drive out the bees and give a little protection.

That night in the village, I took two halves and laid them side by side. The reins and bridle along with some extra grass and leaves filled the empty depression. I had a sleeping bag with me on this return trip. Using the saddle for my pillow, I had quite a good night. The major problem, as usual, was those village dogs that kept barking non-stop all through the night. I was home by two o'clock the next afternoon. This distance as registered on the trail bike was 52 miles from Godare to Teppi. The original trek we made going into Godare nearly fifteen years earlier, before the trail was straightened, was an estimated seventy miles. What took us ten days then, I now did in a long day and a half, riding comfortably on my new horse. The only problem with that horse was that he stumbled much too often. I had wondered why it might be that Sue was able to buy this horse, that is, why they were willing to sell him. It was only a few miles down the trail when I thought I had the answer. I nicknamed him, "Stumbler!" Stumble or not, it was a vast improvement over the bike trip in. Sue Shraeder had done the right thing in that market when she clinched the deal! I've long since forgotten how much she paid!

Within a few days, our hearts were gladdened when MAF came on the radio and reported that the government ban had been lifted and that they'd be able to fly us out whenever we had to leave. We had been trying to figure out how we were going to make it out with just one horse. Some of us were likely to have a long hike. But with MAF again operating, we flew out in one plane, first class. How can we ever be grateful enough for MAF's marvelous ministry?

OUR LAST DAY AT GODARE

On that final day when MAF came in to fetch us for the last time, perhaps as many as eighty or a hundred Mesengos had gathered to bid us goodbye. The afternoon before women came into the house, sat quietly on the floor where they felt most comfortable, and talked softly together. There was real sadness among them as they realized we were going away for a very long time. They seemed to sense that we wouldn't soon return. In the morning, the women were again at the door. They began gathering early in the morning, sitting around as we waited for the plane to arrive. Some of them shared memories of things we'd done together and some spoke of when they had first become believers. Lavina prepared many pots of tea and served ripe bananas and peanuts as she finished off last minute packing.

It was Max Gove who flew in, arriving just after the noon hour. Mesengos helped carry our luggage down the mission road, past the clinic and school buildings, depositing them under those two gigantic trees that formed a gateway between the airstrip itself and the compound. They were incredibly large, stately and tall, measuring between five and six feet in diameter.

It was under these towering trees that the crowd had gathered. But now it was time to get into the plane. Max had finished loading our luggage in the pod located under the fuselage and said it was time to leave. Roket, the man whom we'd ordained, whose finger I'd sewed back on when he was a boy, led us in prayer. In the middle of his prayer he broke down and began to cry. Unable to continue he said, "Muse (Moses), you pray."

Moses finished the prayer. When we opened our eyes we saw that a number of them, along with ourselves, were crying. Even Bakle, chief Balti's son, who had at one time made life difficult for us, was wiping back tears. He had become a brother in Christ and a personal friend, but I never expected to see him cry.

Argeem, who had brought in those first knotted strings, had slipped away behind the big tree to weep there by herself.

We were now in the plane with our safety belts fastened. In a moment the door would shut. People would be warned to move back, the engine would start and be revved up for a final check of the instruments. We'd be on our way for the last time.

THE LAST WORDS FROM THE RAIN FOREST AT GODARE

But before the door of the aircraft closed, Argeem came quickly from behind the tree, thrust her head in through the plane's still-open door and, speaking in English, the language she'd first learned from our daughter, Carol, and the Zudweg girls when they played together as children, said to Lavina, "Nyijobi," (Lavina's African name), "you come back. Okay? You come back." Before Lavina could answer, she continued, "If you don't come back, I'll see you one day in Jesus' house."

These were the last words we heard at Godare! The pilot pulled the door shut and fastened it. Soon we were in the air heading for Jimma and Addis. Argeem's words were God's gift for us to treasure in our hearts forever!

AFTER GODARE

For us, the door to Ethiopia had closed. We had hoped to extend our cassette ministry into other countries in Africa from our base in Ethiopia. But God had larger plans. The cassette ministry was to include India, Asia and other parts of the world as well.

Basing in the United States, we spent five to seven months of each year overseas during the next ten years opening regional centers in Africa, India, Bangladesh, Singapore and Indonesia under the auspices of PRM International. In these centers we trained and equipped nationals to use cassettes effectively. Our vision was to provide on cassettes the translated Scriptures for those unable to read. Scripture on cassette could give the same opportunity for non-readers to learn God's precious Word by listening as those who read have from the printed text.

In 1989 that ministry was enlarged to include providing Scripture on cassette in languages needed to reach ethnic peoples who had left their own countries and were now living among us in America and in Australia and Europe. Audio Scriptures International was organized for that purpose.

PRM International and Audio Scriptures International continue to encourage and assist each other in these challenging, growing cassette ministries.

From Ethiopia come reports of the phenomenal turning of the Mesengo people to Christ. Reliable reports tell of ninety percent of the Mesengo becoming believers. The power of the Gospel is at work among them, being confirmed by miracles of healing and answers to prayer. Merchants in Teppi, the town from which we first pushed off into the forest some thirty years earlier are quoted as saying with astonishment, "What is happening to these Mesengo people? They are no longer killing each other! They are no longer drinking themselves to death? When they are sick, they go off into the forest and pray to their God, and when they come out, they are no longer sick!"

How marvelous, indeed, are the ways of our God. Full of grace and mercy, He closes one door and opens another. He has the master plan. It is His mission. He, graciously uses ordinary people and empowers them to become His missionaries, but when their task is finished, God continues His mission in ways of His own choosing. God is in control. It was God's initiative from the beginning. *"For God so loved the world that he gave his one and only Son, that whoever believes in him shall not perish but have eternal life."* John 3:16

His mission will not fail! Jesus Christ is God's appointed Savior! **"Salvation is found in no one else, for there is no other name under heaven given to men by which we must be saved."** Acts 4:12

How marvelous in our time to witness the dramatic growth of the church where once there were no churches. How tremendous to observe the phenomenal growth in non-western mission organizations among these new churches and to witness the increasing number of missionaries being sent out from Korea, Singapore, India, Latin America and African countries.

Our hearts sing for joy as we remember the word of Jesus when he said, **"And this gospel of the kingdom will be preached in the whole world as a testimony to all nations, and then the end will come."** Matthew 24:14 To have been laid hold of by God to be part of His unfailing mission, has been our unspeakable privilege! To Him be all honor, glory and praise forever and ever through Jesus Christ our Lord! Hallelujah!

"After this I looked, and behold, a great multitude which no man could number, from every nation, from all tribes and peoples and tongues, standing before the throne and before the Lamb, clothed in white robes, with palm branches in their hands, and crying out with a loud voice, 'Salvation belongs to our God who sits upon the throne and to the Lamb!' And all the angels stood round the throne and round the elders and the four living creatures, and they fell on their faces before the throne and worshipped God, saying, 'Amen! Blessing and glory and wisdom and thanksgiving and honor and power and might be to our God forever and ever and ever! Amen!' "

Revelation 7:9-12

VITA

Harvey Thomas Hoekstra was born on November 20, 1920. He was the fourth of six brothers. His boyhood was spent on the farm where he grew up in the atmoshere of a Christian home. He was out of school for four and one-half years between grade school and high school. During this time he had three major operations and spent some forty-five days in the hospital. Through this experience he came to know Christ as personal Savior and was called to the ministry.

He began high school in 1938 and graduated with honor completeing his work in two and a half years.He graduated Cum Laude with an A. B. degree from Hope College, and recieved his B. D. degree from Western Theological Seminary of the Reformed Church. He was student pastor of the Hope Reformed Church in Grand Haven,Michigan for three years while taking his theological training.

Post graduate work included the Summer Institute of Linguistic course with Wycliffe at the University of Oklahoma, a year of post graduate study at Scarrit and Peabody Colleges in Nashville, Tennesee. He also studied during two furloughs, with a term at Princton Seminary and a semester at the Kennedy School of Missions in Hartford, Connecticut.

He recieved the Doctor of Missiology degree from Fuller Theological Seminary in 1978. At that time he was awarded the Donald Anderson McGavran Award in recognition of the excellence of his dissertation on the subject of the World Council of Churches and its 'New Mission.' This study was published in 1979.

While in college, he was married to Lavina Irene Hoffman. With their children they have served as missionaries in the Sudan and Ethiopia for 30 years. In the Sudan he reduced the Anuak tribal language to writing, worked in the area of literacy and evangelism and translated the entire New Testament into the Anuak language which was printed by the American Bible Society. He also translated into the Murle language Mark, John, Acts and Romans which was printed by the British and Foriegn Bible Society using both the Roman and Arabic script.

In Ethiopia he, with his family, pioneered work among the Mesengo forest people in the Southwestern part of the country. Here he developed the use of cassettes in evangelism aimed at reaching a number of previously unreached people groups with the Gospel, each in its own language. Beginning in 1977, the Hoekstras returned overseas annually serving as director of Portable Recording Ministries's (PRM) World Cassette Outreach (WCO) program.

Dr. Hoekstra founded Audio Scriptures International (ASI) in 1989 to provide Scripture on cassette in languages needed by ministries among ethnic peoples who have left their homelands and now live in other countries.

In 1979 Dr. Hoekstra was elected to serve as moderator of the General Synod of the Reformed Church in America. The Hoekstras make their home in San Diego where Harvey continues to serve as President of Audio Scriptures International.

The Hoekstras have six children, five of whom are married. Three of their children are full time missionaries.

******